CHINA ROAD

CHINA ROAD

A Journey into the Future of a Rising Power

ROB GIFFORD

BLOOMSBURY

First published in Great Britain 2007

Copyright © 2007 by Rob Gifford

Map copyright © 2007 David Lindroth Inc.

The moral right of the author has been asserted

No part of this book may be used or reproduced in any manner
whatsoever without written permission from the Publisher except in
the case of brief quotations embodied in critical articles or reviews

Bloomsbury Publishing Plc
36 Soho Square
London W1D 3QY

www.bloomsbury.com

Bloomsbury Publishing, London, New York and Berlin

A CIP catalogue record for this book is available from the British Library

ISBN 9780747588924

10 9 8 7 6 5 4 3 2 1

Typeset by Hewer Text UK Ltd, Edinburgh
Printed in Great Britain by Clays Ltd, St Ives plc
The paper this book is printed on is certified by the © 1996 Forest
Stewardship Council A.C. (FSC). It is ancient-forest friendly. The printer holds
FSC chain of custody SGS-COC-2061

FSC
Mixed Sources
Product group from well-managed
forests and other controlled sources

Cert no. SGS-COC-2061
www.fsc.org
© 1996 Forest Stewardship Council

for Nancy

Hope cannot be said to exist, nor can it be said not to exist. It is just like roads across the earth. For actually the earth has no roads to begin with . . . but when many people pass one way, a road is made.

Lu Xun, '*My Old Home*', 1921

CONTENTS

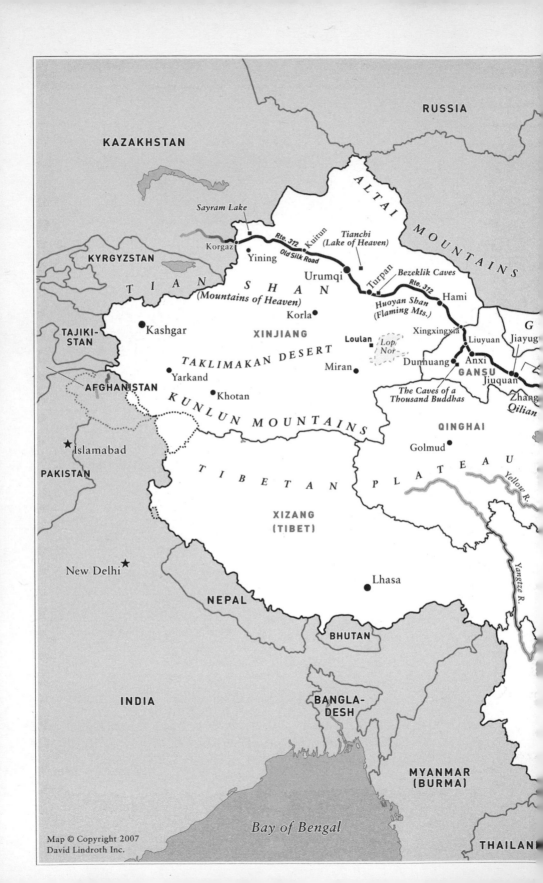

RUSSIA

KAZAKHSTAN

Sayram Lake

Rte. 312
Kuitun
*Tianchi
(Lake of Heaven)*

ALTAI MOUNTAINS

Korgaz
Yining
Old Silk Road

KYRGYZSTAN

Urumqi
Turpan
Bezeklik Caves
Rte. 312

TIAN SHAN
(Mountains of Heaven)

Huoyan Shan
(Flaming Mts.)
Hami

TAJIKI-
STAN

Kashgar

XINJIANG
Korla

Xingxingxia
Liuyuan
Jiayug

G

TAKLIMAKAN DESERT
Loulan
*Lop
Nor*
Dunhuang
Anxi
GANSU

Miran

Jiuquan

AFGHANISTAN

Yarkand

KUNLUN MOUNTAINS

Khotan

*The Caves of a
Thousand Buddhas*

Zhang
Qilian

Islamabad

QINGHAI

Golmud

Yellow R.

PAKISTAN

TIBETAN PLATEAU

New Delhi

XIZANG
(TIBET)

Yangtze R.

NEPAL

Lhasa

BHUTAN

INDIA

BANGLA-
DESH

MYANMAR
(BURMA)

Bay of Bengal

THAILAND

Map © Copyright 2007
David Lindroth Inc.

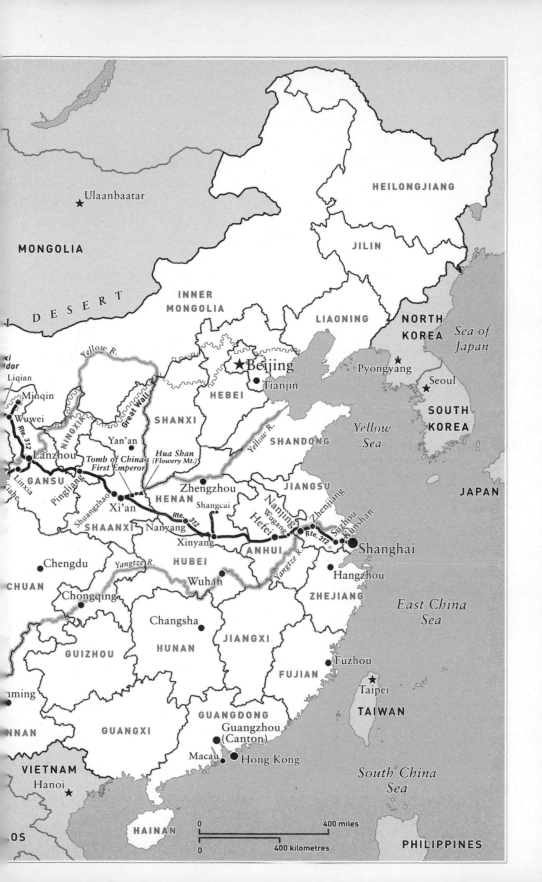

Introduction

THE MOTHER ROAD

The worn black road shoots like an arrow across the desert until it thuds into a low escarpment of rocks, which rises from the lunar landscape of the Gobi's yellow scrubland. The craggy boulders form a ravine that soon encloses the road as it bends for the first time in a hundred miles, then dumps the traveller in a small town that had not been visible from the highway. The ravine gives the town its name, Xingxingxia, which in English means Starry Gorge.

Starry Gorge is a two-horse town, with just a few hundred residents. It caters to the truckers, the long-distance buses and the occasional crazy traveller who chooses to cross the Gobi Desert by road. The town owes its existence to a small freshwater well, the only one for miles around, which has sustained man and beast for centuries on their journeys along this merciless section of the ancient Silk Road. Xingxingxia (pronounced *shing-shing-shyah*) marks the traveller's entry into what used to be called Turkestan but is now the Chinese region of Xinjiang. The gorge to the east and a large tollgate to the west provide the bookends for this shabby jumble of truck stops, houses and one large petrol station that poke out of the scorched desert earth and up into the clear blue Central Asian sky. The hostile sun is high, almost melting the tarmac, and I'm standing beside the road, trying to hitch a ride.

This is not just any old road. This is China's Mother Road, and its name is Route 312. I've been journeying by bus, truck and taxi all the way from the road's beginning in Shanghai nearly 2,000 miles east of here. At the ancient city of Xi'an, it picked up the route of the old Silk Road, which in ancient times ran through the Gobi Desert, through Starry Gorge, to Central Asia, and westward to Persia and Europe. I'm about two-thirds of the way along my 3,000-mile journey, with a 1,000 miles left to ride to the road's end, at the Chinese border with Kazakhstan.

I am unshaven and burned by the fierce desert sun, weary but exhilarated after six weeks' travelling, and weary but still exhilarated after six years of living in China as a journalist. This is my final journey across the country before I leave and move to Europe.

A group of truck drivers has gathered to chat at the petrol station. I wander over to see if any of them will give me a ride west. Word has reached them that, just ahead on Route 312, a patrol car from the small Starry Gorge police station is sitting, waiting. They are all overloaded and will be fined if they are stopped. We stand and make small talk for ten minutes. Most of them are cautious about giving a ride to a westerner. Finally, word comes through that the police car has gone, and the group disperses, each driver to his own truck. I'm left standing until one of them looks back at me and, with a short jerk of his head, motions me towards his truck. I follow, and jump into the cab. He fires up the engine, rolls the big blue beast on to the road and out into the hungry, golden Gobi.

'Where have you come from?' I ask him.

'Shanghai.'

'And where are you heading?'

'Urumqi.'

'What's that huge thing on the back of your truck?'

'It's an industrial filter, going to a company in Urumqi. And last week I was driving from Urumqi to Shanghai, with a truck full of melons.'

It's a symbolic exchange, fresh produce flows east for the consumers of China's coastal cities. Industrial equipment flows west to help with the construction of the less developed regions inland.

Urumqi (pronounced *oo-room-chee*) is the capital of Xinjiang, the heart of Central Asia, and the city furthest from an ocean in the world.

The driver's name is Liu Qiang (pronounced *leo chang*). He travels back and forth along Route 312 from Xinjiang to Shanghai all through the year, driving alternately day and night with his buddy, Wang, who is asleep on the narrow bunk behind our seats. All the trucks have two drivers, so that they can travel twenty-four hours a day, stopping only when they need to use the rest stops along the 3,000-mile road.

'How's life as a trucker these day?' I ask him. 'Can you make money?'

'*Tai nan le*. It's difficult,' he laments, lighting up the first of many cigarettes and tossing his lighter on to the dashboard. 'We have to overload our trucks to make any money, but the police lie in wait and fine us.'

He chain-smokes as he drives and talks with a rat-a-tat staccato.

'I get paid 18,000 yuan [about $2,200] to take a load from Urumqi to Shanghai or back again. I have to pay out about 15,000 yuan in tolls, costs and fines to the policemen. So from a one-week trip, I earn about 3,000 yuan [roughly $380].'

'That's not a bad income,' I say. Many Chinese do not earn that in a month.

'Yes, but there's wear and tear on my truck, and wear and tear on me. And I'm getting paid less as competition increases. Plus the fact that police fines are going up.'

I cannot think of a better travelling companion. Liu is that wonderful mix of modesty and bravado that characterises many

Chinese men. He's built like a boxer, short and muscular, and although he left school at sixteen, he is a one-man philosophy department, with an opinion on everything. One minute he is lamenting the moral decline of China, the next he is telling me about the roadside brothels he visits along the way. He is a coiled spring of energy, with laughter and fury exploding in equal measures. Laughter just at life itself, in all its modern Chinese craziness. Fury mostly at corrupt Communist Party officials and policemen. Like so many modern Chinese people, he is torn between a deep love of his country and a deep anger at the people who govern it.

We travel for hours across the relentless Gobi, talking intensely at first but then with long periods of silence, during which he just drives, and I just sit, and Wang just snores in the bunk behind. The raw beauty of the desert – the implacable desert whose vicious sandstorms used to consume whole caravans of camels and their precious cargoes, the unquenchable desert that used to resist all but the most hardy travellers – rolls past outside.

Though still wild, it is slowly being conquered by an army of blue Chinese-made East Wind trucks. As roads such as Route 312 grow busier, and distant cities such as Urumqi are brought closer to the main centres of population further east, the desert seems a little less dangerous now. An occasional truck whooshes past in the opposite direction, shaking us with its slipstream. Passenger buses rush past too, and occasional cars, but not many.

Liu Qiang talks of the development he sees every day, the transformation of a country changed by the loosening of government controls, by the influx of foreign money, and most of all by the movement of people, untethered from their communist past. But mobility and greater freedom have changed people's characters, he says, and not always for the better.

'In the past, everyone was poor,' says Liu, 'but everyone was honest. Now, everyone is more free, but there is *luan*, there is chaos. Money has made everyone go bad.' He uses the Chinese phrase, a hundred times more illustrative than its canine English equivalent. '*Ren chi ren,*' he says. 'It's man eat man now.'

This is a book about people such as Liu Qiang. Ordinary Chinese people caught up in an extraordinary moment in time. China in the early twenty-first century is, above all things, a nation on the move, as millions of rural people leave their villages and head to the cities, looking for work. Many still travel by rail, but increasingly people are travelling by road. Exact numbers are difficult to gauge, but most experts estimate that 150 million (possibly as many as 200 million) people have left their home villages in search of work in cities around China. It is the largest migration in human history.

Pushed by the timeless poverty of the countryside and pulled by the bright lights of the cities, this army of migrants is fuelling the economic boom that is putting cheap toys, clothes, flat-screen TVs and computers on the shelves of the world's stores.

In China, the common people, both rural and urban, are known colloquially as the *lao bai xing,* literally the 'Old Hundred Names,' who in Chinese legend were made up of just one hundred family names. The lives of Old Hundred Names today are being transformed as never before in Chinese history.

After thirty years of market reforms since the death of Chairman Mao in 1976, China in the first decade of the twenty-first century stands on the edge of something very big, something very different from anything that has gone before. Its unique brand of man-eat-man capitalism (still known officially as 'socialism with Chinese characteristics') has brought unprecedented change to its society. China has overtaken Britain as the world's fourth largest economy; it has accumulated foreign exchange reserves of roughly one trillion dollars and become the workshop of the world. Its hunger for energy and resources is influencing world markets in oil and commodities. Diplomatically too it is growing in importance, with an engaged foreign policy governed by pragmatism rather than ideology. In short, China matters more than it has ever mattered in modern times. Many take it for granted that China will be the next global superpower.

But if you look a little more closely, you will see that dangerous fault lines are appearing too, fault lines which suggest that the country might not be as stable as it seems, and that China's much-vaunted rise may not be as smooth as many imagine. A journey west along Route 312 is a journey into China's frailties. There is a growing gap between the urban rich and the rural poor and this has led to many incidents of unrest in rural areas. The old safety net of free health care and cradle-to-grave provision by the state has collapsed, and this has left a lot of people much worse off than before. In addition, China's explosive development has ravaged the environment. Sixteen of the world's twenty most polluted cities are in China. There is a chronic water shortage, and many of the country's rivers are dangerously contaminated. On top of all that, the whole society is shot through with corruption, the legacy of a one-party state that will not implement political reform and therefore has no checks and balances on its all-powerful officials.

Most westerners who even think about China do not seem to consider the possibility that the pressures building up there could lead to a Soviet-style implosion. But I think the West needs to pay more attention to China's problems, because I think there could well be a crunch coming in China. The less the Communist Party deals with its pressing social and political problems now, the bigger the crunch will be if it comes. China's mobile twenty-first-century society is chafing more and more against its sclerotic Stalinist political system. If the government in Beijing doesn't do more to address the growing inequalities and looming environmental problems, I think that China could be in real trouble.

So as I prepare to set off along Route 312, there's one big

question in my own mind: which is it going to be for China, greatness or implosion? Can the country really become the twenty-first-century superpower that many predict? Or could it all collapse, like the Soviet Union, weighed down by the legacies of the past and sunk by the contradictions of the present? And if it does go on to greatness, what kind of country will China be? Can it ever make the transition to a modern, democratic state?

My plan is to answer these questions as I travel along Route 312, and as I meet the truckers and hookers, the yuppies and artists, the farmers and mobile-phone salesmen whose lives reflect the complexity of modern China. And while I'm trying to answer my questions about China's future, I hope to go some way to answering an equally important question about China today: who exactly are the Chinese people? And what has all this drastic change done to the Chinese psyche, and to the Chinese soul? China's physical landscape is changing as the country is turned upside down by development. But so is its psychological landscape, and its moral universe – what people think, what they believe. In the West, there were more than a hundred years for the dust of the Industrial Revolution to settle before the Technological Revolution came along. In China, the two revolutions are happening simultaneously. The dislocation, both physical and psychological, is immense, and it is tearing at the fabric of society, even as the new roads and railways knit the country more closely together.

In spite of all the change in China, the western world is still stuck in its dangerously outdated, black-and-white view of the country, tripping over its own breathless superlatives about unprecedented growth and progress, or retreating into old Cold War stereotypes and warnings of 'the China threat.' Western images of Chinese people are dated too. The Chinese have always been the faceless masses in the Western mind. Whether the pigtailed coolies of the 1860s or the Maoist Red Guards of the 1960s, they have never been seen in the

West as individuals. Now, though, individualism is emerging in China, as people take more control of their own lives. Chinese people, especially in the cities, have choices, and these choices are creating a whole new generation that is unknown to many people in the West. These are the people I want to meet, the individuals, the new Chinese people building the new China, the tremendous variety of people who live and work and travel along one Chinese road.

My adventure along Route 312 is also the end of a chapter in my own life. I am British, and I read Chinese studies at college in England in the 1980s. I first came to China as a twenty-year-old student in 1987, to spend a year studying the Chinese language in Beijing. After graduating, I became a journalist and spent much of the 1990s reporting on Asian issues. Most recently I have been based in Beijing for six years, as China correspondent for NPR, America's National Public Radio. Now I am leaving China, and within a few months I will be heading for Europe, to be NPR's London correspondent. I could have stayed longer, but six years seemed about the right length of time for a journalistic posting, and I've chosen to leave while I'm still enjoying the party. For twenty years, my life has been entwined with China, and my experiences here have shaped the person I have become. For now, though, it's nearly over. And this road trip is a way of saying goodbye.

I had first travelled a section of Route 312, without knowing it, the previous year, while reporting in the wilds of Gansu province, not so very far from Starry Gorge. I had commented to my travelling companion how good the road was for such a remote area, and he had told me that it ran all the way from Shanghai to Kazakhstan.

I filed the idea away in my mind, waiting for an appropriate time to make the journey, and now that time has come. I packed up our home in Beijing and saw my wife and children to the airport. They flew to London ahead of me, to move into a new house and set up our new life. Now I have the summer stretching ahead of me, two months to explore China in all its contradictions, before I too get on a plane for London and leave it all behind.

Liu Qiang the truck driver drags on another cigarette.

'China is weak,' he says with a grimace, reflecting a widely held view among Chinese people, at odds with the country's emerging image in the West. 'We need decades and decades before we can be called a strong country, before we can compete with America.'

'But China is already a completely different country from what it was ten years ago,' I say.

'That's true,' says Liu. 'Never mind ten years ago, compared with five years ago, it's a different country. But we are still a long way behind.'

Liu's buddy, Wang, has now woken up and is sitting behind us on his bunk. It will soon be his turn to take over the driving, and Liu will take a nap. They are dropping me at the exit that leads into the oasis town of Hami.

I ask Liu if he thinks China can make the transition from a one-party state to a democracy.

'No, I don't think China can ever become a democracy,' he says without hesitation. 'Look at Chinese history. There have always been changes in government, but it's just the history of one emperor being replaced by another. The system never changes, just the people at the top. That is how China is.'

'So what's going to happen?' I ask him.

'I don't know,' he says, shrugging his shoulders and raising his voice above the wind that rushes in through the open windows of the truck. 'We Old Hundred Names, we don't know about these kind of things. But I do know that China will never become like your country.'

Soon after that, we reach the exit for Hami. I shake hands with the two drivers, thank them for the ride, and jump down on to the faded, dirty black tarmac. I stand beside the road looking for another vehicle to give me a ride into Hami, with Liu Qiang's words still ringing in my ears. And I watch as he revs his big blue East Wind truck and accelerates slowly away across the desert.

CHINA ROAD

Chapter One

THE PROMISED LAND

The magnetic levitation train that links Shanghai's gleaming new Pudong Airport with the centre of the city glides out of the airport station and within a few minutes has reached 270 miles per hour. Billboards flash past, almost unreadable. Suspended magnetically along a track that runs some fifty feet above the ground, the train scythes towards the centre of China's most modern city. The landscape is surprisingly American – sprawling, low-rise, newly built. The grey bullet leans lazily to the left as it shoots over one of Pudong's main freeways, past cavernous supermarkets and rows of polished new pink and white apartment blocks.

The maglev, as it is known, cost $1.2 billion to build and is the first commercially run train of its kind in the world.

Six weeks before reaching Starry Gorge and the Gobi Desert, I had arrived by plane in Shanghai from Beijing to start my 3,000-mile road trip along Route 312. I'd been too busy to make many preparations and had only a faint idea of who I might talk to when I got here.

Almost before the maglev's twenty-mile journey has begun, it has ended. The train eases into the terminus, not far from the new jungle of high-rise buildings that make up downtown Shanghai. I look at my watch as I heave my rucksack out on to the platform. '*Bu cuo*. Not bad,' I nod to the smartly dressed female ticket collector standing beside the door. 'Eight minutes.'

'Seven minutes, twenty seconds,' she replies, without smiling.

The streets outside the terminus are a cacophony of noise and motion. There is an intangible feel in Shanghai, an urgency, a hope and optimism that hangs in the air all around you from the minute you arrive. People are pushing forward, with their feet and in their heads, building a future, building a country, moving towards some distant, unseen goal.

I've chosen to stay at the slightly down-at-heel but gloriously historic Astor House Hotel, the first foreign hotel to be established in Shanghai, in 1846. The hotel sits at one end of the Bund, the city's original main thoroughfare, which runs along the Huangpu River. The Bund has for more than 150 years been the interface between Shanghai and the arriving *yang ren*, or Ocean People, as foreigners have always been known.

The Astor House Hotel has witnessed the whole sweep of China's emergence into the modern world, from English opium running in the 1840s through the tea dances of polite society in the 1920s to the excesses of Maoist China in the 1960s. The Art Deco ceilings are high, the creaky floorboards are original, and you could drive a small car down its staircases. Ulysses S. Grant stayed here on his world tour in the 1870s. Charlie Chaplin and George Bernard Shaw and Albert Einstein stayed here too, when Shanghai was the place to visit in Asia in the early part of the twentieth century. Urban myth has it that, in the nineteenth century, you could order opium from room service at the Astor House, and that Zhou Enlai, who would go on to be China's premier, hid in the Astor House when he was a Communist agitator in the 1920s. Shanghai, more than most cities, is suffused with urban myths.

Staying here is also personally nostalgic for me. It was the first hotel I ever stayed at in Shanghai, in the summer of 1988. After my year's language study, I was joined by a beautiful classmate from my university in England. We were going to travel around China for three months by train before taking the Trans-Siberian Railway back through the Soviet Union to Europe.

We stayed in the dollar-a-bed dormitories for backpackers at the Astor House (which still exist) that baking hot summer. We wandered the streets, getting a feel for the new Shanghai as the city slowly crept out of its Maoist cocoon. We sat up late into the night, out on the hotel's old wood-panelled balcony, trying to work out China, the universe and, of course, ourselves. That beautiful classmate is now my wife and has just spent the last six years with me in China. As I lift my backpack up to my room alone, I can't help smiling at her in the faded mirror of the rickety old elevator.

Before going for dinner, I pull on my shorts and running shoes and head out for a jog. If this is a time of change for China, it is also (I hope) a time of change for me, and more specifically for my waistline. I'm trying to get rid of the ten (OK, nearer fifteen) extra pounds that six years of Chinese food have deposited about my person. This need has become more urgent because of what has been happening (or not) on the top of my head. After a relatively hirsute youth, the spiteful Hair Gods (curse them) have begun to pull the rug from under (and over) me. So, resolving not to reach forty both fat and bald, I've rashly signed up to run the Beijing Marathon, all twenty-six-plus miles of it, in the autumn. I'd begun training a few miles a day before setting off from Beijing and am hoping to increase the daily distance as I travel throughout the summer, then run the marathon before finally leaving for London.

I set out with great intentions, despite the heat, but make the mistake of running along the pedestrian walkway between the Bund and the river. The area is so crowded that the jog quickly becomes a game of human pinball. One of the occupational hazards of living in China is that there is not much elbow room anywhere (until you reach the Gobi Desert). I attempt a sweaty slalom through the crowd for about two-tenths of a mile, then decide to leave the remaining twenty-six for the morning and stagger ingloriously back to the hotel for a shower.

My first evening in Shanghai is spent on the terrace of a restaurant called New Heights. It sits atop Three on the Bund, one of the row of venerable colonial buildings that have recently been renovated, a few hundred yards along the waterfront from my hotel. Three on the Bund contains the new flagship Giorgio Armani store, an art gallery, an Evian spa and four swanky restaurants, including New Heights at the very top, with its open-air terrace suspended seven stories above the road. From the terrace you have one of the most intoxicating restaurant views in the world, looking down on the ten-lane highway of the Bund and across the Huangpu River at the extraordinary, newly built district of Pudong.

The word *Bund* comes from an old Hindi word meaning an embankment and was brought by the British from India. The area around the Bund was where the first warehouses (called 'go-downs') were built by the opium traders who flocked to China in the mid-nineteenth century to make their fortunes.

The sun that the opium traders watched setting over the Huangpu is setting for me as I arrive on the terrace with my beer. A gentle, warm breeze floats in off the river, wafting in the same scent of opportunity that it did more than 150 years ago. The go-downs and the junks, the clipper ships and the opium dens have given way to the shiny glass and metal of a twenty-first-century city. Fluttering from several of the neighbouring colonial buildings is the red flag of the Chinese Communist Party, drowned out by the buzzing, capitalist scene below. The clock tower of the old waterfront Customs House, built in 1925 and modelled on Big Ben in London, strikes the hour with Chairman Mao's favourite tune, 'The East Is Red.' But the East is no longer red. The plumage of capitalism is multicoloured, and the view along the Bund is a blaze of green, blue and white light, screaming out an elegy to Marxist economics. News reports say that China is suffering a severe shortage of electricity, but you wouldn't know it from the wattage that sizzles into the hot summer night sky here.

Threading its way through the middle of all this is the river itself, the dark, slow-moving Huangpu, dribbling down the chin of the Yangtze Delta from the mouth of the mother river itself. Three massive barges, laden with coal, are pushing upstream, so low in the water that they almost look like submarines. A larger cargo ship blasts out its horn, as if to remind the postmodern diners high above the Bund that the Industrial Revolution is still taking place down below.

Seated among the many foreign businessmen, the wealthy Chinese diners at New Heights are the new elite, who have gained a taste for miso-glazed tuna, zabaglione and Pinot Noir. People talking about mergers and acquisitions, killer applications, and streaming TV on their mobile phones. People who show how far China has come in thirty years of economic reform. Trendy, wealthy, modern Chinese people, greeting one another over cocktails, joking and laughing with all the confidence of a room full of wealthy New York diners. From the kowtow to the air kiss in less than a century.

Ask any of these people about China's future, and there would be no question. Their natural Chinese modesty might prevent boasting or gloating about China's potential greatness, but for the nouveaux riches of Shanghai, the future is bright.

New York City makes a good comparison. Beijing is Washington, DC, a capital city, too obsessed with politics to be at the forefront of commerce. Shanghai is Manhattan, although in many ways it is Manhattan in about 1910 – a boomtown with immigrants flooding in. There are roughly 13 million people in Shanghai (New York in 1910 had about 5 million). As in New York a hundred years ago, many of these people have just arrived from somewhere else.

There is no Statue of Liberty to welcome them here, but as I stand looking out across the corrugated river to the Elysian Fields of Pudong, it seems to me there should be. Or at least a Statue of Opportunity. Since the city started growing as a foreign trading post, in the 1840s, Shanghai has always been the Mother of Exiles. The difference from New York is that here the exiles are internal, not coming from an old world to build a new, but trying to turn the old world *into* a new one, and that is a much harder task. They are refugees not from ancient lands across the ocean, from Dublin or Kiev or Palermo, but from inland. They are the huddled masses from Hefei and Xinyang and Lanzhou, the cities I will be visiting on my journey along Route 312.

One shiny new office tower on the other side of the river has become a huge TV screen, with advertisements and government propaganda alternately lighting up the entire side of the building, one message replaced five seconds later by another.

Welcome to Shanghai. Tomorrow will be even more beautiful.
1,746 more days until the Shanghai World Expo.
Sexual equality is a basic policy of our country.
Eat Dove chocolate.

After dinner, I wander slowly back down the Bund, avoiding the legion of beggars loitering at the door of the restaurant, heading across the road to the walkway on the waterfront where I had tried to jog earlier in the evening. You can keep Fifth Avenue, and Piccadilly, and the Champs-Elysées. This is my favourite urban walk in all the world. There is nothing quite like it, especially on a hot summer evening. The energy, the atmosphere, the hope, the possibilities, the past, the future, it is all here. Downtown Shanghai makes you feel that finally, after centuries of trying, China may be on the edge of greatness once again.

Thousands of tourists, Chinese and Western, are milling along the pedestrian walkway, their flashbulbs popping like fireflies in the half-light. The westerners are doing what westerners always do in Shanghai, trying to re-create the past as they snap photos of the old colonial buildings. The Chinese are also doing what Chinese people always do, trying to *escape* the past as they snap their photos in the opposite direction, gazing out across the river towards the dazzling ziggurats of Pudong.

Shanghai had been slow to emerge from its socialist slumber in the 1980s. It did not really take off until a group of the city's politicians took over at the top of the Communist Party after the crushing of the pro-democracy demonstrations in Tiananmen Square in June 1989. Then, in the 1990s, Shanghai's economy soared, as the hope and idealism of the 1980s were consumed upon the bonfire of nihilism and cash.

Pudong was just old docks and paddy fields until the early 1990s. Now it has come to embody the modern Chinese zeitgeist, 200 square miles of offices, apartments and shopping malls to add to the superlatives of a city that already boasts the world's fastest train, the world's highest hotel and some of the world's tallest buildings. When you look out at Pudong, it's easy to believe that the nine most powerful men in China (who make up the Standing Committee of the Communist Party Politburo) are all engineers.

I walk the length of the Bund, then cross back under the road, past the buskers and the beggars in the underpass, towards the entrance of the grande dame of the Bund, the Peace Hotel. Formerly known as the Cathay, it was built in 1929 by the scion of one of pre-war Shanghai's famous families of Iraqi Jews, the property magnate Victor Sassoon. The centre of social gravity shifted in the 1930s from the Astor House around the corner to the Cathay. Its jazz was even more jumping, its rooms even more Art Deco a-go-go. Noël Coward, struck down by flu during a stay in 1930, wrote *Private Lives* in one of the suites at the Cathay.

'Roleksu, Roleksu.'

A voice emerges from the shadows, uttering the normal greeting of the hucksters who loiter outside the Peace Hotel as they flash fake watches from their pockets for your perusal. China is, of course, the world centre for fake goods. Gucci bags, Rolex watches, Ralph Lauren shirts are all yours for a few pounds. If it's clear you don't want any of these, the pitch suddenly changes direction.

'Ladies bar, ladies bar,' whispers the man in a broken English without apostrophes. 'You want go ladies bar?'

Communist orthodoxy, and with it Communist morality, have been lifted, and anything goes now. Usually, a few choice words in Chinese persuade the hucksters that you've been here before and you really don't want any of their fake goods or seedy nightclubs. But tonight, as this particularly persistent guy goes through the list of what he has, and I respond with a crisp *bu yao* (not want!) to each one, he eventually comes up with one I haven't heard before.

'*Gol-fu,*' he says. '*Gol-fu.*'

I stop to look him squarely in the face, and can smell the garlic on his breath.

'What?'

'*Gol-fu, gol-fu,*' he repeats, encouraged by my interest, and he points eagerly to his friend, standing beside the entrance to the hotel. There, lined up against the wall, are three complete sets of Callaway golf clubs. Golfing friends inform me you can hardly tell the difference between fakes such as these and real ones. His price? Two thousand yuan for the whole lot, about $250 for a set of golf clubs that would cost at least $2,000 in the West.

I pass the Peace Hotel and head straight on back towards the Astor House. Opposite is the park on whose entrance was supposedly hung the legendary sign of the colonial era: NO DOGS OR CHINESE ALLOWED. (Or is that, too, just another urban myth?)

Then, finally, as I walk to the end of the Bund, I notice an entrance that I have never seen before. It is slightly hidden in the shadow of the elevated motorway that now rises. No buildings inside are visible from the road, but a small sign beside the gate proclaims that this is Number 33, The Bund, the site of the former British consulate. A driveway sweeps back from the gateway and disappears into a clump of trees. It is completely dark, and there is no sign of life except for two night watchmen in a tiny hut beside the gate.

'Can I go in?' I ask them.

'No, sorry,' replies one, a slim man with a shock of black hair and a large mole on his cheek.

'I only want to look. I'm English.'

Even though we poisoned them with opium, stole their land, carved up their country, patronised, humiliated and half-enslaved them, Old Hundred Names, the ordinary Chinese people, are astonishingly courteous and accommodating to foreigners, yes, even to the British. It never ceases to amaze me. And this man is persuaded. 'All right, then,' he says. 'I'll show you very quickly.'

Built in 1872, there are two buildings hidden up the driveway behind the clump of trees, the consulate building and the consul's residence, joined by a zigzag covered walkway. This was for decades one of the centres of colonial rule in Shanghai in the late nineteenth and early twentieth centuries.

The buildings now look run-down and shabby in the shadow of modern Shanghai. The watchman's flashlight dances off the squat two-storey structures, with their colonial-style balconies and green shutters covering huge arched windows. I ask him to shine his light inside, on to the dust and emptiness of the rooms. Suddenly it is one of those surreal moments when, with the buzz of a twenty-first-century evening all around, I can almost hear the nineteenth-century laughter and conversation, the clink of champagne glasses and the braying of the Victorians, the ghosts of colonial Shanghai. So much of what China is today is linked to its need to wipe out the humiliation of those years, most especially the humiliation at the hands of the British.

The two nations had first collided in 1793, when a British envoy named Lord George Macartney arrived in China with a boatful of gifts to request an end to Chinese restrictions on trade. He annoyed the Chinese immediately by refusing to perform the kowtow before the Qianlong emperor, which would have meant prostrating himself nine times and touching his forehead to the floor. Finally granted an audience, he was summarily dismissed by the emperor with a letter for King George III that said much about how China saw itself at that time:

We have perused the text of your state message, and the wording expresses your earnestness. From it your sincere humility and obedience can clearly be seen. It is admirable, and we fully approve . . . Now you, O King, have presented various objects to the throne . . . We have never valued ingenious articles, nor do we have the slightest need of your country's manufactures.

Of course, such a document was like a red rag to the British bull, and British traders spent the next forty years trying to open the China market. They did so by bringing opium from India to trade for the tea, porcelain and other luxuries they wanted. British opium poisoned Chinese society, adding to the many internal tensions that were already developing across the Chinese empire. Beijing's objections to the British trade sparked the First Opium War, which ended with China soundly defeated. Beijing was forced to sign the Treaty of Nanjing in 1842, which ceded the island of Hong Kong to the British and forced open five ports to the foreigners. One of them was a small fishing village called Shanghai. In these cities, the Ocean People were ceded land, known as concessions, on which to build their houses and consulates and churches, where Chinese law did not apply. The area where the former British consulate stands was part of the International Concession of Shanghai.

The Treaty of Nanjing was the symbolic start of China's long and tortuous road to integration with the rest of the world, as the Western powers slowly began to prise the door open. Waves of Ocean People – missionaries and libertines, adventurers and businessmen – arrived in the ports, seeking their future or fleeing their past. Shanghai grew up in the image of a Western city. Its name in the Western mind reeked of the opportunities and excesses, the sensuousness and mystery of the East. In the Chinese mind, by contrast, Shanghai bore the stench of humiliation and contamination by the West. It was the bastard child of China.

Everything the Chinese did after 1842, from initial moderate efforts at reform, through the revolution that overthrew the imperial system in 1912 to the adoption of Communism and its final victory in 1949, was about reclaiming Chinese land from the colonialists and restoring China's greatness. Now, more than a century and a half later, that is finally starting to happen.

The watchman grins at my interest in the history that drips from the old consulate. He doesn't care about this place. What is it to him but run-down buildings that represent China's past humiliation? Perhaps he thinks they should be knocked down. Why not put up something better, something modern? A few months later, I hear the site is being refurbished by one of Hong Kong's venerable hotel groups, to be turned into the Shanghai Peninsula Hotel.

We wander, following the beam of his flashlight, back down the long driveway.

'Sorry about all that stuff with the opium, and the whole colonisation thing,' I say to him. 'We're not very proud of all that, you know.'

'*Mei shi*.' He laughs. 'Don't worry. That's history. You can't change history.'

Chapter Two

DISLOCATION

The gnomes in the neon mines of Borneo must be working overtime to keep Shanghai lit.

Apart from Las Vegas (and possibly Tokyo), I have rarely seen so much hot, tubed colour. Walk along Nanjing Road in downtown Shanghai, and you are blinded by every kind of neon sign, the louder, the brighter, the better as far as Chinese businesses are concerned.

Quite apart from the many types of goods and foods being advertised, all that neon is flashing out some very important messages about modern China. First of all, plain and simple, there is the amazing consumer boom that is going on in cities large and small. When I first arrived, in 1987, many everyday items could still be bought only with ration tickets, and you couldn't even purchase milk over the counter. Now, anything you can buy in the West can also be bought in a Chinese city such as Shanghai. You want an MP3 player? You can buy an iPod or any other brand in any department store. Food processor? Exercise bike? It's all here. Caviar? Champagne? KitKats? Special K? You name it. Stores in China's coastal cities stock them all.

The second thing that is noticeable as you walk around a city such as Shanghai is rather obvious, but not to be underestimated in the broader context of the nation's history. China is at peace. For the first half of the twentieth century, it was in chaos – collapsing internally, and being devoured by fierce colonial wolves. Peace seemed finally to arrive with the Communist takeover in 1949, but the country then set about devouring itself, amid the madness of Mao's political campaigns. Now, though, the watchwords of the Communist Party are peace internationally and stability domestically. Its policy of stability *über alles* causes many problems, but it also provides an environment in which many can prosper.

And finally, the third thing lit up by all this neon is that urban Chinese people now have space to live without government interference in many areas of the lives. After the killing of the students in Tiananmen Square in 1989, the Communist Party leaders made an unwritten, unspoken deal with the people of China: stay out of politics, and you can do anything you want. During the 1990s, for the first time in more than forty years (or perhaps four thousand), the Chinese government began to retreat from people's everyday lives.

This was a very clever move by the Party. The tiny bird cage in which Chinese people had previously lived became an aviary. You cannot yet fly up into the clear blue sky, and they can still catch you if they want to, but there is plenty of room to fly around. After more than forty years of being forced to participate in politics, the majority of Chinese were only too happy to disengage from it completely and get on with the business of making money.

Now stop just a moment, and look at those three developments from a different angle.

First of all, yes, there is a consumer boom, but the majority of people have no access to it. If in the US you need money to get power, in China you need power to get money. China's prosperity today is just a patina of wealth, accessible mainly to the corrupt and the very fortunate at the top, which disguises a seething mass of urban social problems, such as unemployment, crime and outdated housing. And don't even mention the countryside. Just go a mile from the neon of the Bund and Nanjing Road and you will find thousands of people living on $40 per month, severance pay from their former jobs at now-defunct factories. They have no health insurance, and if they become really sick, all they can do is go home and die.

Sections of the big department stores are permanently empty, as are many of the new office blocks and shopping malls, built as a result of corrupt deals, giving a veneer of affluence that makes the city look more prosperous than it is. For every member of the emergent middle class who drives her family to Pizza Hut in her new Volkswagen, there are perhaps a hundred who can barely afford a bicycle.

Second, yes, China is at peace with most of its neighbours and at home, but it is an uneasy peace. By the Party's own estimates, there are more than two hundred incidents of rural unrest *every day*, many of them the result of the economic inequalities that have emerged since reform began. Then there's the anger felt by many Chinese citizens at the bribes and extortion that go on throughout the one-party state, against which they have no recourse because there is no independent legal system.

Looking further afield, there are more than seven hundred missiles, not to mention plenty of bellicose rhetoric from Beijing, aimed at the island of Taiwan, which China claims as its own. China keeps Tibet and its Muslim northwest from seceding only through sheer brute force. It enforces claims over islands in the South China Sea by building military outposts on coral reefs that are nowhere near Chinese territory and maintains relations with nations such as Iran, North Korea and Sudan, which are condemned by many Western countries for their nuclear activities and their human rights records.

And third, again it is true that there has been some loosening of social controls, but Chinese people still enjoy no protection from their own government, and there is nothing even approaching a functioning system of checks and balances on Communist Party power in China.

Religious groups, such as 'house church' Christians, who refuse to be part of the government-sponsored church, and members of the spiritual group Falun Gong, are still persecuted relentlessly by the Communist Party, and any case that even sees the inside of a courtroom is manipulated by the Party, which appoints all the judges. Chinese courts have a conviction rate of over 99 per cent. Beijing still runs a system of labour camps, to which any member of society can be sent, at any time. Tens of thousands of people are still sentenced to 'reform through labour' every year.

Everything that I have just written, from both points of view, is true. It just depends on how you look at it. Is the glass half empty, or is it half full? How foreigners see China often has as much to do with their own characters and their own prejudices (or the character and prejudices of the reporter who writes the article or book they read) as it has to do with the reality on the ground. For every fact that is true about China, the opposite is almost always true as well, somewhere in the country.

This dichotomy has led to a division among China watchers between the panda huggers, who say China is doing great and won't be a threat to anyone (while admitting, of course, that there are a few peripheral problems), and the dragon slayers, who say China is a threat to everyone and needs to be contained (while noting that there have been a few small improvements).

What do I think? It depends which day you ask me. China messes with my head on a daily basis. One day I think that it really is going to take over the world, and that the Chinese government is doing the most extraordinary thing the planet has ever witnessed. The World Bank says China has lifted 400 million people out of poverty since 1978. That's more than the entire population of South America.

The next day it will all seem built on sand and I expect it all to come tumbling down around us. I'll be disgusted at the way the Communist Party treats its people, and shocked at the sheer cost of it all, the human cost, which seems acceptable to the government in everything that it does.

To my mind, though, one of the key things is choice. Whatever our own prejudices, we simply cannot deny that there is more choice in China now than there used to be. And I am of the opinion that where there is choice, there is often change for the better, and that includes the possibility of political change. You can now choose where you work in China. You can choose whom you marry. You can choose paper or plastic to wrap your groceries, full fat or skimmed milk for your cappuccino. It's not happening tomorrow, but I think that once you allow people to choose their pizza toppings, sooner or later they are going to want to choose their political leaders.

'Shanghai has 300 miles of elevated motorway.' My taxi driver has a glint in his eye as he hits the slip road leading up to one of the city's most modern roads. 'How many miles of elevated motorway are there in New York?'

I tell him I don't have that fact at my fingertips. He gets beyond the slow-moving traffic in the centre of town and accelerates at a crazy speed westwards, a sort of Fu Manchu does *Blade Runner*, which has me reaching for a rear seat belt that isn't there. I notice, as one notices bizarre things in times of danger, that on the back of the headrest of the front seat is an advertisement for breast enlargement surgery.

'Don't worry,' he shouts back at me, with a grin. '*Anquan diyi*. Safety first.'

If you survive the driving, the roads in Shanghai are extraordinary. A series of elevated motorways race through the city at varying heights above the ground. Swathes of beautiful colonial villas had to be demolished to make way for some of these roads. Some of the villas that remain now stand just yards, sometimes inches away from the six-lane motorway, kissing the road as it slashes their face.

I'm heading to meet the host of a radio phone-in show, whose name is Ye Sha. Her show, called *Shanghai State of Mind*, goes out from midnight till 2 a.m. every night, and has been popular among the city's residents for years. You can call Ye Sha (pronounced *yeah shah*) with any problem and ask her advice, live on air, and thousands of people do.

I want to talk to her about the huge dislocation that is going on in people's minds. Shanghai may make the visitor feel that China is on the verge of greatness, but the speed of the changes has left psychological and spiritual confusion in many people's minds. After the convulsions of the Maoist years, and now the convulsions of the reaction *against* the Maoist years, there can be few countries more in need of therapy than China. Yet for most Chinese there are few places to turn for refuge and advice amid the blizzard of change. Untethered from both Confucian and Communist morality, many young people find Ye Sha is the closest thing they have to a guiding voice not laden down with parental disapproval (although she knows how to dish out some of that when necessary). A friend had given me her number, so I called her on arriving in Shanghai and set up a meeting over dinner.

We meet in Pizza Hut and order Diet Cokes and pepperoni pizza. She is probably in her late thirties, with a round face and thoughtful eyes, and wearing a floral blouse and white linen trousers. She tells me as we sit munching on pizza that she is planning her first trip to Europe. I ask her about her radio show.

'Generally speaking, callers to my programme have three types of problems,' she says. 'First, emotional problems, mainly to do with love. Second, work problems and relationships at work. And third, relationships within the family.

'I started hosting the show soon after I graduated from college, in 1992. At that time, the main emotional issue was people starting to have extra-marital affairs. They knew it was wrong, and they wanted to know what they should do once it had happened. Now, there are even more people having affairs, but many of these people don't really think it's wrong. They think it's reasonable, and understandable.'

Her tone is measured and mature, and as she nibbles her pizza, I can imagine why people would want to call her on air for advice.

'There has been a huge change, especially among women. Women want their independence. They think they have the right to do what they want. And now, they have so many choices of lifestyle, and choices of things to enjoy.'

Ye Sha says many people now believe that if there's no law against it then it's all right. To many in the cities, she says, morality – a sense of what is right and wrong – doesn't matter any more. 'I think a lot of young people are simply confused by all the change. They call up and say they are unhappy, but they can't even articulate why.'

This matters to Ye Sha a great deal. Suddenly she becomes quite emotional. Her bottom lip quivers. She stutters as she speaks, as though she were talking about the death of someone close to her, which in a strange way perhaps she is.

'People, especially young people, are *mishi le*. They are lost.' She repeats the word 'lost' in English.

There is a pause while she regathers herself.

'Why, after all that Mao did to ruin people's lives, do you sometimes hear older people reminiscing fondly about the Maoist era?' she asks. 'Because, despite the problems, there was still a morality, and an ethical framework to life. There was right, and there was wrong. Now . . . what is right, and what is wrong?'

Ye Sha doesn't have any easy answers, but she is trying to raise the questions for a deracinated generation, which she says is drifting in a moral vacuum. Having struggled for a century to escape the strait-jacket of family ties and social obligations, some young people in China's cities are now foundering in the isolation of individualism.

'And people can't keep up with the machines,' she says, as we finish our pizza and prepare to leave. 'The previous pace of life was too slow, for sure. But now it's too fast. In traditional China, people were taught *zenme zuo ren*, how to be a person. In fact, we emphasised it too much. The morality, the rituals, the ethics. Now it isn't emphasised enough. No one knows how to be a person anymore. We are training technicians. We are not training people.'

Months later, I come across a quote from the 1990s by a famous China scholar, Myron Cohen of Columbia University, that seems to sum up what Ye Sha is saying very well.

For much of China's population, being Chinese is culturally much easier today than it ever was in the past, for this identification no longer involves commonly accepted standards of behavior or belief. Existentially, however, being Chinese is far more problematic, for now it is as much a quest as it is a condition.

*

Shanghai consumes me for four whole days. I could have stayed four weeks. I meet lawyers who are working to build China's legal system, I meet businesswomen who do all their deals on the golf course, and I meet young entrepreneurs at an Internet start-up. I meet a fifty-year-old former peasant who spent the first fifteen years of his adult life planting rice, then travelled along Route 312 in 1986 and made millions in the construction industry. He now owns four apartments, and his daughter goes to college abroad. I visit a factory, typical of so many along China's coast, packed with hundreds of rural women working in Dickensian conditions. They will never be millionaires, but they are sending half their salaries home to their villages and helping to spread some wealth inland.

I visit the old Jewish ghetto, to which more than 20,000 European Jews escaped in the late 1930s because Shanghai – open, international Shanghai – was the only place in the world that didn't require them to have a visa. And I meet a diplomat who tells me the city is now transforming itself again, moving away from manufacturing to become more of a service economy. Everywhere, people seem to have put the horrors of Maoism behind them. Those years are rarely mentioned. Everywhere, there is an energy and a focus on the future that seems to spring from the knowledge of how many years, and how many lives, were wasted.

On Sunday I attend a service at Mo-En Church on Tibet Road, built in the 1920s, when Shanghai was still a centre of missionary activity. As I climb the stairs to find a seat in the gallery, I am greeted by an old Chinese lady with silvery hair and sparkling eyes, who says 'Good morning' to me in strong, clear English. I want to stop and ask her, 'What have you *been* through in your life? What, in God's name, have you *seen*?' But I just smile back at her and continue up the stairs. The church is packed with people.

I sit in McDonald's and observe the new middle classes bringing their chubby only children to gorge on Big Macs and McNuggets. The parents sit, watching their children eat, perhaps subliminally hoping that by bringing their child to McDonald's, that same child may be swept up into the stream of globalised culture that is coursing through urban China, and somehow end up at Harvard Business School.

I wander down the back alleys in the poorer parts of town, looking for the flip side of all the optimism and the downside of all the globalisation, looking for some angry people, some losers in the economic food chain. I find plenty of people who lament the wealth gap, as they grind out a living in their low-paid jobs on the building sites, in the kitchens, in the markets of the city. But even in the most squalid alleyways, where people live crammed into tiny, dirty rooms, you hear the story over and over again: 'Yes, life is hard, and our work is hard, but it's a million times better than life in the countryside.'

That's the problem with Shanghai. You don't really see many of China's problems. Of course, you notice that the maglev from the airport is no more than a quarter full at best. And you notice there are some empty stores in the shiny new malls, and an increasing number of beggars on the streets. But the speed and the glitz and the sheer exhilaration of being in the legendary city mean that Shanghai blinds the visitor to what lies beyond. If you only visited Shanghai, you would leave thinking that China is undoubtedly bound for greatness.

One afternoon I visit Lu Xun Park in northern Shanghai, a beautiful oasis of green, that honours China's most famous writer of the early twentieth century. Lu Xun (pronounced *loo shoon*) is buried there in a large mausoleum. Nearly a hundred years ago, he was at the forefront of trying to diagnose China's problems, and prescribe a remedy. He wrote searingly about the weaknesses of Chinese culture, and of the Chinese character. He wrote of antiquity and modernity and tried to find a path between the two.

Lu Xun's literary vehicle of choice was the short story, and his most famous selection came out in 1921, the same year that the Communist Party of China was formed. Its title was *Na Han*, which means 'Call to Arms'. Not a military call, but a metaphorical one, a cultural one, a call to wake up from the arrogance and conservatism that the Qianlong Emperor embodied in his response to Lord Macartney, and which was still, more than a hundred years later, preventing China from waking up to the need for deep psychological and cultural change. In the introduction to *Na Han* he wrote this paragraph, describing his homeland and its culture:

Imagine an iron house without windows, absolutely indestructible, with many people fast asleep inside who will soon die of suffocation. But you

know since they will die in their sleep, they will not feel the pain of death.
Now if you cry aloud to wake a few of the lighter sleepers, making those
unfortunate few suffer the agony of irrevocable death, do you think you
are doing them a good turn? But if a few awake, you can't say there is no
hope of destroying the iron house.

Thus Lu Xun gave literary form to a call to arms that has echoed
down through the twentieth century and into the twenty-first.
The stories in *Na Han* all followed this theme: that the Chinese
lived in an iron house of Confucianism and needed to escape.
They needed to wake up and not just overthrow the emperor
and change the political system, but change their whole way of
thinking.

There are many problems and imperfections in China's recent
urban development. But the fact that Shanghai has the world's first
commercial magnetic levitation train can be traced directly back to
the call to arms issued by Lu Xun in 1921, and to other writers like
him, who wrote about China's need for a psychological revolution.
It is the logical progression of those calls. The whole of Shanghai's
development, the roads, the skyscrapers, the high-speed Internet,
they are all answers to those calls. Finally, finally, after a century,
Shanghai is rising, as China is rising, on the back of a century of
humiliation before 1949, and then a half-century of Communist
chaos that came after it. The question of whether China will open
to the world seems to have been answered forever with a resound-
ing 'yes'. But what a tortuous, painful, winding road it has been to
get here, and what a road there is still to travel.

The day before I leave Shanghai I meet two young members of the
Communist Party. I want to ask them about what it means these
days to be Party members, and to find out if they are as confused as
the radio host Ye Sha suggests.

We meet in Starbucks, not far from the house where the Chinese Communist Party (usually referred to as the CCP) was founded in 1921. The old house has been turned into a museum — actually more of a shrine to the Communist Party — but it is largely empty, located as it is next to one of Shanghai's most popular modern shrines, a shopping mall called New Heaven and Earth.

The Party members, both women in their twenties, are typical of the smart, connected younger generation, a million miles from the militant Red Guards of their parents' generation. Both have chosen English names.

Lucy works for a large multinational corporation. She has long dark hair and a polite, responsible air that suggests she might have been head girl at school. She is a study in modern urban confidence and success. She speaks excellent English and clearly thinks deeply about important subjects.

'Yes, Communism collapsed in Eastern Europe, but that was because they weren't doing it right,' she says. 'I know, you westerners think that after capitalism, there will still be capitalism. We Chinese think that after this stage of capitalism, there might eventually be Communism.'

I open my eyes wide. 'Really? You really believe that?'
She nods.

Emily looks over. She is smaller, with thick dark hair and big eyes. 'Many people grow up in this educational environment,' she says, which I take to mean that she thinks Lucy has been brainwashed. 'I believe less than Lucy,' she says. 'I'm quite unsure about it all.'

'Why did you join the CCP?' I ask them.

'My grades were good. I was a responsible student. I have no regrets at all,' says Lucy. 'I believe this Party can bring us a stable society.'

'Now, the Communist Party members have nothing to do with ideology, they are simply the best students,' explains Emily. 'It is considered an honour to join the Party, and all the best students are asked to join. That was the same with me.'

I point out the irony of this, which Emily has already seen. But Lucy is still in earnest. She is the perfect example of how the best-educated people are often the most pro-government.

'We need to study what the leaders are thinking,' she says. 'We feel good about studying this. It's good. And as for Communism, you should understand it in your own way. It means you should be a good and helpful member of society.'

Lucy then relates how, at a recent meeting of the Communist Party members within the big American multinational where she works, two books were handed out. One was published by the Communist Party and contained all the latest Party directives. The other was a company book on how to be a better sales-person.

Lucy and Emily are typical members of the new, young, urban middle class. They are not out on the streets demanding more democracy, as their predecessors in the late 1980s were. They are enjoying the fruits of prosperity. They support the Party because they say it has given them opportunities they could not otherwise have had. Although they are very patriotic, they are not ideological in the least. They are individuals. They believe in romantic love. They have chosen their own jobs, their own boyfriends, their own lifestyles. The pursuit of happiness has been deeply enshrined in their minds, if not yet in their country's constitution. In short, they are not unlike two young women in any country in the Western world. I put to them what the radio show host Ye Sha says, that the young generation of China is lost and confused and doesn't know what to believe in or how to behave.

'Why do you say that about China?' asks Lucy. 'What about the West? Do Western people have anything to believe in?

'I'm not lost,' she continues. 'I don't believe in Jesus or Buddha, but I believe in self-struggle, an effort to improve myself and my country. You don't have to have a faith to have a meaningful life.'

Again Emily, the more pensive of the two, is not so sure. 'I had a period when I felt lost, confused, when I was in college,' she says. 'Now I've come through it. But there is some confusion generally among young people. For example, everyone watches Western TV programmes, like *Friends*, like *Desperate Housewives*, and we're totally aware of how people live in the West. Lots of girls, for instance, want to live with their boyfriends, but that clashes with their parents' wishes.'

'But our generation is completely different from our parents' generation,' says Lucy. 'It's a different world now. We have to look after ourselves.'

Emily nods. 'We are the *ziwo yidai*, the Me Generation,' she says, a little wistfully. 'We believe only in ourselves.'

My final interaction with the Me Generation of Shanghai occurs that evening. While searching for the International Cemetery in the west of the city, I stumble across Shanghai's first branch of the restaurant chain Hooters.

Hooters, for the uninitiated, is a chain of restaurants in the US whose waitresses tend to be somewhat underdressed and, shall we say, rather buxom. But to make sure no one thinks the name is referring to anything risqué, the symbol of the restaurant is a large owl. Consequently, the name in Chinese has been translated as 'The American Owl Restaurant' (there are some double entendres that just don't translate).

Having never dined at Hooters in the US I felt slightly sheepish stepping inside, believing it to be the home of stag parties and sad single men. The only people looking as sheepish as me, though, are the other single white guys, of whom there are not many. Everyone else is having a fantastic time. Three

Japanese women are there with their children. Some Chinese guys seem to have brought their dates; a couple of businessmen appear to be discussing some kind of deal, oblivious to the Hooters girls in their skimpy orange shorts and skimpier white T-shirts. There seem to be far fewer sexual overtones than you might find in an American Hooters. Somehow, the whole thing has been transformed into a rather wholesome family dining experience.

It's somebody's birthday, so the Hooters girls do a little dance, calling for some audience participation, which I manage to avoid, and soon two sensible, suited Chinese businessmen are standing on chairs waving their arms in the air alongside the scantily clad Hooters girls.

The young woman serving my table appears to be the only one of the ten or so waitresses who doesn't seem comfortable, nervously smiling at the customers she is serving. We get chatting as she serves me my burger and fries. She is from the city of Wuhan, 400 miles inland.

'Do your parents know you're working here?' I ask her.

'No, they don't,' she replies with a nervous laugh. '*Tamen bu hui lijie.* They wouldn't understand.'

'Don't worry,' I tell her. 'My wife doesn't know I'm here. She wouldn't understand either.'

Chapter Three

THINGS FLOW

The next morning I climb into a taxi at the Astor House Hotel, and tell the driver to take me to the start of Route 312, in the far west of the city. It takes about an hour. I have that feeling I always have in Shanghai, of being sad to leave. But at the same time I'm excited to be getting on the road at last. Who will I meet today? Where will I stay? I have a few ideas, but have arranged very little in advance.

Route 312 makes an inauspicious start. The road creeps out from under the shadow of Shanghai's outer ring road, a huge, elevated motorway that encircles the city. A slip road brings traffic down from the ring road on to 312 as it emerges from among the forest of concrete pillars that support the motorway. Two men in white coats are standing giving haircuts for fifty cents on the traffic island around the pillars.

I get out of the taxi, hitch my rucksack on to my back and start to walk. As I wander along the pavement of the first segment of the road, I am approached by three women, clearly from the country-side. Each has a small baby strapped to her back.

'DVD,' they mutter, as they gather around me. 'DVD.'

They hold out a selection of DVDs with pornographic scenes printed on them. I shake my head and move on. Another young woman holding a baby is begging, the story of her woes laid out on a piece of paper in front of where she sits on the pavement. Her

31

husband has leukaemia and has no money for treatment. No one is throwing money into her paper cup.

The two-lane highway rapidly gathers confidence as it leaves behind the shadow of the motorway. Beside it runs a bicycle lane, separated from the main thoroughfare. Beside the bicycle lane lies a broad pavement and behind that a long row of stores, continuing along the roadside as far as the eye can see. There's a carpet store, a car showroom selling Volkswagens, a huge furniture store called Homemart and a branch of Kentucky Fried Chicken, of course. (There are already a thousand branches of KFC in China. A new one opens every other day.)

The road itself is a crazy mélange of mobile humanity. Every type of human transport is here, heading in both directions, as though a conference on the history of road transport is being held somewhere and representatives of every era are hastening to attend. It's like one of those evolutionary diagrams of man, emerging from the transportational ooze. People walking with their knuckles scraping the ground (not really), a scavenger pulling a three-wheeled cart, ringing a bell and shouting out to no one in particular. Men and women on simple, rickety bicycles, going barely faster than the pedestrians. Men and women, helmetless, zipping past on little scooters. Men and women with helmets on, clearly further up the evolutionary chain, buzzing in and out of the traffic on bigger scooters. Cars, pick-ups, cement-mixers, local buses, long-distance coaches, superdeluxe long-distance coaches are all here too. Then, pulling up at a traffic light is the *Homo erectus* of this Darwinian scene. A shiny white 7-series BMW. Where are you going, Mr BMW Man? And where did you get the money to buy that car?

Route 312 itself used to be the main road west from Shanghai, but for decades it was little used, because only government officials had cars, and most freight travelled westwards by rail. It is not a motorway, but what's known in Chinese as a *guodao*, a national road, with turnings off to residential areas or stores, just like a normal, busy city road. Since the frenzy of road-building began in the 1990s, the equivalent of UK motorways have now been built, and one of them, known as the A11, runs almost parallel to Route 312. But its tolls are high, so Route 312 is still by far the busier road.

Beside the entrance to a huge wholesale vegetable market, two Tibetan women are selling jewellery out of a suitcase. Nearby, Muslim Chinese belonging to the Uighur ethnic group from northwest China stand at long charcoal stoves, turning over lines of *yang rou chuanr*, lamb kebabs, sprinkled with bright red spices. And of course ethnic Chinese traders are here too, dominating the scene, running the small stores beside the road or selling shoes or clothes or belts or ties, laid out on pieces of cloth on the pavement, selling ice creams and candy, and pineapple slices hygienically placed inside small plastic bags to protect them from the fumes of the road. A sign on the eastbound lane says PEOPLE'S SQUARE 15 KM. Nine miles to the centre of Shanghai. In the other direction a sign announces my first destination. KUNSHAN 48 KM (30 miles).

A truck goes by with the name of a company painted on the side in large Chinese characters: RUI XUN WU LIU, it says, which means 'Rui Xun Logistics'. A few minutes later I see another truck, this one belonging to Wang Jing Logistics. Every few minutes another 'logistics' company truck drives past. It's the boom business in today's China: removals, relocation, moving anything of any sort is covered by *logistics*. The word in Chinese, such a wonderfully logical language, is *wu liu*, which translates literally as 'things flow'.

In the Western mind, a road trip conjures up images of the 1950s and 1960s, of Jack Kerouac, of beatniks and hippies hitting the road to find themselves, or lose themselves, whichever they needed to do. In China, travelling by highway is a very new phenomenon, and Chinese people have not yet fallen in love with the open road. Rather, it is a marriage of convenience. They are travelling mainly out of necessity, to find work, in order to feed themselves and their families. To come up with a more appropriate comparison, you have to travel back to the 1930s and the Okies of John Steinbeck novels, fleeing westwards from the Dust Bowl to California. Most road trips in China these days are still more John Steinbeck than Jack Kerouac, and in celebration of the fact, I have brought along a copy of Steinbeck's classic *The Grapes of Wrath*, which is tucked into the top pocket of my backpack.

Tian Yabin has never read Steinbeck or Kerouac. He's a 27-year-old advertising executive, who says he earns about $6,000 per month. That's about sixty times the wages of the average factory worker in Shanghai. He has a shaved head and a slightly squeaky voice, and he smokes a pipe, giving him an air of eccentricity unusual even among the nouveaux riches of Shanghai. Tian's friends call him Tintin, after the French cartoon character. Well educated and well connected, Tian has flourished in the new China. He has bought his own apartment, travels abroad for holidays, and keeps up with the latest technology. But his real passion is his Japanese-made jeep.

I've found Tintin through the Shanghai Off-roader Jeep Club, of which he is a member, and have hooked up with him just near the start of Route 312. Each weekend, the Jeep Club members get together and drive out of the city for a day or two, exploring the surrounding area. Our convoy today is only three cars. The week before there were eight. As well as Tintin, the group includes another twenty-something jeep owner named Little Liu, a software programmer whom everyone calls Camel, and a fifty-something businessman called Old Zhang. Liu's jeep has an engine problem, so he is riding with Tintin and me.

Most of the movement along Route 312 is eastwards, towards Shanghai, as migrants flow into the cities to find work. These four fine representatives of the new Chinese middle class are going against the flow, heading west.

Tintin weaves in and out of the traffic, as if he's trying to lose the others, not lead them. As we move further out of Shanghai, factories line the road. This is the city's industrial hinterland, which fuels its growth, pollutes its air and keeps the price of consumer goods around the world ridiculously low. Everything is made here, everything that the West buys – from Barbie dolls and Christmas tree lights, trainers and clothing, to laptops and mobile phones.

Entrances to factories, showrooms and markets flash past in a blur of dull industrial grey. The Xijiao Wood Market, the Donghua Building Materials Market, the Fengbang Horticultural Village are selling everything you might need to build a country from scratch. One store is simply selling pillars. Ionic, Doric or Corinthian, take your pick. All along the road are yawning building sites where more factories will soon spring up.

There is so much earth being moved on these vast construction sites it is a wonder the world isn't tipped off balance. Vehicular representatives of every earth-moving equipment company on the planet have been sent to participate. Kobelco, Komatsu, Hyundai, Sumitomo, Caterpillar, they are all here, almost outnumbering the cars, gorging on the rich soil beside the road. Cranes rise out of building sites too, wrestling with the hulking electricity pylons along the route, competing to form the ugliest backdrop.

To a postmodern foreigner, travelling westwards along this road is a journey back in time, to an industrial past that his own country has largely left behind. The whole scene feels like desecration. To the premodern Chinese migrants, travelling east-wards into an industrial future they have never known, the chimneys and the factories announce salvation, symbols at last of modernity and an opportunity to earn more than they have ever earned before.

'I like your car,' I tell Tintin, genuinely impressed.

He adjusts his sunglasses, looks at me in his rearview mirror, then basks in the praise of his foreign passenger. 'It's a smooth ride,' he concurs in his squeaky voice, clearly feeling nothing more need be said.

He chats to Old Zhang on the CB radio and flicks on his Global Positioning System. 'Most of the roads in China are now on GPS,' he says. 'They've been mapping it for years now. If I get the time, I want to head out to the Muslim northwest next summer, and really make use of it.'

Tintin has heard about that trip from his friend, Little Liu, who drove there last year. 'You can do it in five days if you drive non-stop,' enthuses Liu.

The Muslim northwest of China, at the far end of Route 312, beyond the Gobi Desert, is where I am heading. It is clearly also the cool destination for any self-respecting, SUV-owning yuppie these days, like heading for California on Route 66 in the 1950s. Many of China's new rich are fascinated by the wilder corners of their country, partly because those areas are so different from eastern China. And if you can say you have been to Xinjiang or Tibet (or even better, Thailand or America), your neighbours know that you have money to travel.

'There are lots of interesting ethnic groups who are part of our country but not like us,' Little Liu explains. 'The Uighur Muslims, the Tibetans. They're very wild, you know.'

Route 312 is just one of several roads heading west, but it's the only one that goes all the way to Kazakhstan. There is something rather satisfying about knowing that it stretches three thousand miles, that I'm at the start of something very long and symbolically very grand. Small white concrete posts appear beside the road, with NATIONAL ROAD 312 inscribed in red, and the number of kilometres from Shanghai written underneath.

Suddenly, the road widens. Now it is three lanes each way, but the concrete barrier down the middle disappears, and the enforced order evaporates. Cars pull out from factory gates without warning. Others do U-turns across the road. An old man on a bicycle suddenly appears, pedalling against the traffic in the fast lane in front of us. Tintin doesn't even comment but simply swerves to avoid him, as though this is a normal occurrence.

'This doesn't feel very Communist,' I suggest, gazing out at mile after mile of factories. It looks how I imagine Manchester, or Pittsburgh, might have looked in about 1890.

Tintin laughs, as if to say 'Who cares?' and we talk about how practical and unideological the Chinese are. I tell them of the time I visited a racecourse outside Beijing where people were clearly placing bets on the horses. I was astounded to discover that this was going on, since gambling is illegal in China. I thought I would give it a try too, so I approached what looked like the betting window and said that I would like to place a bet. The woman told me that I couldn't place a bet (betting is illegal in China, she confirmed), but if I wanted to, I could place a guess on one of the horses.

A guess! I could place a guess on a horse! So I put down twenty yuan ($2.50), and stood cheering the horse on, hoping that my guess would win me some money. The horse didn't win, but it didn't matter. I would have paid a lot more than $2.50 for the experience and what it told me about modern China. That a race course (not some secret basement gambling joint but an out-in-the-open, everyone-can-see-you race course) was able to operate openly, taking bets on horses simply by *calling* the bets something else is quite fantastic. And so it is with China's political or economic system. Call it 'socialism with Chinese characteristics'. Call it whatever you want. If the Communist Party needs a semantic fig leaf, that's fine, even though everyone knows that, in many parts of China, it is in fact raw industrial capitalism.

I can't work out where Shanghai ends and Kunshan begins. Kunshan is a city of more than a million people in its own right, originally the hometown of one of China's most famous ancient opera styles. Now, though, it is a sprawling mass of factories and development, completely joined to Shanghai in the east and to the city of Suzhou in the west. Eventually, the signs confirm that Kunshan has arrived, and I pull out my mobile phone and make a call to a Taiwanese factory manager, a friend of a friend I had spoken to the day before. We drive around for a while trying to find his place. Everywhere you look, it is just factory after factory, all of them annoyingly similar. A large retractable metal gate, in front of a long, squat building clothed in white tiles, from which comes the sound of whirring machinery.

Eventually, we find the one we are looking for, and the manager comes out to meet us. He is a friendly, relaxed type named Mr Yang, who has left his wife and family back in Taiwan and joined the tens of thousands of Taiwanese businessmen who have invested billions of dollars in Kunshan. The city is known locally as Little Taipei, after the Taiwanese capital.

I jump out of the jeep, thank Liu and Tintin for the ride, and head back to where Camel and Old Zhang are parked just behind to shake their hands too, wishing them well on their day out, heading west. They drive off back towards Route 312, to continue their adventure.

Mr Yang's factory is making that most essential of exports, artificial grass for golf driving ranges around the world. It is a standard Chinese factory of which there are thousands along the coast, from Shanghai down to Hong Kong. There are of course some shocking labour rights abuses in Chinese factories, where workers are locked in and forced to toil in near-slavelike conditions. The conditions at this factory are more typical: basic but not bad. The workers have all travelled here from inland, by road or rail, and they receive $120 a month, plus the possibility of overtime.

Stop at any factory here, and you will hear the same stories. 'I'm a farmer. I earn more here in a month than I did in a year growing rice. Yes, it's hard work, but it's worth it. I'm putting my brother through college. My wages are helping to support my parents back home.'

Multiply this factory by thousands upon thousands upon thousands, and you have the start of the transformation of a nation. The area known as the Yangtze Delta, or sometimes in Chinese as the Golden Delta because it is producing so much 'gold', comprises hundreds of factory towns like Kunshan that together cover an area around Shanghai slightly larger than Portugal. Chinese statistics say that this sea of factories produces goods that make up roughly 20 per cent of the value of the Chinese economy. That would mean that if the Yangtze Delta were an independent country, its economy would rank as the world's seventeenth largest, just below Indonesia and Australia, and above South Africa, New Zealand and Thailand.

Mr Yang is not thinking about such macroeconomics. He is just trying to get more orders from the golf ranges of North America. He seems to have excellent relations with his staff. We all sit laughing and joking over a basic but tasty dinner in the factory cafeteria. I had planned to head for Nanjing tonight, but after dinner Mr Yang suggests we go to sing some karaoke, which seems like too good an invitation to decline. So, with several of his workers, we jump into Mr Yang's van and head for the centre of Kunshan.

In China, wherever there are people, there are karaoke bars. In fact, where there are no people, there are karaoke bars. There is probably a karaoke bar on the Chinese side of Mount Everest.

Mr Yang drives us to a very fancy one nearby, and I pay for a room, which is upholstered with purple velvet. The favoured songs are Taiwanese, and not just to please their boss. Just as the Pakistanis love Indian films, so for Old Hundred Names, music bridges the political divide with the arch-enemy across the Taiwan Strait. All of the workers sing a song, some sing two, as I manage to put off taking part myself. Soon, though, they will not let me defer any longer, so I flick through the menu, past the Carpenters, the Backstreet Boys and the Jackson 5, and past George Michael's 'Last Christmas' (which I secretly *really* want to sing), until I find a song that suits the occasion. The workers applaud politely as a sad, out-of-tune, but singularly appropriate rendition of 'Desperado' by the Eagles croaks out into the hot Wild West summer night.

The next morning I find a taxi and head towards Zhenjiang, a city about three-quarters of the way between Shanghai and Nanjing, a hundred miles to the west. Taxis are cheap and convenient in China and, of course, have the advantage over buses of allowing you to stop when you want. I plan to make only a brief stop in Zhenjiang, a sort of personal pilgrimage to visit memorials to two Ocean People whose involvement with China has had an impact on my own.

The coastal megalopolis of Shanghai, which has sprawled to encompass the ancient city of Kunshan and then the garden city of Suzhou, has extinguished the agricultural past of southern Jiangsu province. But as Route 312 leaves Suzhou behind, a little greenery begins to appear between the towns. We pass the grimy industrial cities of Wuxi and Changzhou before reaching Zhenjiang (pronounced *jun-jyahng*), which turns out to be a wonderful place, full of surprises. It is famous for its production of vinegar, the smell of which lingers everywhere. and there is a surprisingly good museum of traditional Chinese art, porcelain and bronzes. This is also the first place where you can see the Yangtze River, which has run parallel to, but out of sight from, Route 312 since Shanghai. The river is a beautiful sight to behold from the high ground at the centre of Zhenjiang, as wide here as an inland sea, glistening timelessly beyond the changing city.

Zhenjiang (formerly spelled Chinkiang) was in the second wave of treaty ports that were forced open by the European powers after the Second Opium War, in 1860. Its name means 'Garrison on the River', and it is still one of the busiest ports on the Yangtze.

The city had been home to two Ocean People who were crucial in shaping foreigners' views of China, and especially in bringing the lives of Old Hundred Names, the ordinary Chinese people, to the attention of the Western world. I had read both their writings as a student and they had both drawn me deeper into my fascination with China.

The first was the American author Pearl Buck, who moved here as a baby in 1892 and grew up in Zhenjiang, the daughter of Presbyterian missionaries. The grey brick house in which she lived with her parents, Absalom and Caroline Sydenstricker, still stands, preserved as a museum by the city government. It has a wonderful view out over the city to the mighty Yangtze. You can almost imagine little Pearl Sydenstricker and her brother playing in the garden, chatting away with their Chinese nanny. Pearl went to boarding school in Shanghai from 1907 to 1909, then returned to the United States to attend college in Virginia, graduating in 1914. She then returned to China and spent most of the next twenty years here.

Buck's writing on China brought the country into the Western mind in a way it had not been described before. Chinese writers in the 1920s and 1930s were caught up in the internal politics of the country, trying to stir China to revive itself, and so were not widely read in the West. Many Western writers at that time still took a condescending, colonial tone towards China. Buck's novel *The Good Earth*, by contrast, painted a largely sympathetic picture of an ordinary Chinese farmer and his family, and their attachment to the land. Like many people, when I first read it, I was struck by the dignity with which Buck portrayed the Chinese people, and a realistic tone that I had never before encountered in Western writing about China. Here was an author with a deep love for the

41

Chinese people. *The Good Earth* is a story about the lives and loves, the hopes and fears of Old Hundred Names, but it is also a universal tale that connected their lives with ordinary westerners in a new way. The book sold 1.8 million copies in its first year and won Buck the Pulitzer Prize for Fiction in 1932. She went on to win the Nobel Prize for Literature in 1938.

The other notable westerner linked to Zhenjiang is James Hudson Taylor, an Englishman who had come to the city as a missionary almost forty years before Pearl Buck's family. Taylor felt a divine call to China from a very early age. He arrived in Shanghai in 1854, aged twenty-two, and went on to spend most of the next fifty years here, founding the China Inland Mission in 1865 with the aim of evangelising the interior of China. Taylor was a revolutionary figure in the missionary community of the Victorian age. He caused a stir in the 1850s, when he decided not to live in the foreigners' compounds, as missionaries had done up to that point, but to live among the Chinese people. Taylor was one of the first Western missionaries to adopt Chinese dress, and he insisted that all members of the China Inland Mission do the same. He too cared deeply about Old Hundred Names, and about bringing both their spiritual and their material plight to the notice of the West.

Though sometimes criticised as being the 'spiritual arm' of the imperialists, many of the missionaries were deeply committed to China and had a great love for the country. Their impact was immense, and not just in conversions. They were a progressive force, bringing modern education and medical expertise to China, and emphasising the need to teach girls, who were largely denied education in traditional China.

Taylor's wife, Maria, died in Zhenjiang from cholera in 1870, when she was only thirty-three. Two of his children also died there. But Taylor stayed on in China for most of his life. He died in 1905 in the city of Changsha, and his body was brought downriver to Zhenjiang by boat to be buried next to his beloved Maria.

During the madness of Mao's Cultural Revolution of the 1960s, when anything foreign was attacked, the small international cemetery in Zhenjiang was desecrated by Red Guards and the tombstones torn down. They lay abandoned until recently, when some local Christians found Taylor's tombstone, restored it, and placed it in a specially built little mausoleum beside their church.

Before I leave Zhenjiang, I drop by the beautiful little nineteenth-century church and ask the young minister if I can see Taylor's rebuilt tomb. The pastor is gracious and welcoming, and goes to get the key. He tells me that so many people come to church on Sundays that they have to hold several services.

Once upon a time, long ago and far away, in the first flush of youth and the first flush of faith, I had read Taylor's biography, and it had affected me deeply. I was already considering whether to enter the ordained ministry, and reading the book made me think perhaps I should be involved in some kind of church work in China. I went to talk to the minister of my church in England about it. He is still the person outside my family whom I admire more than anyone on the planet, and knowing of my interest in international affairs, he said to me, 'I think that sort of canvas might prove a little small for you.' I remember his words exactly. They surprised me, because I had always thought that the human soul was as large a canvas as you could find. In the end, though, for many and varied reasons, my pastor's perception proved correct, and the flow of my life changed completely. But, like your first love, you never really forget your first hero. Nor do you ever forget the road not taken. I often look back at the fork in the road at which I stood, and the choice I made, and what might have been. And I stand for a very long time that hot summer day, just looking at the tombstone of James Hudson Taylor.

Chapter Four

THE UNFINISHED REVOLUTION

History hangs heavy over China. Like a vapour that used to be sweet but has somehow imperceptibly turned bad, it seeps into every corner and silently makes its way into the mind of every Chinese person. Sometimes you feel the Chinese don't know quite what to do with their 5,000 years of continuous history.

In the Western world, we love history. A visit to St Paul's Cathedral, or the Colosseum in Rome, or to colonial Williamsburg in the US, is a positive experience that fills us with undeniable satisfaction. There are no doubt many reasons, but I think the main one is simply that we won. History for Ocean People led to the two most crucial elements of our societies: democracy and prosperity.

In China, by contrast, there seems to be a great tension in people's minds about history. All Chinese people know that their history used to be magnificent. Chinese civilisation began its rise to world dominance in the seventh and eighth centuries, and reached its zenith in the twelfth century, while Europe was still in the Dark and Middle Ages. Many people in the West know about the Big Four inventions, which China came up with long before the West: paper, printing, gunpowder and the compass. But the Chinese were also responsible for a whole treasure trove of other inventions which found their way into Western life: the sternpost rudder, the iron-chain suspension bridge, deep drilling techniques, canal locks, the kite and the crossbow to name but a few. At that time, China was vastly more powerful, wealthy and technologically advanced than Europe or anywhere else. In fact, it was China's advancement, and the desire this created in Europeans for luxuries they so clearly lacked, that was one of the preconditions for Europe's rise. When British envoy Lord Macartney arrived in 1793, China was the export superpower, its silk, tea and porcelain in demand around the world (especially in Europe). It was the European powers who, though the Industrial Revolution would soon make them strong, were desperate to buy Chinese luxury goods at that time with cash and narcotics such as opium.

Historians say the problem was that China peaked too early. It founded a very successful Confucian system of bureaucracy under an all-powerful emperor and, for a premodern society, attained an amazing degree of stability and relative prosperity. But by the late eighteenth century, China's population had grown so much that it was putting strain on the land. There was bureaucratic corruption too, of course, and over-taxation, and towards the end of the eighteenth century, China began to sink under the weight of its own success. And then, as we have seen, along came the hairy barbarians from the ocean, and everything that Chinese people previously thought was magnificent, and a sign of their superior culture, suddenly became a symbol of backwardness and humiliation, as the Ocean People semi-colonised China. The legacy of this psychological tension still plays out in the minds of Chinese people and is one of the reasons they are so obsessed with making their country strong today. There is no better place to see the different layers of modern Chinese history, and the evidence of China's decline, than the ancient capital of Nanjing.

If, like most sensible people, you had driven along the shiny new motorway from Shanghai to Nanjing, it would have taken you only a couple of hours and deposited you at the east gate of the ancient city. If, however, you are determined to take the slow road, you will have seen tombs of missionaries, caught a glimpse of the Yangtze River, and bought a teapot you didn't need, but you'll have to scramble through the northeastern suburbs for a while before you get into Nanjing proper.

Route 312 from Zhenjiang has expanded considerably by the time it hits Nanjing, and now it is not the slow road at all but four lanes wide in each direction. You can accuse the Chinese government of many things, but neglecting road building is not one of them.

Nanjing is a very pleasant city, despite being known as one of the three *huolu*, or furnaces, of central China, on account of its hundred-degree summers. Located mostly on the south bank of the Yangtze River, it has a population of more than 6 million people, and as with Shanghai, the overall atmosphere is one of energy, of people moving and looking forward. The market economy is gaining the upper hand over the planned economy here, too. The streets are busy and the shops are full, of food and clothes, of toys and books, of electronic equipment and every brand of mobile phone. Many people in Nanjing have now emerged, in twenty-five short years, from the tyranny of poverty into the (admittedly more manageable) tyranny of choice.

The city is less heavily industrialised than the towns such as Kunshan that line Route 312 as it leaves Shanghai, and Nanjing's main streets are lined with graceful *wutong* (or Chinese parasol) trees. Their silvery trunks divide uniformly in two, and their branches spread over the pavements, providing shade from the scorching summer sun.

The name Nanjing (formerly spelt Nanking) means nothing fancier than 'Southern Capital'. (Beijing means 'Northern Capital'. Tokyo is called Dongjing, which means 'Eastern Capital'. There is no Western Capital.) The city rests on layer upon layer of Chinese history within its crumbling fourteenth-century walls.

For centuries, Nanjing was a symbol of China's strength. It was the capital of the Ming dynasty, founded in 1368, which had kicked the Mongol hordes out of China. Soon afterwards, that city wall was constructed, one of the longest ever built in the world, measuring twenty miles in all.

In 1405, it was from Nanjing that the famous admiral Zheng He (pronounced *Jung Huh*) set off on the first of his extraordinary maritime journeys to Southeast Asia, Arabia and Africa. This was nearly ninety years before Columbus sailed for America. Chinese sources say Zheng He's fleet consisted of 300 boats and some 28,000 men. The same sources say his flagship was more than 400 feet long, although some experts question whether it was possible to build such a huge wooden ship at that time. In 1492, Christopher Columbus took just eighty-eight men on his three tiny ships to the New World. His flagship, the *Santa Maria*, was just under a hundred feet long.

Historians have long debated the what ifs of Zheng He. What if the Chinese had continued to explore? What if *they* had become the Ocean People and gone on to conquer other lands? But they didn't. The emperor who had supported Zheng died in 1424, trouble grew at home, and the maritime expeditions fell foul of court infighting. In an extraordinary reversal, a later emperor ordered the destruction of all oceangoing ships. The Ming navy of the early fifteenth century went from 3,500 vessels to almost none, a move that would later prove fatal.

Fast forward to 1842, when Nanjing rapidly became a symbol of China's weakness. The British Royal Navy sailed up the Yangtze River, and the Southern Capital, with no modern navy to protect it, quickly succumbed, ushering in what historians call China's 'century of humiliation' at the hands of the Western powers. That lasted until the Communist Party victory in 1949.

Nanjing holds a special significance in this century of humiliation, because of what took place there over seven weeks beginning in December 1937. It was one of the most shocking events of twentieth-century warfare and has come to be known as the Nanjing Massacre.

Soon after the Chinese had refused to open their country to the Ocean People in the 1830s, the Japanese had made the exact opposite decision. They set about major political, economic and social reforms, pushing education, industrialisation and active engagement with the outside world. Because Japan had borrowed culturally in the past (not least from China), the decision to borrow again (this time from the West) was perhaps not so problematic. Japan did not see itself as the cultural centre of the universe, as China did, so was able to shed a skin. China, on the other hand, was forced to change its soul.

Until 1895, Japan was actually seen as an example by many Chinese reformers – in that year, Japan defeated China militarily and imposed humiliating conditions on Beijing, just as the Western powers had done decades before. The defeat was a huge shock for the Chinese, who saw (and still see) Japanese culture as derivative from, and therefore inferior to, Chinese culture. The defeat was one of a number of humiliations that finally convinced the Chinese court after 1900 that it had to reform. But by then the Chinese revolutionaries were gaining as much support as the reformers, and indeed the wave of reforms after 1900 led not to a reformed imperial state but to revolution and the overthrow of the last emperor in 1912.

The leader of the revolutionaries was a Western-educated doctor called Sun Yat-sen, who wanted China to become a modern, liberal republic. Sun laid out his goals in what he called the Three Principles of the People. These principles are often translated as People's Nationalism (that is, making China strong), People's Livelihood (that is, putting food in their stomachs) and People's Rights (that is, giving them rights). There was just one problem. No one in the country had any experience of governing a modern, liberal republic. As the Soviet Union found out eighty years later, and the US found in Iraq in 2003, it is much easier to overthrow an old order than it is to establish a new one. So when the last emperor abdicated, in 1912, Sun and the other revolutionaries had none of the mechanisms of modern government with which to rule the new republic. In 1916, one by one, the provinces declared independence from the capital, and the country simply fell apart.

So the revolution led by Sun Yat-sen was really only half a revolution. The old order was swept away, but the building of the new order failed. China descended into chaos, presenting resource-poor Japan with an opportunity to expand into its resource-rich neighbour. And that is exactly what happened.

'The Japanese troops used to have competitions to see who could kill the most Chinese civilians in a day,' says the tour guide matter-of-factly.

She is standing in front of about fifteen Chinese tourists, pointing to a pit that is separated from the visitors by a sheet of glass. Lying in the pit, still encased in the soil in which they fell, are dozens of human skeletons.

'See that skeleton over there?' The guide points. 'That's a middle-aged woman with a bullet in her skull. Over here is a child with its skull smashed.'

The Nanjing Massacre Memorial is in the southwest of the city, close to the southern bank of the Yangtze River. It is built upon one of the sites where Japanese soldiers, in an orgy of violence, executed some of their victims. Known as the Pit of Ten Thousand Corpses, the site spares no detail of the killings. Silence reigns among the crowd of Chinese visitors.

After fifteen years of collapsed central government in China and amid continued internal chaos, the Japanese invaded Manchuria — that's northeast China — in 1931, and this became a fully fledged invasion in 1937, with Japanese troops landing at Shanghai that summer. Nanjing was then the Chinese capital, so the city was a special prize for the Japanese soldiers who, when they reached it in December, embarked on seven weeks of murder, torture and rape. Casualties were hard to measure, and the number may be lower, but the figure seared into the minds of all Chinese people is 300,000 killed by the Japanese. The number is carved in huge figures in the courtyard of the Massacre Memorial.

The museum is especially disturbing to me, because only nine months before, I had visited Japan and interviewed the infamous right-wing mayor of Tokyo, Shintaro Ishihara, who had denied to my face that the Nanjing Massacre ever took place.

After the pit comes an exhibition that contains photos of Japanese troops burying Chinese victims alive and using live Chinese prisoners for bayonet practice.

A man of about thirty is loitering at the back of a group being led through the exhibition. He is wearing a jacket, despite the heat, and large glasses, and is standing very close to the pictures, squinting slightly, seeming to search the details of each one.

'What do you think about the Japanese now?' I ask him.

The man may be moved by the exhibition, but he is pragmatic. He pauses, then shrugs. 'Of course we should not forget the past,' he says, 'but it is impossible to ignore the Japanese in this globalised world.'

'But do you have Japanese friends? *Could* you have Japanese friends?'

'I could be friends with a Japanese if he admitted the past. If he didn't, it would be difficult,' he says slowly. He tells me his name is Wu. He is on business from Beijing and has taken the opportunity to visit the museum.

The wounds of the massacre are still raw for Chinese people for two reasons. First, most of the victims were civilians. Second, the Chinese don't believe that the Japanese have apologised sufficiently for what they did. The Japanese have in fact expressed regret and remorse many times, but certainly they have not been as repentant as the postwar Germans. And the fact that former Japanese Prime

Minister Junichiro Koizumi and other senior politicians have continued to visit the Yasukuni Shrine in Tokyo, where several Class A war criminals from World War Two are enshrined, makes the Chinese apoplectic with rage. 'What if German leaders paid respects at Hitler's tomb?' they ask.

It is no coincidence, though, that the rise in anti-Japanese sentiment in China has coincided with the decline of Communism as an ideology. The ideological glue that held the Chinese people together under Mao has disappeared, and the Communist Party's legitimacy has become largely economic. Now nationalism, especially virulently anti-Japanese nationalism, is providing another bond between Chinese people, and a new legitimacy for the government, which casts itself as the champion of Chinese nationalism.

The Communist Party is very good at controlling the official Chinese memory, playing up Japanese crimes against the Chinese people, and playing down the Party's own crimes against its own people. The Party, which never allows street demonstrations on other issues, permitted protests in the spring of 2005 in opposition to the publication of a Japanese textbook that the Chinese say whitewashes the history of the war. Allowing anger at Japan is a useful way of channelling frustration over domestic issues away from the Party itself and towards an outside enemy.

'This is the reason why China must grow strong,' says Wu, standing in front of a particularly gruesome photo. 'So that this never happens again.'

When you see the exhibition, you can begin to understand the Chinese obsession with becoming strong. You can also understand why many Chinese put up with the Communist Party. There is a mountain of problems in modern China, many of them caused by the Communist Party itself. But after all the humiliation, it is clear that the Party, for all its faults, has gained China a lot more respect in the world.

The debate about Japan is as much about the future as it is about the past. Asia has never had a strong China *and* a strong Japan. The Japanese talk about becoming a 'normal' country now, and amending their pacifist postwar constitution to be allowed a functioning military that can play a more active role in international peacekeeping missions. Their main motivation is long-term concern about China's rise. China, for its part, insists its rise will be peaceful, but it is equally concerned about a return to militarism in the Land of the Rising Sun.

'Some people in Asia, and in the West, are afraid that China could become like Japan in the 1930s,' I say to Wu. 'You know, after industrialising, with all this growing nationalism, and needing oil and other resources, that China could invade its neighbours just like Japan did.'

'*Bu keneng*,' says Wu softly, echoing the words of every Chinese person I have ever talked to on this issue. 'That is not possible. Chinese people could never do this. The Chinese character is completely different from the Japanese character. They are warriors, *samurai*. We love *ren*. We love compassion. We love peace. And besides, we know what it is like to be occupied and killed.'

I thank Wu for chatting to me and move slowly towards the exit, stopping to look at more of the photos on the way. It is all too horrific for words, but as well as saying a lot about Japan, it also says something about China, especially in the tone that comes through in the museum. It's a tone you hear a lot in China, when history or the country's role in the world is discussed, and it's the tone of the victim.

China *was* the victim, there is no doubt, and has been for too long. The western powers and Japan are guilty as charged of terrible military aggression. But now China is becoming a Great Power. Economically, diplomatically, internationally, it is on the verge of greatness. And yet it still tends to think and speak like a victim.

I don't know what will change that. What does it take to change your psychological identity as a nation, when for so long you have been a loser and then suddenly you become a winner?

I return to my hotel, pull on my shorts and running shoes, and head up the hill towards the tomb of Sun Yat-sen. It's a steep hill, and a real test of my new fitness regime. I stagger all the way up without stopping, coming to a halt outside the entrance to the tomb. A group of Chinese tourists, who have clearly never seen a foreigner expire in real time, gather to stare at me, doubled over with my hands on my knees.

In my sweaty state, I decide not to go in and look around, saving that for the following day. You can visit Sun's tomb at the top of a magnificent flight of shining white stone steps, surrounded by some rather beautiful gardens. There are exhibits and historical displays discussing the 1912 Revolution and its ideals, though there is little about its failures, which seems to me a rather serious oversight.

Nearly a hundred years later, no one seems to have learned the lessons of the 1912 Revolution or, for that matter, the 2,000 years before it, or the tragedies of the twentieth century that followed it: that a corrupt one-party state can't go on for ever, and that if you don't want a revolution and subsequent collapse, you had better start planning some proper political transition. Modern-day China has disturbing echoes of the situation in China a hundred years ago.

I turn and head back to the hotel, letting my legs freewheel downhill in the heat, returning the waves of the giggling gaggles of Chinese tourists struggling up the hill. I run past the tomb of the first emperor of the Ming dynasty (a man who certainly never tried to establish a republic), then past the entrance to the Nanjing Botanical Gardens. It's late afternoon, and as I'm looping back towards the hotel, I see a small iron gate almost in the shadow of the old city wall, and a large sign beside it. I almost don't stop, but something about it seems unusual. From the gate a path winds round the edge of a garden, with a handrail running beside it. All types of trees and shrubs and flowers have been planted along the path, so that a blind person can walk, holding the rail, and feel the leaves and branches and buds of each one. The sign says BLIND PEOPLE'S ARBORETUM.

I stand, still out of breath, dripping sweat and marvelling at such a beautiful concept – in China, of all places, where disabled people are still often considered flawed and superfluous. I have never seen anything like this, even in the US or Europe, and yet here, hidden away on the edge of a noisy, bustling, modernising Chinese city, someone has taken the effort and expense to plant this beautiful, tree-hugging garden – an island of stop-and-rest in a sea of smash-and-grab.

Chapter Five

'A SINGLE SPARK CAN LIGHT A PRAIRIE FIRE'

Three taxi drivers are standing smoking outside my hotel, waiting for a fare.

'I want to go west into Anhui province,' I tell the first one.

'Anhui?' The word drops from his tongue to the pavement, weighed down by five millennia of urban disdain.

'Yes, Anhui' (pronounced *An-hway*).

He repeats the name, then inhales audibly through his teeth, the sort of sound that is always followed by a dollar sign and a large number.

'Where in Anhui?'

'Hefei.'

He lightens up slightly. The regional capital is at least urban.

'Eight hundred renminbi.' About $100.

'*Tai gui le.* Too expensive.' The mantra of the foreign traveller.

The next guy in line says the same, as does the next, so I decide to bypass their little three-man union and flag down a taxi on the street. He's willing to do the journey for 500 yuan. Cheaper, but there's one condition. His friend must come with him. In most countries, that is an immediate red flag to the traveller, so I ask him why.

'Because it's too dangerous.'

'But there are no bandits on the roads. China is totally safe!'

'I'm not worried about bandits. I'm worried about the police,' he explains.

'The police?'

'Yes. They're vicious. They stop any car from out of state, and it's just safer if there are two in the car.'

This seems vaguely plausible, and so, tired of standing around, I agree. A deal now struck, we pull out on to Nanjing's beautiful tree-lined streets, drive over to pick up his friend, and head towards the Yangtze River.

It's early morning. The rising sun embraces Nanjing in its heat and light, looking for all the world as though it belongs to China and not to its mortal enemy across the sea to the east. Morning is the best time in China, before all the layers of impossibility have piled themselves upon each other. Everything seems possible as a hot summer sun rises on a modern Chinese city.

Route 312 leaves Nanjing across the massive Yangtze River Bridge. Completed in 1968, the bridge enabled trains (and cars if there had been any) to travel in a straight line between Beijing and Shanghai for the first time. The lower level, holding the railway, was always busier than the upper car level. Now that is reversed, and there's a bottleneck as we wait to get on to the bridge.

We cross, the rolling, roiling Yangtze, which has swept down more than 2,700 miles from the Tibetan Plateau. Upstream, the Yangtze has been dammed by the largest hydroelectric project in the world, but here the river's flow seems timeless and unchanging, passing frame by frame, in slow motion almost, hundreds of feet below the soaring bridge. The activity on land, by contrast, seems to be moving in fast forward.

'Property south of the river is too expensive,' explains my driver, motioning to the huge construction site on the north bank. 'Everyone's buying apartments north of the river now.'

The industrial smog lifts completely when you leave Nanjing behind. The air begins to smell different, a mingling of manure and woodsmoke. The sky is bluer, the leaves are greener. Suddenly this is rural China, and to the visitor, its colours and smells and rhythms are soothing after the organised chaos of the coastal cities and their suburbs.

Route 312 runs just south of an invisible line that cuts across eastern and central China. The line runs roughly along the thirty-third parallel, and divides the country into two very different geographical regions: the dry wheat- and millet-growing areas of north China and the moist rice-growing areas of the south. The two regions are strikingly different in terms of rainfall, temperature, soil and land usage.

The road itself divides as it enters Anhui province, like a river flowing in reverse, upstream into its tributaries. The shiny new four-lane Route 312 has taken much of the traffic off the old road. The old 312, one mile to the south, narrow and potholed, built for an earlier age, looks relieved that all the trucks heading west now take the motorway and it only needs to deal with local traffic.

The two roads are in many ways symbolic of the two Chinas that are emerging across the country. The new motorway, which cuts through the green fields without engaging with them in any way, is the road that the government wants everyone to see and use and marvel at. The old road, intimately connected with the lives of the villagers, is the one that tells the real story of rural China, and it's a very different story from the dazzle camouflage of Shanghai and Nanjing.

Anhui is what the Chinese call a *nongye dasheng*, a 'big agricultural province', which is usually just a polite way of saying a place is very poor. It has been called the Appalachia of China.

Just after turning on to the old 312, we pass a man on a bicycle with a tall red flag attached to his saddle that waves in the wind as he rides, and a huge yellow sign attached to his back wheel. I ask my taxi driver to pull over, and I jump out to talk to the man. He tells me that his name is Wang Yongkang. The title on his big yellow sign reads ANTICORRUPTION JOURNEY ACROSS CHINA. He says he invested $100,000 in a hotel in southern China but was cheated in the deal by corrupt government officials. The hotel was never built. With no way to get his money back, he says there is nothing he can do except protest in this way. Wang is cycling from the very south coast of China to Beijing, and our paths happen to have intersected. He says people support him wherever he goes and often stop him to offer encouragement.

'Every dynasty is the same,' he says. 'It starts off well but then becomes corrupt. Everyone suffers. That's why we need political reform.'

'Otherwise?' I raise my eyebrows, surprised at his frankness.

'Otherwise, the Party and the country will collapse in about ten years.' He wags his finger at me to emphasise his point.

'You see, in the West,' he says, 'people have a moral standard that is inside them. It is built into them. Chinese people do not have that moral standard within them. If there is nothing external stopping them, they just do whatever they want for themselves, regardless of right and wrong.'

This is something that foreigners often feel in the Wild West atmosphere of boom-time China, though they are careful to whom they say it. We stand and chat a little longer. Then Wang climbs back on his bike, and I climb back into the car, and we both head off down the road.

Wang is playing out a certain role in Chinese history. Throughout the ages, there have been honest people, who have not wanted to follow the corrupt ways into which every dynasty eventually descends. They try to stand up against it, and they inevitably lose. They don't change the political culture of China, they are crushed by it. One sign throughout Chinese history that the end of a dynasty is coming, or that a revolution is brewing, has always been honest officials or citizens performing brave but useless protests against the state. The other sign has always been angry peasants.

In 1926, an angry peasant named Mao Zedong left the central city of Wuhan and travelled back to his home province of Hunan, south of Anhui. Born into a moderately wealthy peasant family in 1893, Mao (whose name used to be spelled Mao Tse-tung) had seen China's attempts at republican government come to nothing and witnessed the collapse of the country after the 1912 Revolution. He was angered by China's continued status as the Weak Man of Asia. Mao looked west to Russia and, in 1921, became one of the founding members of the Chinese Communist Party. But he then saw the Party struggle to gain support in Shanghai and other cities, partly because there were few urban proletariat to mobilise, and partly because the entrenched Chinese and foreign interests did not want to see grassroots activism on their streets and in their factories. As he travelled around rural Hunan in early 1927, Mao saw the desperate conditions inherited generation after generation by Chinese peasants, and they caused him to rethink completely how to spark the Communist revolution.

Mao realised that Communism would only work in China if he took it to the peasants. When he returned from that visit, he wrote a prophetic report, parts of which have become legendary in the history of Chinese Communism:

Within a short time, hundreds of millions of peasants will rise in central, south and north China with the fury of a hurricane. No force, no matter how strong, can restrain them. They will break all the shackles that bind them and rush towards the road of liberation.

Mao took Marxism and adapted it to the Chinese reality. There were few workers, but there were many peasants. They were oppressed by the landlords of the old ruling classes, and were starving and downtrodden, ripe for revolution. 'A single spark can light a prairie fire,' wrote Mao in 1930.

It wasn't the classic Marxism of urban revolution, but it worked. From 1927 until the day Mao stood in Tiananmen Square in 1949 and proclaimed the founding of Communist China, everything was about the peasants. During the 1930s and 1940s, even when the Communists were fighting against the invading Japanese, the peasants were the primary base of support for the revolution.

After 1949, Mao's rural revolution went well for a few years. Landlords were overthrown, amid general rejoicing. But the land was never really given to the peasants. The Communist Party, insisting that it represented the people, became the new landlord, herding the peasants into communes.

Then, in the late 1950s, Mao launched his harebrained scheme to industrialise China at lightning speed in the movement known as the Great Leap Forward. Some 30 million people *(30 million people!)* are thought to have died simply because everyone had been mobilised to work on massive infrastructure projects and the production of steel, and so the peasants were unable to gather in the harvest. Most of the steel produced was of such poor quality that it was unusable. Then, in 1966, Mao launched the Great Proletarian Cultural Revolution, in which he encouraged the young to rise up and attack the old, the foreign and the bourgeois. Millions more lives were destroyed, but the importance of the peasants as models of loyalty and self-sacrifice was maintained throughout, and millions of urban intellectuals were sent to the countryside to learn from them.

Now, though, after more than thirty years of market reforms since Mao's death in 1976, the cycle of Chinese history has come round again. In the 1990s, the Communist Party began to abandon the farmers and ally itself with the new moneyed classes, the entrepreneurs and businessmen, the urban elite, for whom the farmers are just migrant factory fodder. Now, in the new century, even the urban taxi drivers look down on the rural people once again.

The small town of Wugang feels empty, as though residents must have heard us coming and fled just a few hours before, leaving everything in place but untended. It's a typical town along the old Route 312. Beside the road is a fading sign painted on to a wall in the Maoist era, which reads SERVE THE PEOPLE. Above the street, a bright red banner with white characters on it has been hung. STRICTLY CRACK DOWN ON FAKE DOCTORS, it says. Rubbish blows along the pavements as the road tumbles through the centre of town and out again into the countryside.

Here, as in much of rural China, there are new houses as well as the old mud and brick ones. The new residences are often built with remittances from relatives working in the cities. They are usually slightly futuristic, two-storey buildings, almost always clad from top to bottom in white tiles, and sometimes boasting blue-tinted windows. They stand out like spaceships amid the greens and browns of rural China, proclaiming a new-found prosperity and a very symbolic break from traditional rural architecture. Their only nod to Chinese tradition is two small dragons facing each other at the apex of every roof, the humps of their long bodies rising and falling like a pair of Chinese Loch Ness monsters.

'If you don't build a new house, you won't be able to find a wife,' says my driver.

Just beyond Wugang, I ask the driver to pull over when I see a man harnessing a water buffalo to a plough a few yards from the road.

His name is Wu Faliang. He is sixty-six years old and has lived here all his life. His taut, wiry body looks twenty years younger, the legacy of decades in the field. His lined, weary face looks twenty years older, the legacy of his daily struggle to make ends meet. I walk up and down talking to him as he ploughs his field. Never mind the Industrial Revolution, this scene hasn't changed in centuries. Wu's shirt is ripped and soaked with sweat. His hands are calloused. When he should be thinking of retiring, he must still come out to his half-acre of land and plant and harvest yellow beans.

Pity the poor, long-suffering Chinese peasants. This was supposed to be their revolution. They form the majority of the Chinese population (some 750 million people), and they have suffered longer and more deeply than anyone. They were promised so much. They were supposed to be liberated by this great experiment in social equality called Communism, but they have ended up back at the bottom of the pile. It is a betrayal of monumental proportions, considering the roots of the Communist revolution and its original aims, and a betrayal that could end up having monumental consequences for the Communist Party.

'Life is poor here,' Wu says. 'You can't make a living off the land these days. Both my sons and their wives have gone to the city. I'm left looking after my grandchildren.' One of them, aged about seven, is standing nearby, watching his grandpa talking to me.

Wu Faliang whips the water buffalo as he walks it up and down the field and says there are two issues that most characterise the betrayal of the peasants by the Party: crushing taxes and land seizures by local officials. Because China is urbanising so rapidly, its cities are expanding fast. In order to expand, the cities need land. Farmers rent land on a long-term basis, but officially all Chinese land belongs to the state. So local officials, as representatives of the state, have the final say in what happens to the land within their jurisdiction. Now they are taking the land by force from the farmers and selling it to developers. Officials of the party that came to power promising to give land to the peasants are taking land *from* the peasants for their own personal gain.

The central government is opposed to the practice, knowing that it creates anger towards the Party among rural people. But without any checks and balances in the system, it is difficult for them to rein in the predatory local officials. Not without reason have the Chinese said for centuries that 'the strong dragon is no match for the local snake'. Beijing launches occasional campaigns to try to persuade officials to be honest, and it will sometimes select particularly corrupt officials for punishment, but otherwise, land seizure continues on the outskirts of almost every city in China.

The farmers are offered compensation for their land, but usually far below market rates, and if they object, local officials and developers hire thugs to beat them up and force them off the land. In 2005, a rural activist handed the *Washington Post* correspondent in Beijing a videotape that showed a pitched battle not far from the capital between a group of peasants and a band of thugs. The video looked like a scene from a medieval battlefield, with both sides wielding hoes, pitchforks and other farm implements. The peasants had resisted official demands to give up their land to a state-owned power plant, and they accused the plant of hiring the thugs to clear them off the land. Several people were killed.

Wu Faliang's biggest problem, however, is not land seizure, but taxes. Road tax, population tax, grain tax, every kind of tax, applied rigidly, enforced ruthlessly. The loosening of Beijing's direct controls on the provinces since the early 1990s has meant fewer central government subsidies for local officials, so if they cannot supplement their income through land seizure, they do so in the time-honoured manner of squeezing the peasants for more taxes.

Occasionally, here in Anhui, the farmers who have not left for the cities rise up. The Communist Party's own statistics admit that there were more than eighty thousand incidents of rural unrest in 2005, four times the number reported ten years before. From a few grannies demanding the payment of their pension to tens of thousands of people protesting some huge construction project on their land, it is happening all over China. In 2006, the number decreased for the first time in a long while, suggesting a clampdown on rural demonstrations as the party leaders become more and more concerned about the powder keg of discontent in the countryside.

Wu Faliang takes a break from his work, leans on his plough, and points a dirty finger towards a nearby town beyond Wugang. Last year a group of farmers marched on the mayor's office there, he says, demanding that their taxes be reduced. Scared by the possibility of unrest, the government used its usual carrot-and-stick approach with the protesters. Concede to some of the demands but round up the ringleaders once the situation has died down. 'The leaders are still in prison,' says Wu.

Aware that the extraction of higher taxes was starting to cause major problems in the countryside. Beijing has announced with much fanfare that the hated agricultural tax – the money peasants pay to the central government based on the amount of land they work and the number of people in their families – would be eliminated. The policy was just being put into effect as I made my journey along Route 312, and some peasants I spoke to were very pleased with it. Wu Faliang admits there has been a reduction in taxes, but he brushes the sweat from his lined face and dismisses the policy with a flick of his gnarled brown hand. 'You can reduce some taxes,' he says, 'but there will always be others to pay. There is no respite.'

'We, the people, Old Hundred Names, get no benefits from the Communist Party. It brings nothing good,' Wu goes on with a sneer. 'And if you complain to the local officials, they will lock you up.'

For Americans, so much about their country is summed up in the first line of the Constitution: 'We the people . . . do ordain and establish this constitution of the United States.' 'We the people' is what America is all about. For all the complex, money-soaked and frequently messy nature of democracy, power in the US is in the hands of the people. The Chinese have a direct equivalent of 'We the people', and you hear it every day of your life in China. *Wo men, lao bai xing*, they say. 'We, Old Hundred Names.' But 'we, Old Hundred Names' is never followed by grandiose statements of individual empowerment; it is usually followed by a lament of helplessness, like that of Wu Faliang.

The plight of Wu's family is typical for a rural Chinese family in the early twenty-first century. There has been an almost complete breakdown of government subsidies for essential services in rural China. 'If you want to educate your children, you have to pay,' Wu says. 'If you need health care, you must pay too.'

The Communist Party now gives almost nothing to the people it claims to represent. The Party only takes. From each according to his ability, to each . . . nothing. In terms of social welfare, it is fair to say that Chinese society today is less socialist than Europe.

The early reforms of the 1980s, which allowed Wu Faliang to sell some of his produce on the open market, did lift his poverty a little, and that improvement lasted into the 1990s. But in recent years, he says, the situation has become much worse again because prices for his produce have stagnated, while the cost of living (especially of education and basic health care) has skyrocketed. Mao's work report of 1927, in which he predicted the Chinese peasantry would rise like a hurricane, is starting to look increasingly relevant as the cycle of Chinese history turns once again.

Back in 1989, one of the reasons the Tiananmen Square demonstrations failed to spread beyond the cities, and therefore failed to cause major problems for the Communist Party, was that the peasants were not angry. The protests were an urban move-ment, of intellectuals joined by some workers. The peasants had emerged from the wreckage of rural Maoism in abject poverty, and in 1989 they were still moving up. Now though, they are angry again, and the Party knows that hundreds of millions of angry peasants is a much more serious problem than a few thousand angry urban intellectuals. By lowering taxes and trying to rein in corrupt local officials, the Party is doing everything it can to prevent the same kind of rural revolution that it once led.

There are now two main issues for the Communist Party in the countryside. First, can it improve the lot of farmers before they become too angry? Realising the extent of rural anger towards the Communist Party, in 2006 Beijing declared rural reform a major goal of its new five-year economic programme. As well as abolition of the hated agricultural tax, it has promised free public-school education for rural children and a new rural insurance system to help subsidise medical care for those who are too poor to pay to see a doctor.

And second, can it prevent the farmers who are angry from organising themselves and linking up with other disillusioned elements of society, such as the disaffected urban intellectuals and the laid-off factory workers? This kind of cooperation is already starting. I have spoken to intellectuals and lawyers heading out to the countryside to advise the farmers in their disputes over land and taxes, and to try to use the law to gain recourse for Old Hundred Names. The state is still strong, but the grass on the prairie is very, very dry.

'What will he do?' I ask Wu, pointing at his grandson. 'What kind of China will he live in?'

'He'll go to the city, of course, to work and to make money,' Wu replies.

'And never come back here?'

'This will always be his ancestral home, his *lao jia*. But there is no future here.'

For rural Chinese, there is only one real means of empowerment, and one source of hope, and that is escape. They have an exit, along Route 312 to the coast, or increasingly to the inland cities that are starting to boom.

Several days before, I had read in my already dog-eared copy of John Steinbeck's *The Grapes of Wrath* a section about the Dust Bowl in the US Midwest of the 1930s. 'A half million people moving over the country, a million more, restive, ready to move – ten million more, feeling the first nervousness.' Those numbers are too small even to describe the single province of Anhui, and its army of migrants moving, or preparing to move, to the cities. There are twenty-seven provinces and 'autonomous regions' in China, and you have to multiply Steinbeck's numbers for Oklahoma by twenty, or thirty, or fifty to reach the number on the move in China today. Of course, some of the issues in Anhui are different from those of 1930s Oklahoma, but what Route 66 represented to Steinbeck's Okies would sound very familiar to the peasants living beside Route 312.

66 is the path of a people in flight, refugees from dust and shrinking ownership, from the desert's slow northward invasion, from the twisting winds that howl up out of Texas, from the floods that bring no richness to the land and steal what little richness is there. From all of these the people are in flight, and they come into 66 from the tributary side roads, from the wagon tracks and the rutted country roads. 66 is the mother road, the road of flight.

Wu Faliang is old. He will never leave his home village now. He has seen everything: the civil war and chaos of the 1940s, when he was a boy; the hope of Communist land reform in the 1950s, ruined by collectivisation; the hopes of economic reform in the 1980s, dashed by the corruption and stagnation of the early twenty-first century. His life mirrors the tumult of twentieth-century China, which after a sixty-year cycle has come to rest, in many ways, where it began. People are not starving, and that should not be forgotten, but life as a Chinese peasant is a constant struggle.

Wu's seven-year-old grandson stands beside him, fiddling with a short piece of rope. His grandpa's whole life was decided for him by the Party. Now, amid the many problems of rural China, for perhaps the first time in Chinese history, peasant children in fields across China are being untethered from their ancestral homes, and from the day-to-day control of the state, and can decide for themselves what to do when they grow up. The choices are not great, the conditions are basic, but they are something. And perhaps that is the real new revolution, meagre and slow though it is.

As I head back to the car, a huge red lozenge of a sun is starting to set, dragging the day behind it. The boy follows at a distance, and after I climb into the car and we drive off, I look out of the rear window. Wu Faliang has gone back to ploughing his field. But the boy is standing, motionless, watching as we drive away along the dusty road.

Chapter Six

SILICON VALLEY

There are nine cities in the US with more than one million inhabitants. In China there are forty-nine. You can be travelling across China, arrive in a city that is twice the size of Houston, and think, I've never even heard of this place. That is how it is for many foreign visitors to Hefei (population 4.2 million). I have been travelling to China for nearly twenty years and had only visited here for the first time the previous year. There had never really been any reason to come. But as in so many cities in China, the local government is trying to change that. After centuries of inland poverty, Hefei (pronounced *Huh-fay*), like all Chinese cities, is opening up to the world.

Like dye dripped upon a piece of cloth, a moderate level of wealth is seeping to cities inland. The new Route 312 has been a part of the change, dramatically cutting the journey time for people and goods going to Nanjing, Shanghai and the coast. The spread of factories and companies inland in search of lower costs has helped too, as have the remittances from migrants working near the coast. This growing wealth in turn is changing some of the patterns of inland migration. Shanghai is still the Promised Land for migrant peasants, but there are now more mini Promised Lands around the country, regional capitals such as Hefei, other cities further inland, such as Xi'an and Lanzhou, to which people are travelling to find work simply because there is now work available. For the first time, some factories on the coast say they have a labour shortage, and one reason is that people can now find jobs (albeit not so well paid) in China's interior. This emergence of the inland cities is actually a re-emergence. The countryside has always been poor. But for centuries Chinese cities were far more prosperous than their counterparts elsewhere in the world.

The government is doing everything to encourage it. In recent years it has introduced an old Confucian concept into its propaganda. The word it uses is *xiaokang* (pronounced *shao-kang*) and it means 'moderate prosperity'. It's hard to imagine thousands of Red Guards marking through Tiananmen Square chanting 'moderate prosperity'. But that's the point. The old slogans – and the old thinking – are dead. The new slogans promoting *xiaokang* are everywhere, another sign of the metamorphosis of the Communist Party from persecutor of the bourgeoisie to its ardent promoter. Economists say we should not refer to what is going on in China as 'capitalism', and that a more appropriate term for it is 'Leninist corporatism'. It is not a true market economy, they say, but still very much guided and managed by the Communist Party. Either way, the Party in Hefei, as throughout China, knows that the market economy, however much a work in progress, could be its salvation. But the Party also knows that the inequalities of the emerging market economy could be its downfall too.

The demise of cradle-to-grave health care, education and employment has created large groups of losers as well as winners in reform-era China, from the peasants I have just met to the workers laid off from the factories of China's cities. So alongside the campaign promoting 'moderate prosperity', another campaign has been launched, promoting something called *hexie* (pronounced *huh-shyeh*), which translates into English as 'harmony'. Signs encouraging citizens to build a more harmonious society have sprung up all over Hefei and most other Chinese cities, sometimes just yards away from signs promoting 'moderate prosperity', the contradiction in their aims apparently lost in the maelstrom of development.

Located just 250 miles west of Shanghai, Hefei is the first city of any size that you hit as you enter the rural heartland of China. In the 1930s it had a population of just 30,000, but in 1949 the Communist Party made it the capital of Anhui province. The city became part of the Communist attempt at high-speed industrialisation in the late 1950s, which has left it with a none-too-inviting industrial feel.

The city gained a degree of notoriety in 1986 as one of the first sites of post-Mao student unrest. The demonstrations in favour of more political change would spread to other cities before being (peacefully) stopped by the Party, but they presaged the bigger protests of 1989, which were brutally put down by the government with the loss of hundreds of lives. The demonstrations of 1986 had been encouraged by the vice-president of Hefei's top seat of learning, the University of Science and Technology, an astrophysicist and well-known political liberal called Fang Lizhi. After the crushing of the Tiananmen protests three years later, Fang took refuge in the US embassy in Beijing and eventually gained asylum in America.

Neither political reform nor political protest has come back on the agenda, in Hefei or anywhere else, since China switched its focus to the economy. Hefei has traditionally been so far off the pace of change that it didn't even benefit from the 1990s boom. 'What a dump,' said an acquaintance of mine who had lived there as a teacher in the early 1990s. 'Terrible place,' said another friend who had travelled there to adopt a baby girl in 1996.

Now, though, things are looking up a little. After the three-hour journey from Nanjing across a sea of rural poverty, it feels as if you have climbed on to another island of moderate prosperity when you reach Hefei. The British giant Unilever recently moved its entire manufacturing base here from Shanghai. The city government is trying to persuade other companies to do the same. The rhythm of life is picking up. There are building sites all over, the shops are full of all kinds of consumer goods, and some of the wealthier citizens have begun to buy cars. Undoubtedly most ambitious of all, the Hefei government says it is trying to turn this unknown city in central China into a major centre for global high-tech companies.

The next day, I am met in the lobby of my hotel by Mr Wang and Miss Zhu from the Foreign Affairs Office of the Hefei government.

Until I reach Hefei, I have been flying completely beneath the radar as far as Chinese officialdom is concerned. I have neither sought out nor been troubled by officials of any sort. It's very easy to do that in China these days. Just take off, and talk to whom you want along the way. Here in Hefei, however, because I am hoping to visit a high-profile government project, I have contacted the government in advance.

Every province, every city, every town in China has a so-called Foreign Affairs Office, known as a *waiban* (pronounced *why-ban*), and visitors, especially foreign journalists, are supposed to contact the *waiban* if they visit. Few people ever do, though. I travel around China all the time talking with all sorts of people and rarely contact the *waiban* unless I want official interviews. There's no guarantee you won't run into problems if the police catch you, but the birdcage for foreign correspondents has also become an aviary.

Mr Wang, or Section Head Wang as I'm careful to call him, is probably in his late forties and speaks no English. He is an affable guy, not at all like the kiss-up, kick-down types who are so common in the Chinese government hierarchy. Miss Zhu (pronounced *jew*) is probably in her late twenties and speaks English very well. They are both typical *waiban* officials in a provincial capital, a little cautious in what they say, but friendly and helpful. They both respectfully call me Journalist Qi (pronounced *chee*), using the Chinese family name given to me long ago by my first Chinese teacher. Foreigners have many identities in China. I am respectfully called *Lao Qi* (Old Qi) by Chinese friends who are younger than me. I am affectionately called *Xiao Qi* (Little Qi) by Chinese friends who are older than me. And I am called *Qi Dixiong* (Brother Qi) by my friends within the Chinese church. The Chinese for 'Journalist Qi' is *Qi Jizhe*, which means 'The One Who Writes Things Down Whose Name Is Qi'. It's a moniker that I like very much.

Section Head Wang has set up an itinerary to show visitors how his city is going to take over the world technologically. Technology is the new religion of urban China, and no longer just in the coastal cities. Having wasted decades, centuries almost, overcoming traditional objections to progress, and then wasted thirty years convulsing to a Maoist revolutionary tune, the Chinese have finally got themselves into a position where they can develop technology and begin to take on the world. Everywhere you see signs that say REVIVE THE NATION THROUGH SCIENCE AND EDUCATION.

Whether it is space travel, computer software, or medical research, scientific progress is a national obsession. Many Chinese-born scientists have returned from abroad to continue their research, not just out of patriotism but because Chinese research facilities have become so cutting-edge. The Communist revolution's annihilation of traditional thinking has also made for an astonishingly free approach to areas such as medical research: scientists can try things that are banned in the West by strict ethics laws. (I would not be surprised if the first cloned human being is already lurking somewhere along the banks of the Yangtze River.)

Hefei's focus, though, is nothing quite so controversial. The city is simply aiming to become a centre for high-tech companies. Mr Wang and Miss Zhu take me first to an industrial park where the city government has been offering free office space to high-tech start-up companies, of which there are now dozens. We visit a company developing voice recognition software, and another one

73

doing online conferencing. The second was set up in the US by a Chinese graduate student. When he returned to China, he chose not Shanghai, not Beijing, but Hefei as the location of his Chinese headquarters. Costs are much lower, there are plenty of very well-trained engineers graduating from the University of Science and Technology and other universities here, and the Internet means it doesn't matter where they are actually sitting. The building is shiny and modern, the open-plan office humming quietly with the gentle sound given off by a roomful of software engineers.

I am not a techie by any stretch of the imagination. In fact, it is all I can do to get online and check my e-mail. But walking through that office in a city in central China that no one in the West has ever heard of, I was struck by the uneasy feeling you sometimes get in China. I felt for a moment that I could see the future. Here are 300 software engineers, all probably just as good as their counterparts in the US but earning perhaps twenty or thirty times less.

This is not to say that Hefei will immediately achieve its aims. It still has a long, long way to go, and wishful thinking and hot air are attached in equal measures to the government's efforts at turning it into the new Bangalore. But things are moving here at a rather startling pace, and the aspirations of some of these regional governments are incredible.

Section Head Wang suggests that I haven't seen anything yet, and after a brief lunch, we head out to the west side of Hefei. On the edge of the city, right on Route 312 as it rolls out of town, is a development known as Science City, another good example of a massive state investment. The site will eventually cover twenty square miles, and planners are hoping it will become one of the biggest high-tech parks in China, attracting Chinese and international companies. Part of the area being bulldozed to make way for the first buildings was formerly a government-owned pig farm, but it will now incubate high-tech firms, not piglets. We all have a good laugh about that.

Here I get a full PowerPoint presentation, with a dazzling array of maps, figures and plans. 'We want Hefei to become the Silicon Valley of China,' says an appropriately youthful manager called Jin Rui. 'Through hard work over the next fifteen years, we think we can do it. The project has already attracted $2 billion of government investment.'

I'm not kidding. That is the figure he gives. And he gives it in US dollars. He has many more – so many statistics and superlatives, in fact, that I have trouble keeping up.

'The start-up phase is from 2004 to 2007,' Jin Rui says as he turns off the PowerPoint projection. 'The implementation phase is from 2007 to 2010. And 2011 to 2020 is the improvement and completion phase.'

I write down the dates of the phases in my notebook and wonder how likely it is that they will be met. Certainly the Chinese government, when it sets its mind to a construction project, can generally achieve it with time to spare. But there is also a lot of aspirational building in China, a sort of 'build it and they will come' approach in projects like this and in the attitude toward constructing the nation's extraordinary system of new roads. There's a lot of smoke and mirrors. Build enough shiny buildings, and hope that they will reflect one another and make the place *look* like Silicon Valley.

Will Hefei fill up its buildings? Or have they overbuilt, as other cities have overbuilt malls and office buildings up and down the country? Will international companies want to come here? Are the skills of Chinese software engineers *really* as good as those of their American counterparts? Is there more to it than just the latest hardware? What about the software in people's heads? Can you become a player in the 'knowledge economy' if you restrict the teaching and flow of knowledge?

I think these questions matter not just for Hefei but for the whole country. If the government can improve the lives of rural people while consolidating the economic growth of inland cities such as Hefei, it may be able to keep China on an upward trajectory. But the questions touch on more than economic growth. They're about creativity and innovation and the freedom of thought that feeds them, which China at present will not allow. It can build all the skyscrapers it likes, but if it wants to cross over from being a growing economic power to being a creative super-power, it will have to allow something more than just the construction of shiny new buildings.

My pre-dinner run takes me right into the centre of Hefei, which is surprisingly pleasant. A narrow river runs through it, and there are small lakes and a number of attractive parks. As usual I am the only one exercising. Perhaps it's just the heat, but for a country that regularly ranks among the top three medal winners in the Olympic Games, there always seem to be precious few spontaneous sports activities going on in China. Sports officials say they are hoping to dominate many more Olympic disciplines in future. They have announced, for instance, that they are pushing to become gold medal winners in women's field hockey. I have no doubt they will win gold in every women's field hockey event from now until kingdom come, but I have never met a single Chinese person who even knows what field hockey is. Sports in China, like capitalism, are noticeably government-led. In the park, I run past a knot of grannies doing a variety of shake-your-booty two-steps to the sounds pushed out by a portable CD player, but that's about it.

For dinner, I had been planning to try the revolving restaurant at the top of the Holiday Inn, but I discover that the hotel also houses an Indian restaurant. Sure enough, there is an Indian manager at the door, and several Indian chefs making naan bread behind a big glass window in the kitchen. I wave at them, and they grin back. The restaurant is about half full, and as the manager shows me to a table,

I ask him how the chicken tikka masalas are going down among the diners of central China.

'Yes, Chinese people are getting the feel for Indian food.'

I invite him to sit with me while I wait for my dinner.

'What do you think of China?' I ask him.

He smiles and says, 'It's developing very fast.'

'Faster than India?'

'Oh yes,' he says.

'But do you think it is improving the lives of people here more than the Indian government is improving the lives of Indians?'

'Well, in India there is democracy,' he says, putting his finger on the point of my question.

'But does that make it better to be an Indian peasant than a Chinese one?' I ask.

He smiles again. 'I think democracy is important.'

'But is Indian democracy helping to raise the standard of living of the people on the bottom rung of society?' I press him.

'Yes, I think so,' he says defensively.

He doesn't really want to have the discussion, which is a shame, because it's a discussion I really want to have, especially here in Hefei, where the Chinese government-led model is so much on display. China and India are both huge countries, with populations of more than a billion people, trying to lift tens of millions of farmers out of poverty. Is the more ordered, government-backed, scorching-growth rate model of one-party China a better one for a developing country than the slightly chaotic, laissez-faire, slower-growth-rate, democratic model of India?

Most westerners seem to side with India, I think, simply because of that word 'democracy'. Certainly, democracy has provided checks and balances in India that have prevented the crazy political and economic campaigns that destroyed China in the 1950s and 1960s. That in itself was enough to win the argument for India in some areas during those years.

But it feels to me as if the word 'democracy' leads us to attribute certain advantages to India that do not necessarily exist. Similarly, the word 'dictatorship' leads us to attribute terrible things to China, that do not *necessarily* exist there. We judge because of the images in our minds and not because of the reality on the ground.

If the existence of democracy in India meant there was real democracy, with all the checks and balances, and the reduction of corruption, and the freedom to choose, and the delivery of crucial services such as education and health care, then India would probably still win the argument. But India, like China, is hugely corrupt, and although Indian peasants can help to kick the highest leaders out of office, it appears that the new leaders who come in each time consistently fail to lift the millions out of poverty.

There are certain improvements in life that go beyond the political system, such as the chance that your child will live to see adulthood, the likelihood that your daughter will get an education, and the probability that you yourself can find a job which does not involve wading up to your knees in a rice paddy for the rest of your life. Chinese statistics are notoriously unreliable, but in many of these areas, even allowing for a 10–15 per cent exaggeration, China still comes out better than India.

You're twice as likely to lose a child in India before the age of five. If you are Indian, there is only a 60 per cent chance that you can read. If you are Chinese, the chance is 93 per cent. If you are an adult woman in India, that goes down to 45 per cent, whereas in China, according to Chinese government statistics, 87 per cent of adult women can read. Income per capita is double in China what it is in India. The life expectancy in India is lower than in China (sixty-three to seventy-one). The list goes on.

In China in the early days of reform of the 1980s, people used to say, 'To get rich, first build a road,' and the instruction, though a crude over-simplification, has much truth in it, as I'm finding all the way along Route 312. China's infrastructure is decades ahead of

India's. In 2005, China invested seven dollars in infrastructure for every dollar that India spent.

In short, the Chinese government has till now, in some areas of life, undeniably *delivered* basic services and provisions in a more complete way than the Indian government. (One brief footnote, of almost no importance alongside the life or death discussion of infant mortality, though it is of passing interest: the model also applies to sports. China's government-led sports programme achieved sixty-three medals at the Athens Olympics, thirty-two of them gold. India won one medal in Athens, a silver in shooting.)

There are now two big questions for China, though. First, is it all crumbling? The peasants such as Wu Faliang, with whom I had spoken the day before, say that it is, that Old Hundred Names must now pay for health care and education, and that the government has stopped providing the very services which speak so well of its development model. The rural boom of the 1980s and 1990s has ended, and despair is creeping back. One sign of it is the increase in the suicide rate, especially among rural women. China now has the highest rate of female suicide in the world, and suicide is the number one cause of death among women aged between eighteen and thirty-four.

The second question is this: *Is it all worth it?* The cost of a government having absolute power to push through its policies is immense. Of course, it's admirable that the Communist Party has been able to implement extensive vaccination programmes and literacy drives, even though they may make their statistics look better than they are. But the flip side is that the government can push through policies that are not necessarily to the benefit of ordinary Chinese people. It can still decide how many children its citizens may have. It can destroy historic parts of ancient cities for redevelopment. And it can approve and build projects such as the Yangtze River Dam, which required the relocation of more than a million people. Even more controversially, it can still engage in a murderous campaign to suppress a relatively harmless spiritual group such as the Falun Gong. In most areas of Chinese life, there are few constraints on the power of the state if it really wants to intervene, so everything depends on whether the individual policy the state wants to pursue is beneficial to the people or not.

In India, the cost of some restraint on the government is a slower growth rate, and many Indians seem prepared to put up with that, if it means that lunatic political movements like the Cultural Revolution can be avoided. Indian democracy may not be perfect, but at least independent trade unions are allowed, and some of them have teeth. India also has a free press, which can act as a watchdog on governmental bad behaviour. In China, the press is more free now on social and economic matters, but it can easily be muzzled by the government on any sensitive issue.

In the end though, there is one crucial difference between China and India, and a perfect example of it is coated in black tarmac and runs east and west through Hefei. China is a brutal place to live if you are on the bottom rung, but there is an exit. And, just as important, there is a real possibility of a job at the other end. India's 1.1 billion population is rapidly catching up with China's 1.3 billion. But India has only about 10 million manufacturing jobs, compared with about 150 million in China. So there are simply more opportunities in China to improve your life. (And I haven't even mentioned India's restrictive caste system.) The growing service sector in India – in software development, in call centres and service centres – is great if you are already middle class and speak English. But what about possibilities for the hundreds of millions of illiterate peasants? It seems to me that India is trying to reach modernism without passing through the Industrial Revolution.

Now, as the cost of manufacturing rises in China, we are starting to see some manufacturing relocating to India. The country's retail sector is opening up too, and India is in the midst of other major economic changes. So it may be that, in the near future, more opportunities of escape from rural poverty will be provided, in which case the balance will tip in India's favour.

I'm really disappointed that one of the few Indians in central China does not want to have this conversation with me. So in the end, I have the conversation with myself over dinner, and I conclude that I do not want to be a Chinese peasant *or* an Indian peasant. But if I have to take a side, despite all the massive problems of rural China, I'll go for the sweet and sour pork over the chicken biryani any day of the week.

Chapter Seven

'WOMEN HOLD UP HALF THE SKY'

'How old are you, boy?' asks the policeman.

'Twenty,' replies Little Wang.

'Let me see your driving licence.'

We have both stepped out of the car, and the policeman glances suspiciously at me as Little Wang leans back in to find his documents.

'You're going to have to come to the police station,' says the officer. 'Get back in your car and follow me.'

Little Wang glances at me, but we realise we have no choice.

A hundred miles west of Hefei, the four lanes of Route 312 have become two as the road crosses into Henan province and the traffic thins out. There are plenty of long-distance buses and blue trucks on the road, plus the occasional minivan on local business, and a few sleek black Audi A4s, the modern-day palanquins of government officials. But there are few personal cars. The landscape is green and flat.

Little Wang was trying to drop me at the city of Xinyang, 250 miles from Hefei, and return to Hefei in one day, so as we entered Henan, he had put his foot to the floor. Soon, a siren wailed and a police car appeared behind us, flashing us to pull over.

He is kicking himself for breaking the speed limit. 'It's always dangerous crossing into another province,' he says as we follow the police car along the road. 'The police just lie in wait for you, knowing they can find something wrong with your car and fine you.'

I point out that he was exceeding the speed limit by quite a lot, and he admits he was but says they would have found something wrong anyway. 'That's how they supplement their salary,' he says.

Little Wang is very concerned as we approach the police station. I tell him not to worry, to be extremely penitent, and to let me do the talking. I have been arrested several times around China for reporting without permission, and the bottom line is the police might shout a bit, but they will never harm a foreigner or his driver if they are together. Here, they do not even know I am a journalist.

When I arrived in China as a reporter, I imagined a great web of officials, all in contact with one another, the customs people at the airport who check your bags talking to the public security people who tap your phones, who talk to the local officials in the places where you visit. In fact, it is nowhere near as sophisticated. The Chinese state security apparatus is very decentralised and quite disjointed. It can be unpleasant to a foreigner when it wants to be – if you are caught investigating something very sensitive – but even then, local officials often choose not to report you further up the chain of official command, for fear that they will look bad for having allowed you to be there in the first place.

At the police station, there is more surprise at the arrival of the foreigner with the funny sandals and the dirty feet. I can't imagine there have been many passing through here lately. Certainly there seems hardly any reason for a foreigner to come to this part of China.

The police chief, clearly the bad cop of the outfit, takes over the case from our officer, saying immediately he may have to confiscate both the licence and the car of my young driver. Little Wang is sitting fretting in the corner.

'Confiscate the car?' I exclaim, trying to strike a tone somewhere between Please-sir-don't-do-that and I'm-a-foreigner-don't-even-think-of-doing-that.

He starts to write down what happened while we sit there watching.

The other policemen want to talk to me, and as the chief is writing, one of them asks if I like basketball.

'Yes, I do,' I reply.

'Who is your favourite player?' he asks me.

'Oh, Yao Ming, definitely,' I say.

'He's good, isn't he?' says the officer. 'We like him too.'

'He's better than any of the Americans,' I say, realising that flattery may be the quickest way out of this particular hole.

His buddies join in, with their analysis of the ups and downs of the NBA, and then we switch to European soccer, and how Manchester United are doing, and, as always, they want to talk about the former England captain David Beckham, who they all know is married to Victoria, otherwise known as Posh Spice from the Spice Girls.

The mood lightens a little, so I launch into another apology to Mr Bad Cop on behalf of Little Wang and explain how it was all my fault. Foreigners get a lot of leeway with Chinese police. Ordinary Chinese people get none. Bad Cop points out again how serious an offence it is and even pulls out his rule book.

'Do you read Chinese?' he asks.

I nod. He opens the book at the page where it is actually written, enshrined in Chinese law, that the fine for speeding is 'between 500 and 2,500 yuan' ($70 to $300), thus conveniently leaving it up to each policeman how much to charge and pass along and how much to keep for himself.

In the end, it takes two hours of humility on my part, and form filling on his part, not to mention further discussions about the Houston Rockets' defence and the Arsenal offside trap, before we are released. Bad Cop forces Little Wang to sign a form admitting his guilt and stating that the fine is 1,700 yuan. That's roughly $200, more than a month's salary for Little Wang. I pull out my wallet, pay the fine, and we politely thank the police and leave before they change their minds.

We pull back on to Ronte 312 and Little Wang drives much more slowly after that, but his hopes of dropping me in Xinyang and getting back to Hefei before nightfall have gone.

Chairman Mao once said that 'revolution is not a dinner party', and he wasn't kidding. Mao destroyed China. Quite apart from the staggering number of deaths caused in the Great Leap Forward, and the lives ruined by the Cultural Revolution, he decimated the intellectuals, annihilated China's cultural heritage, and encouraged parents to have large families, resulting in a population explosion that is still being dealt with today. The census of 1953 found the population of China to be just over 580 million people. Now, at around 1.3 billion, it has more than doubled.

However, in two areas there is no denying the overall improvements Mao made. The first was public health and life expectancy. The edge that China has over India in basic health statistics is largely attributable to the campaigns in the early years of Maoism. In 1949, average life expectancy was just thirty-five years. By 1975, it was sixty-three. Today, it is seventy-one. The infant mortality rate was halved in the first five years of Mao's rule and today is one-eighth what it was in 1949.

The second area in which Mao improved life was the status of women. He famously said that 'women hold up half the sky' and set about making sure they did. Right up until the Communists came to power, in 1949, women were being bought and sold as wives, as they had been for centuries. It was not unusual for wealthy men to have three or four wives. But suddenly, all of that changed. Women were given jobs in factories. Some earned positions of responsibility. The propaganda machine saturated society with posters of women standing shoulder to shoulder with men in the revolution. The reality was not as perfect as the propaganda made out, but it was a huge improvement.

Now, though, the wheel is turning again. It's clear that five thousand years of male domination takes more than sixty years to change. The Communist revolution is over. The status of women in China is certainly much higher than it was sixty years ago, and to the Western visitor it definitely seems higher, proportionately, than it is in much wealthier Asian countries, such as South Korea and Japan, where women sometimes seem to be treated like a lower form of life. But while their place in society may be higher, the death of Communist equality has meant that, as in the former Soviet Union, Chinese women are struggling to hold on to some of the gains of the Communist years. The death of Communist ideology also means that the strict morality the Party enforced has lost its grip on people's behaviour. Studies estimate there are between 10 and 20 million women involved in the sex trade in China.

Which all leads to the karaoke bar on the seventh floor of my hotel in Xinyang (pronounced *shin-yang*), a rather nondescript city in the flat agricultural heartland of southern Henan province. Karaoke seems to be the biggest boom industry in Xinyang (possibly the only one). And where there is karaoke, there are invariably what are known in Chinese as the *sanpei xiaojie*. Literally, that means 'the young ladies of the three accompaniments'. For a small fee, they accompany you to drink, to dance and to sing. There is, of course, a fourth accompaniment, but that costs extra.

Two institutions exist in almost every mid-size or large hotel in China that show the radical changes in public morality. One is known as the 'sauna massage' facility, which, as its name suggests, provides every type of sauna and every type of massage, often, I'm told, at the same time. The other is the karaoke bar. Both are advertised openly, and unashamedly, and both are generally just fronts for prostitution. Although there are regular clampdowns on such institutions, if the management has good relations with the local police (or, more likely, offers them free visits), the authorities will leave them alone. Indeed, it is well known across China that the police and the military have been some of the biggest sponsors or owners of brothels.

I have interviewed several Chinese prostitutes during my years in China. Not surprisingly, these women frequently have the most compelling and tragic tales of life at the bottom of Chinese society. But I still feel slightly uncomfortable going to karaoke bars or places where they work. There is something about looking for a prostitute, even just to interview, that annoys me, because doing so only feeds the Chinese stereotype of Western men as sexual predators. I always call my wife in Beijing to tell her what I am doing ('Hi, darling, I'm just going out looking for hookers'), in case I get detained by the police.

By the time the elevator door opens on the seventh floor, though, I have transformed myself into the stereotype of a Western man, looking for a Chinese woman for the night. I am greeted by a middle-aged woman who looks as though she is trying to fulfil a stereotype too. Wearing a traditional red Chinese *qipao* dress that probably fitted her perfectly five years ago, she dominates the entrance with the presence of a woman who enjoys being in control. Her smile is a little too tight, her bow a little too polite. She is the *mami,* the madam who runs the karaoke bar. She motions with the slightest flick of her head to two girls who hover quietly behind her, then motions to me with her hand, and an even more unctuous smile, that I should follow them. They take me down a darkened corridor covered in green wallpaper towards one of the karaoke rooms. Several Chinese men in different rooms are wrestling with high notes of love songs, and the corridor echoes with the discord. It's a good sign. As a general rule in China, the worse the karaoke, the more interesting the story.

As we pass, one of the doors is just being pushed shut, but I manage to see inside a room full of young, attractive women, sitting, chatting, many in skimpy clothing, applying make-up. These are the girls of Xinyang, preparing for a night's work, and if you want proof that the Communist revolution is over, it is here.

I'm led into a large room with a green and purple couch in an L shape, along two walls. There is a large low table in front of the couch and a huge television on one wall. The girls disappear, and I am left alone, feeling too small for the room, looking at the menu of songs for the Chinese karaoke.

The smiling *mami* reappears, leads four girls into the room, and asks me to choose one to sing with me. The girls all stand, looking ashamed, avoiding eye contact with me, and I feel embarrassed to be putting them through the ordeal. I point to the girl on the end, and the *mami* and the three others file out.

'*Qing zuo*. Please sit down,' I say with a friendly smile that is trying to tell her, 'don't worry'. She picks up on my friendliness and sits down, still a little nervous, on the green and purple couch.

'Your Chinese is very good,' she comments, having only heard me say two words.

She says her name is Wu Yan, and she's twenty years old, although she tries to exude the confidence of someone older. She is not very tall, with shoulder-length black hair, and is wearing a short fake-silk black dress. Her nails are painted red. Her job is to play dice and sing and drink with men who come here, and sometimes offer the fourth accompaniment too.

I encourage her to sing, so she picks up the microphone and sings a syrupy Chinese ballad in a sad, lilting voice, pouring her whole being into the song.

Watching karaoke in China is a wonderful pastime. As a radio journalist, I found over the years that persuading Chinese people to speak frankly into a microphone is a real problem. The country has loosened up a lot since Maoist times, but there is still hesitancy about speaking frankly, especially to a foreigner and especially to a foreign reporter. Of course, there is the fear of saying something that might lead to political problems, but there is also just an inbuilt Chinese reluctance to speak frankly to strangers.

Thrust a karaoke microphone into a Chinese person's hand, though, and he or she needs no second invitation to sing, no matter how badly. Karaoke is the ultimate socially acceptable vehicle for Asian people to say the things that are hidden deep inside them. Wu Yan just said a whole lot of things to me, and to the large empty room, which I didn't really understand.

Most westerners (including most of those in China) would rather stick needles in their eyes than sing in public. Perhaps we are so used to speaking our minds, frankly asking questions and expecting frank answers, that little remains hidden to come out in such an embarrassing, indirect manner as public singing.

The truth of this point is brought home even more sharply when it is my turn to sing. It's hard for a happily married father of two to say too many hidden things to a hooker he's just met and doesn't want to sleep with, in a karaoke bar in central China, while singing Rod Stewart's 'Sailing' at the top of his lungs. I try not to embarrass myself, but my poor performance is all too clear. Wu Yan grabs the microphone and sings another, slightly more upbeat number, again infusing it with all sorts of dark emotions, perhaps things she has never told a soul, and here am I, hearing it all poured out but not understanding.

The second song over, she produces dice. Once again, I'm the dumb foreigner. It's a game I don't understand, and she can't believe I don't. She rattles the dice and throws them on to the table with a confident laugh, and whatever it is you have to do to win, I manage not to do it several times. While we're playing, I tell her what I am doing here and ask her if she will answer my questions. She looks at the door to check that the *mami* is not coming in and then, after a long pause, agrees to talk, as long as I don't use her real name.

She is paid twelve dollars for accompanying a man to sing and chat and dance, and if the man wants the fourth accompaniment in his hotel room, he must triple the price, to nearly forty dollars. That seems a lot of money for this part of China. A third of that sum she must then give to the *mami* who runs the karaoke bar.

Sixty years ago, and throughout Chinese history before then, there were prostitutes like Wu Yan on every street, in every town. When the Communist Party rose in the 1930s and 1940s, with the aim of reuniting China and making it politically strong, it also set about wiping out gambling and opium and prostitution, and after it came to power, it largely succeeded. After 1949, society was transformed. At the height of Maoism, Wu Yan might have been a young factory worker, toiling alongside young men to build socialism, cared for from the cradle to the grave by the state.

Now, though, socialism is dead and prostitution is back, and so are gambling and drugs. The intense, enforced morality of Communism was just a blip in the country's long history. Sheer market forces have killed it off.

Wu Yan's story is most interesting, though, because it is not just about money. I was expecting what she said about her father dying when she was young, and about her having to live with her grandmother, and how she had to leave school early because there was no money, and how she couldn't get a proper job when she left school. Life is tough on the bottom rung of society in modern China, and the tragedies are legion.

But there is a dangerous tendency for everything in modern China to be given an economic impetus, as though financial pressure is the only reason anyone ever does anything. We often fail to see that Chinese people are living, breathing, loving, hating individuals, who do things for complex psychological reasons, just like westerners. And as Wu Yan sits talking about her life, her story doesn't have that standard tone which says 'I must do this or I won't be able to eat'. She is slightly laconic, and cynical and angry.

'So why are you working here?' I eventually ask her.

There is a long pause.

'There was a boy . . .' She pauses again for a long time, rattling the dice in the cheap plastic cup. '*Wo ting xihuan de* . . . who I liked a lot.' She is looking at the floor.

'But he liked another girl.' She stops shaking the dice, then looks up at me with large, hurt eyes. There is a long silence as I try to compute what she is saying.

'So . . . you're . . . doing this to punish him? . . . Or to punish . . . yourself?'

She doesn't answer but reaches out her arm to me, the palm of her hand facing up. There are two jagged scars on her lower arm, as though her wrist had been cut. She looks angrily into my eyes.

'It's difficult being a person, isn't it?' she says finally.

I look at her and nod slowly. She shakes the cup with the dice inside and slams it down on the glass table.

Chapter Eight

'PUT THE PEOPLE FIRST'

The next morning I rise early, feeling a slight sense of trepidation. So far on my journey, I have not really done anything, or been anywhere, that I shouldn't. It is perfectly easy to do that in China, to travel around, marvel at the phenomenal change, chat to all sorts of people, and never really be aware that, lurking underneath, there are still some terrible things going on. Today I am going to investigate one of them.

As a radio journalist in China, I have reported on a fair number of sensitive stories, and there is a checklist of three things that I always make sure I have before setting off. First, an excellent local guide or driver, who knows people and can whisk you in and out of your destination before the police find out you're there. Second, a safe mobile phone SIM card that the authorities don't know about. And third, the right type of underwear.

The most important parts of any reporting trip for me are my minidisks, the three-inch-by-three-inch digital disks on which I record all my interviews. If I return from a trip without them, then I have nothing to broadcast. When you go to places you are not supposed to in China, you are running the risk of being detained and searched by the local police, who, needless to say, do not want you snooping around their turf and reporting on things that make them look bad. And if they detain you, they will invariably search you and your bags very thoroughly, and take your minidisks, camera, videotape, and notebooks if they find them.

So I have developed a strategy, which I will be using today (because I intend to record my interview), that means I am well prepared should it become clear I am about to be arrested. It involves having a decoy minidisk in my pocket, which I can switch at the drop of a hat with the minidisk in my machine (containing the sensitive interviews I have just done). With the dummy disk safely in the machine, the sensitive disk then disappears down my pants, where even the most belligerent Chinese cop is unlikely to venture.

Now, if you have ever tried to hide a minidisk (or anything else that shouldn't be there) in a pair of boxer shorts, you will find that, sooner or later, it will be slipping down your leg towards your ankle and, if you are unfortunate, spilling out on to the floor. If you happen to be standing in front of several fierce Chinese policemen, your goose will be cooked, and you will be led off to the cells (and, more to the point, so will your Chinese interviewees). So, take my advice. If you're planning any sensitive journalistic missions in China, pack your briefs.

The province of Henan definitely has an image problem. Henan (pronounced *huh-nan*, not to be confused with the province of Hunan, pronounced *hoo-nan*), is roughly the size of North Dakota, but whereas North Dakota has 642,000 people, Henan's population is 92 million. That's right. The single Chinese province of Henan has nearly 150 times more people than North Dakota, and in fact has a larger population than any country in Europe.

Where there is a farm in North Dakota, there is a village (or two) in Henan. This means that plots of land here are very, very small and margins of subsistence very, very slim. Perhaps the squeeze on land is why so many people find their way into scams of every kind.

Henan is the province that other Chinese people love to hate. It is amazing how often you will hear people say, '*Henan ren hen huai.* People from Henan are very bad.'

Henan's reputation has not always been bad. Quite the contrary. The province used to be synonymous with the glory, not to mention the robustness, of Chinese civilisation, and consequently it was considered a most wondrous place, nestled in China's heartland, far away from the dangers of any frontiers. The Shang dynasty, (1750–1014 BC) had its capital near Anyang, in northern Henan. The Shang cast fantastic bronze vessels and developed the first known system of Chinese writing. The Longmen grottoes, southwest of Anyang, are world-famous for the 100,000 Buddhist images carved into rock faces in the sixth and seventh centuries AD. And Henan's very own Shaolin Monastery has, since the fifth century, been the centre of martial arts in China. Everybody was kung-fu fighting in Henan when Europeans were still living in caves. And I haven't even mentioned the extraordinary story of the Jews of Kaifeng, long-lost descendants of the Israelites who somehow found their way to Henan in the twelfth century, or before.

But alas, all of those finger-licking venues will have to be the subject of someone else's story, for they lie too far north from Route 312, and out of reach of this particular traveller, who must limit himself to the south, where there are fewer signs of the glory of past Chinese dynasties and more evidence of the horrors of the current one.

I'm heading for what are known as the AIDS villages of southern Henan. Foreign non-governmental organisations estimate that there are at least 300,000 people infected with HIV in Henan province alone, and the epidemic has been entirely caused, exacerbated and then covered up by the local Communist Party government.

AIDS is a problem that, in the Western mind, has not been largely associated with China. The epidemic that has decimated southern Africa has not yet reached such proportions in Asia, although the United Nations has warned that there could be 10 million cases in China by 2010 unless serious action is taken. China does have problems similar to those of the rest of the world when it comes to the drugs and sex trades, which are both growing rapidly. But Henan province has been the centre of another, perhaps even more shocking, source of HIV/AIDS: government-run schemes encouraging farmers to sell their blood.

When central government subsidies came to an end as China moved from the planned economy towards a more market economy in the early 1990s, local governments had to think of ways to raise their own money. The Department of Health in Henan came up with the idea of paying ordinary farmers to give blood, from which plasma could be extracted and sold to Western and Chinese pharmaceutical companies, who use it for making vaccines. The schemes were set up in other provinces too, but Henan's was on the largest scale, and consequently the worst affected.

Blood selling stations were set up in small towns, and large mobile clinics travelled to villages, where farmers discovered they could make more money than they earned in a month every time they sold their blood. The news spread like wildfire. Unfortunately, so did the HIV virus.

A farmer would be taken into the blood donation van, and a needle would be placed in his arm. The extracted blood would go directly into a vat in the middle, where it would be mixed and the plasma extracted. Then, because Chinese people traditionally do not like to lose blood from their bodies, the blood would be pumped back into his arm.

When, in the late 1990s, strange rashes began appearing on the farmers' skin, local health workers had no idea what they were. Then, in 2000 and 2001, these peasants started to die. The local government would not allow any media coverage of what was going on, but in China's more open social climate, it is much more difficult these days for government officials to keep secrets. A few reports were published by the more daring Chinese media, and soon foreign journalists, including myself, were visiting the villages undercover and gaining interviews with the AIDS sufferers. For several years, the central government refused to accept that there was a problem, but suddenly, at the end of 2004, the leaders in Beijing changed their stance and launched an initiative to tackle the problem head-on. That, however, has by no means solved the AIDS issue in Henan, because of the age-old difficulty of enforcing central government policies at the local level. Henan authorities don't want to look bad, so they do all they can to restrict any kind of access to the AIDS villages, even trying to stop doctors and officials sent by Beijing from doing their work.

To help me navigate around the AIDS villages, I have arranged to meet an AIDS activist named Hu Jia. He is travelling down specially from Beijing to meet me, and to help me avoid being arrested. Hu Jia is one of the new breed of Chinese activists. After the killings in Tiananmen Square, in 1989, many dissidents went into exile or were jailed. When the jailed ones were released in the 1990s, it became clear to them that their cause of political reform was hopeless. Some gave up political activity altogether and threw themselves into business. Younger activists, such as Hu (who is thirty-three), know they would immediately be arrested if they campaigned for political reform, so they have turned to activism on *non*-political issues. After years campaigning to protect the environment, Hu now works full time for his own AIDS non-governmental organisation. He has some room to manoeuvre, because the aims of his organisation are largely in line with government policy, but he still treads a fine line.

Despite the easing of social controls in China, any kind of activism attracts attention from the public security forces, and

Hu Jia is under constant surveillance in Beijing. You won't necessarily be put in jail for being an activist, but you'll certainly find plenty of people smoking cigarettes and reading newspapers under the streetlamps outside your apartment. Hu's home and mobile phone numbers are tapped, and every time I want to contact him, I have to text him asking for a safe number. He finds a public telephone and texts me back the number. I write it down, then change the SIM card in my phone to my back-up phone number, which the Public Security Bureau doesn't know about, and call him on the pay phone he is standing next to.

For several days, I have been messaging Hu Jia using cryptic vocabulary about where to meet and when. We have previously discussed, on a safe phone, the names of a number of HIV-infected towns, so in order to save continually changing SIM cards and finding public phones, I just write messages 'I can be in S on Sunday around 9 a.m., can you?'

'*Yue zao yue hao*. The earlier the better,' he messages back.

I had walked around Xinyang the night before to find a taxi with smoked glass windows and a driver who was willing to set off early the next morning. Hu Jia says I should wear a hat and sunglasses so I won't be immediately recognisable as a foreigner when I jump in and out of cars and walk in and out of houses to meet the people who have been infected with HIV as a result of local government policies.

There are at least thirty AIDS villages in southern Henan, and a cluster of them is located roughly two hours' drive north of Xinyang on Route 107. That is the north–south equivalent of Route 312, which runs from Beijing to the very south of China. The two roads intersect at Xinyang. The position of Henan as a crossroads in the middle of the country goes some way to explaining the initial AIDS cases. The disease is believed to have been brought by truck drivers from the Golden Triangle area in China's southwest, near the border with Laos and Burma, who became infected through sex or drug use and then brought the virus up along China's road system. Once a few people had become infected in Henan, the unhygienic blood-selling programme caused the epidemic to explode.

My taxi driver, when I tell him our destination is Shangcai, is not very happy, even though I say simply that I am going to meet a friend.

'It's a bad place,' he says.

'Why?' I ask.

'There are just a lot of bad people there,' he says, but offers no more.

Hu Jia has arrived from Beijing the night before, and as we approach Shangcai (pronounced *shang-tsai*) at around eight-thirty that morning, he calls on my safe phone card and tells my driver where to meet, at a petrol station just outside town. A small three-wheel motorised rickshaw pulls up alongside us, and Hu Jia jumps out, ushering me out of the taxi. The rickshaw is simply a motorcycle pulling a little covered trailer that can squeeze four people inside.

Hu has strung a piece of cloth across the back of it, so that no one can see in. I tell my taxi driver to meet me back here in three hours.

There are many police cars on the roads, and Hu Jia firmly holds the tiny flap of cloth that is covering the back of the trailer. At one point, we stop at a traffic light, and I can see through the flimsy curtain that a police car has pulled up behind us, just five yards away. I raise my eyebrows at Hu Jia as he struggles to hold the tiny cloth curtain in place. He grins mischievously.

The trailer bumps along a dirt track, with us bouncing around in the back, before arriving in a tiny alleyway in a village a few miles outside Shangcai. The driver lifts the wheels over the wooden lintel of a traditional doorway and into a small courtyard, where several children are playing. I insist Hu shoo away the children before I step out. One small child seeing a foreigner and telling his mother can destroy the best-laid plans. Hu shuts the courtyard gate, and there is silence.

I climb out, shake Hu Jia's hand and give him a hearty pat on the back. I always like seeing him. He gives me hope for China. Hu is short and stocky, with a military-style buzz cut, and he wears, unusually for a Chinese man, a pair of shorts, with a large bum-bag around his waist. Inside he has a digital camera, a small video camera and three mobile phones. He is connected to a web of sources around the country, constantly talking to friends and contacts, ducking and diving, sailing much too close to the wind sometimes, occasionally placed under house arrest, but often managing to stay one step ahead of the forces of darkness.

Three men emerge from the rundown one-storey brick house. They usher us inside, and I sit on one of the filthy couches in the dark, musty room to hear their stories. All three men, and their wives, had sold blood at the mobile blood stations in the mid-1990s.

'My wife got sick in January 2002 and died in August the same year,' says 32-year-old Li Zhengda.

Li has a mop of black hair and a tiny growth of stubble on his chin. He did not even get himself tested until August 2004. 'I didn't want to know,' he said, even though in his heart, he said, he knew he would be HIV-positive.

He now takes a cocktail of drugs that is being provided by the local government, following pressure from western NGOs in Beijing. 'I take the medicine, but it has very bad side effects that make me feel sick,' he tells us.

'Eighty per cent of the farmers don't take their drugs on time, because they make them feel so sick,' interjects Hu. 'It's a real problem.'

Sitting beside him is Li Yonglong, who is forty-three. (He is no relation to Li Zhengda. There are more than 90 million people in China whose family name is Li.) He says he and his wife only sold blood three or four times in the mid-1990s, but they are both HIV-positive.

'They gave us 45 yuan [nearly $6] each time we sold blood,' he says. 'That is a lot of money.'

The third man, Zhang Hongda, has a similar story.

When I ask about the local government, all three men just sit and say nothing. There is nothing for them to say. Li Yonglong shakes his head slowly. 'The government has now been forced to give us something,' he says finally. 'They give us these drugs, and they give 10 yuan [$1.20] every month as a kind of silence money.'

'The main reason we sold our blood is *pinqiong*,' says Li Yonglong, his rural Henan accent spread thick across his vowels. 'Poverty. That's the reason. And the main reason for our poverty is that local taxes are too high. Local officials tax everything. All they want to do is make money.'

'For local officials, everything is seen as a way to make money,' Hu Jia explains. 'It's the Chinese tradition. You become an official, you make money. Officials get fat, the people get thin.'

Here in Henan, the problem is HIV. Elsewhere in China, there are other deadly (and less deadly) issues. Everywhere, though, the underlying problem is the same: corrupt, all-powerful local officials creating a cauldron of hardship and anger in the countryside.

Li Yonglong says it's the same with every area of a farmer's life. Family planning, for instance. Many rural people want more than one child, he says, and are prepared to break the one-child policy. 'But if your wife does get pregnant again, and they find out, they will force her to have an abortion. If you escape the family-planning officials and give birth to the child, you will be massively fined. When my second child was born, I had no money to give them, so they took my tractor, which was worth several years' wages.'

The other two men simply sit with their heads bowed.

'Is there anything you can do to reason with the government, to make them answerable for what they have done here?' I ask.

'Nothing,' says Zhang. 'If you oppose them on anything, they simply put you in jail.'

I have to ask them one more question, even though I'm sure I know the answer.

'The central government is starting to talk about rule of law. It says it wants to encourage it. How about if you went and hired a lawyer?'

'There is not a single lawyer in the whole county,' says Li Zhengda. 'And even if there were, they wouldn't speak up for the ordinary people. They would just be hand in glove with the officials.'

Hu Jia tells me there are more people he wants me to meet, which means crossing town, so I climb into the back of the motor rickshaw with him, not knowing exactly how to say goodbye to three men who may be dead within a year.

We head over to another peasant home, where Hu jumps out again and checks that the coast is clear. Here there is a whole roomful of AIDS sufferers. It is a shocking sight. About fifteen of them, sitting there, in silence. Ordinary farmers who are under a death sentence because of official corruption, and now official negligence. Hu introduces me to Deng Xiaoming, a 34-year-old man whose wife died of AIDS in 2000. He too is infected. His six-year-old daughter died the previous week, and he is completely disconsolate. He says his daughter was very sick with AIDS. One night she began to vomit, and he took her to the hospital. On her second night there, she died.

Deng confronted the hospital authorities, and in an act of desperation and anger at the destruction of his family, he blamed them for his daughter's death. He says he placed her body in the lobby for all to see. The hospital told him to remove the body or he would be arrested. He summoned family and friends as reinforcements, but later that evening, he says, fifty police came to take her body away – to cremate it, they said. Hu Jia says there was a virtual tug-of-war over the corpse of the little girl.

Deng is too disturbed by the experience even to be emotional any more. Hu has to complete the story. The local government is simply waiting for them to die, Hu says, so that they will stop causing problems and making Shangcai look bad.

I sit there hating China and everything about it. I ask Hu if we should just go to the hospital to confront the authorities, but he advises me we would get nowhere. The farmers we are visiting would immediately be arrested, he says, and we would end up spending the night in some police station. All the other people in the room have horror stories of run-ins with officials, never mind their anger at how they were infected in the first place.

'None of us can find work, so we have no money for our children's education,' says a middle-aged man named Huang.

'Even then, when our children go out to look for work, it's difficult,' says a forty-something woman named Zhang. 'When employers hear they come from Shangcai, they never want to hire them, so they have to lie about their home town.'

We talk for a little longer, and then I leave the village the way I arrived, in the back of a covered rickshaw, which pulls up alongside my waiting taxi driver on the outskirts of Shangcai. I jump in quickly to avoid being seen, but roll down the window just enough to reach out and grasp Hu Jia's hand. He smiles at me, a conspiratorial grin, full of fire and compassion. Then he jumps back into the rickshaw and is gone.

Just in case, I take the mini-disk containing my interview out of the recorder and slip it down my briefs, replacing it with the dummy one. Then, once out of Shangcai and beyond the local capital, I text-message Hu that I am safely out. He replies to say he is heading north to the provincial capital, Zhengzhou, to catch a train back to Beijing. A few days later, Hu e-mails me to say the local public security heard about our visit after we had left and went to interrogate the people we had met. But no one owned up to meeting us, so the police were unable to take any action.

I ride back to Xinyang, still fuming. The taxi driver is complaining again about how backward the area is. 'The roads are bad, there are no modern buildings,' he grumbles.

Certainly I never thought I'd be glad to get back to Xinyang. As Route 107 hits Route 312 at its age-old intersection, there is a sign that reads pathetically:

Preventing AIDS is everyone's responsibility.

And then, a little further on, the ultimate insult. The new consumer-friendly Communist Party slogan:

Yi Ren Wei Ben. Put the People First.

Chapter Nine

POWER

On 15 June, in the year 1215, a group of twenty-five barons gathered in a field in southern England. They were some of the most senior representatives of England's feudal classes, men given power to rule over regions of the country in return for their allegiance to the king, and their commitment to levy taxes on his behalf. The barons had come to force John, the King of England, to sign a document that would place legal constraints upon his power as monarch.

The King was in trouble. In the years before, he had picked a fight with the Pope and been excommunicated. He had lost great swathes of formerly English land in France and was in dire need of funds that could be raised only through the barons. But they were angry, and for what it was worth, many of the common people supported them. Broke and almost broken, the king knew he had no option, if only to buy himself time, but to place his seal upon the charter drawn up by the barons.

The name of that field in southern England was Runnymede, and the document that King John signed that fateful June day was, of course, Magna Carta.

Although it meant less to the serfs and villeins of thirteenth-century England than it would to men and women of later times, Magna Carta has rightly been called the cornerstone of the freedom and democracy enjoyed in the Anglo-Saxon world and beyond. There were other important elements of European life that contributed to checking the absolute power of the king, notably the very considerable power of the church, but Magna Carta became a rallying point against monarchical oppression. Many laws in the UK and the US, implemented centuries later, that protect our freedom as individuals, have emerged directly from clauses in Magna Carta. If you want to trace the origins of the human rights eventually enjoyed in the West, the origins of the jury system and the idea that a monarch could be bound by law, it is no exaggeration to say that all roads lead through Runnymede.

So the question that has always troubled me is this: If China was so developed and so civilised and so advanced before its time (which it was), why was there no Chinese Runnymede? I raise this question not in order to criticise or condemn Chinese tradition, or to ask arrogantly why other cultures can't be like ours. There are many ways in which China was far ahead of Europe, in terms of technological development and prosperity. But for some reason their system never developed any real checks on state power, and since in the West these checks did emerge, it has become a point of real contention between the two sides. The subject of human rights, which overshadows much of China's dealing with the West, at the heart of it comes down to the unrestrained power of the Chinese state.

As far as I can work out, the reasons for this continuing political set-up are threefold: one reason is political, one ideological, and one social, and all of them have their roots in the ancient capital of China, Chang'an, which is now known as Xi'an.

During the Tang dynasty, in the seventh and eighth centuries, when Europe was a fractious mess of feuding kings and princes, Chang'an (whose name means 'perpetual peace') was the largest and most cosmopolitan city in the world, with a population of more than a million people. Even at the height of the Renaissance, more than seven hundred years later, major European cities such as Venice contained no more than about 180,000 people. During the Ming dynasty (1368–1644), after China's capital had been moved east, the city was renamed Xi'an (pronounced *shee-an*), which means 'Western peace'. Recently, looking to appeal to the tourist dollar, Xi'an's local government has taken a leaf out of the Roman book and started calling itself the Eternal City. When you look around at the legacy of 1950s city planning, it feels as though that might be stretching it a little. But historically, politically, philosophically and artistically, for a thousand years, until about the tenth century, Chang'an was Athens and Rome combined.

I'd arrived at the Xi'an bus station late the night before, after a nine-hour ride from southern Henan. That's about as long as you want to spend on a crowded Chinese bus, especially when the driver is trying to break the land speed record. In the dark. On winding roads.

The section of Route 312 between southern Henan province and Xi'an is the first time the road has encountered hills of any sort. Nothing too mountainous, but hilly enough for the first rice terraces to be seen on either side. After leaving the buzz of the coast behind, the road through China's agricultural heartland had been a sober, solid, almost boring companion across a landscape of matching temperament. Now, on this leg of the journey, it had become a little more adventurous and gained some character as it climbed into the hills of southeastern Shaanxi province, heading towards the ancient capital.

I had checked into the Xi'an YMCA, surprised to see a Bible verse inscribed above the front desk, and even more surprised to find a packet of condoms placed beside my bed and listed on the minibar price list. After a good night's sleep, I got up and headed out to see the sights of Xi'an.

With a population of nearly 3 million, Xi'an today is, on the surface, just another large Chinese city, trying to pull itself up by the bootstraps. Throughout the city, though, glimpses of the past poke through the veneer of modernity: the original city wall, for instance, down which you could still march an army, and the old mosque, built with flying eaves and archways and without minarets, completely in the Chinese architectural style. Xi'an's modern architecture is somewhat less pleasing. Architects here, as in every Chinese city, seem to have outdone themselves in overlooking their own marvellous heritage and putting up some monstrous pastiches of what they think is modern. Despite that, though, it's a pleasant enough city to walk around, another island of moderate prosperity in a sea of rural problems. After a morning's wandering, I head off to see Xi'an's main tourist attraction, an hour's bus ride northeast of the city, a site visited by thousands of people every day.

The Terracotta Army was created to guard the grave of Emperor Qin Shihuang, a crucial figure in Chinese history. Qin was the first man to unify China, in 221 BC, and as such is remembered as China's First Emperor. He standardised China's writing system, its weights and measures, its coinage, and began to build parts of the Great Wall. It is from his name (pronounced *chin*, and previously spelt Ch'in) that the English name China derives.

The army of Terracotta Warriors has been turned into one of China's major tourist attractions and is displayed in three massive buildings. There are tourists from every land, and many Chinese too, crammed on to the long metal walkway that skirts the edge of the largest exhibition hall. The hall is a hangar as big as a football field, and the life-size figures of the soldiers, all made from clay, are lined up in rows in the huge open area below the walkway.

There are about 8,000 warriors in all, and they make a spectacular sight. They stand in the long corridors in which they were found, dug like trenches into the red earth, their heads in line with the tops of the trenches, some of which are up to ten feet wide.

Some soldiers have fallen, some have been smashed, but the majority of them are standing up, as though in military formation. There are several types of figures – archers, infantrymen and crossbowmen – each assigned his place in the ranks, and each figure has a different facial expression, which strikes me as a startling degree of individualism for the third century BC.

The terracotta figures were discovered in 1974, inside an underground chamber, by a group of farmers digging a well. Subsequently, two more vaults were found, which are housed in neighbouring hangars. There are terracotta horses too, and richly adorned chariots made of bronze. Weapons were also found, cast from an unusual thirteen-element alloy, which means they are still sharp today. They are all extremely impressive, like works of Roman art that leave you thinking how advanced those ancients were, all those years ago.

Archaeologically speaking, the Terracotta Army was just the appetiser. The main course of the feast is reputed to be the tomb of the emperor himself. The tomb is said to be a vast underground palace that took 700,000 conscripted workmen more than thirty-six years to complete, with models of underground palaces and pavilions, and even seas of mercury to emulate the Yangtze and Yellow rivers. I say 'reputed to be' because, for some strange reason, it has not yet been excavated, even though the authorities know exactly where it is.

Anyway, the point is not so much what the tomb is like, because the First Emperor of China was clearly going to give himself something more than just a quiet funeral for close family and friends. The point is that this man Qin succeeded in carrying out one of the crucial acts of early Chinese history, namely the uniting of China for the first time.

In 230 BC, he was the ruler of just one of seven states that existed in Northern China, states that had themselves been formed from dozens of smaller ones. China as we know it today had never been unified, and in fact the period from 403 BC until Qin's unification, in 221 BC, was known as the Warring States period. His unification is still hailed by the Communist Party.

I'm not convinced it was such a wonderful event, though. Qin's unification is the first reason, the political reason, why China's system never developed the checks and balances that eventually emerged in Europe. Qin unified the states not through skilful negotiation nor with cunning diplomacy but by banging a lot of heads together rather hard and with a less than selective use of those thirteen-element-alloy weapons. The doctrine he espoused in both conquest and ruling was known as Legalism. Not a doctrine of laws in the modern sense, it was more a doctrine of rules, rewards and punishments that brought about obedience. Qin's violent, heavy-handed means of conquest, however, did not prove the best method for ruling the newly united territory, and when he died suddenly, aged forty-nine, in 210 BC, the Qin dynasty ended after just eleven years.

But Qin Shihuang (pronounced *chin shuh-hwahng*) had set a very important precedent, which has survived to this day: that China *should* be united. It has fallen apart many times between then and now, but each time, someone has said, 'China must be reunified', and set about doing so. Chairman Mao was just the most recent in a long line of reunifiers, and if Emperor Qin were to return to China today, he would recognise the mode of government used by the Communist Party.

I have to say I find this idea rather scary, that two thousand years of history might have done nothing to change the political system of a country. Imagine a Europe today where the Roman Empire had never fallen, that still covered an area from England to North Africa and the Middle East and was run by one man based in Rome, backed by a large army. There you have, roughly, ancient and modern China. The fact that this set-up has not changed, or been able to change, in two thousand years must also have *huge* implications for the question, Can China *ever* change its political system?

The Roman analogy is an apt one. The tendency is to think of contemporary China in terms of the United States, because of their similarity in geographical size. Actually, to understand China today, the best comparison by far is Roman Europe two thousand years ago: lots of people with different languages and dialects, different customs, different artistic styles, even different cuisines, all with a shared heritage, but ultimately held together by force. It makes no more sense to say you're going out for a Chinese meal than to say you are going out for a European one.

The laments you constantly hear in China, that the country is too big and that there are too many people, can both be blamed on Qin Shihuang. At one fell swoop he not only created both of these problems but made sure they would be perpetuated throughout Chinese history. He created a 'country' that *needed* a strong man at the top in order to hold it together, and that requirement precluded any constraints on his power. On top of that, he burned all the books of the scholars, then killed the scholars themselves, thus setting another precedent for how to deal with anyone who challenged the power of the ruler. This is, of course, an attitude to dissent that still holds today. The only times when intellectual comment and discussion were possible were when China was not unified (such as during the Warring States period before Emperor Qin, or during the 1920s and 1930s, after the failed 1912 Revolution). At all other times, including now, intellectual orthodoxy has been enforced.

The second reason that restraints upon the power of the Chinese state never developed is more of a philosophical one that emerged during the Han dynasty, which followed Qin. The Han also had its capital at Chang'an, current-day Xi'an, and lasted until AD 220. Aware of the problems that ruling too harshly had caused, the Han took elements of Qin's Legalism, necessary for control, and added an ideology that, crucially, could legitimise the power of the state. That ideology was Confucianism. In 124 BC an imperial academy was established that taught the Confucian classics and made them the basis for written examinations used to choose scholars to serve in the civil service.

This philosophical double-act of Confucianism plus Legalism was an early Chinese version of speaking softly but carrying a large stick. It put down roots throughout the Han dynasty, took even deeper root during the Tang dynasty, in the seventh and eighth centuries, and lasted for another 1,200 years after that, until the beginning of the twentieth century.

One of the crucial consequences of this philosophical fusion was that, unlike in Europe, just about all educated Chinese men were in the direct service of the state. This was achieved through the examinations on the Confucian classics and also by the weakening of the power of the Buddhist church. (The existence of the Christian church in Europe, often outside the power of the kings, was crucial in the development of checks and balances on European royal power. It also created educated men who were not sworn in loyalty to the monarch.)

Philosophically, Confucianism distrusted the concept of law. Based on the teaching of a man named Kong Fuzi, or Master Kong, who died in 479 BC, a decade before the birth of Socrates, its premise was that society should be brought into harmony with the cosmic order by adhering to certain ethical principles. These principles were supposed to be exemplified in the behaviour of rulers and officials. Western historians have called this 'rule by virtue', or 'rule by example', and it was directly in contrast to the courts and juries and the focus on 'rule by law' and then 'rule *of* law' that grew up in the West. Confucius said, 'When a prince's personal conduct is correct, his government is effective without the issuing of orders. If his personal conduct is not correct, he may issue orders but they will not be followed.'

Leadership in China has always been more about trying to live your life as a moral example and less about standing up and telling people what they should do. The written word has always had more power than the spoken word. It's probably why there have never been any great Chinese orators. Even today, public or television addresses by leaders are rare, and important policies are more likely to be propagated through an editorial in the *People's Daily* than through an address to the people by the president.

One of the big problems with Confucianism as a governing philosophy, though, was its insistence that man is by nature good, and therefore educable and perfectible. The individual should police himself ('rectify himself' in Confucian terms) in order to become more virtuous. An admirable goal, no doubt, but human nature being what it is, the lack of *external* checks and balances on power led to the gradual corruption of dynasties all through history, down to the Communist Party of today. The Party is rotten to the core with corruption, but of course it can do nothing about it, because if it instituted any independent checks and balances, it would lose its monopoly on power.

The other major problem was the nature of Confucian orthodoxy. Unlike Christianity, which looks forward to a Judgement Day sometime in the future, Confucianism looks backwards to a Golden Age in the past and tries to mimic and re-create that time. Whereas Christianity, especially Protestant Christianity, wants to overcome evil and put an out-of-kilter world back on track, Confucianism tends to accept the world as it is and try to order human relations within it. So although the Tang dynasty saw many amazing inventions, they remained what China scholar Joseph Levenson called 'a brilliant cluster of scientific *aperçus*, but not a coherent tradition of science flowing into the universal stream.' Explaining why Chinese scientific discoveries didn't flower into a scientific revolution, Levenson wrote, 'It is not because their forebears were constitutionally unable to nurture a growing tradition of science, but because they did not care to.' Science had no social prestige, he says, and it would never have occurred to traditional Chinese scholars that kudos was to be gained from claiming discoveries or inventions. The ancients didn't turn such inventions into world-chamging technologies, so why should we?

If it's even permissible to look for a silver lining to the very dark cloud of Chinese Communism in the twentieth century, you could say that it has acted as Reformation and Enlightenment for the Chinese, destroying the constraints of the old orthodoxy and setting them free to develop. Perhaps it is *not* permissible to say that, because the cost has been so very high, but it was easier for China to ditch its orthodoxy than it is for, say, the Muslim world to do so, because Chinese orthodoxy was not believed to be divinely inspired.

With the power of the church reduced and Imperial Confucianism in place, there remained just one problem group of people, who might try to cramp the style of the emperor and his Confucian elite: the aristocracy themselves, China's equivalent of the pesky barons who had stood over King John and forced him to sign Magna Carta at Runnymede. And this, finally, is the third reason, the social reason why no checks arose on imperial and bureaucratic power. The emperor and his mandarins destroyed the aristocracy.

The barons could only challenge King John at Runnymede because they had substantial power, as a result of the feudal set-up of thirteenth-century England. Eighth-century China was the same, and the Tang dynasty was initially an age with a powerful aristocracy. But regional rebellions and general aristocratic misbehaviour persuaded the emperor and his bureaucrats in the later Tang dynasty, and the Song dynasty which followed (960–1279), to break the strength of the aristocracy, which never again regained power. Amazingly for such a hierarchical society, the government decreed that a family's land be divided up equally at the death of a father to prevent the consolidation of large landholdings in private hands. This is why there are no big country houses and estates in China as there are all across Europe. After the Tang dynasty, such families were simply not allowed to emerge.

Europeans built not only country houses but different roads to prosperity and respectability – the church, the law, business, the military. But in China by the end of the eleventh century, despite the fact that China was the most commercialised and urbanised civilisation on the planet by far, becoming an official through the Confucian examination system became the primary, and almost only, route to prosperity and respectability.

Although China is criticised for its history of autocracy, ironically the erosion of aristocratic power and the establishment of the Confucian bureaucracy meant there was a lot more social mobility in China than in medieval Europe. Power was not hereditary. It was allocated through examinations, which anyone could take.

This must be one reason why there is still so much attention paid to education (and exams) in China and in all Confucian-based societies, just as there is in the similarly meritocratic society of the US. This is very different from Britain and Europe, where the university was historically just preparation for the church or a finishing school for the (hereditary) upper classes. When I told people in England that I was going to the US to attend graduate school, the response was generally 'Why? Haven't you been a student long enough already?' No Chinese or American would ever ask such a thing.

The big question now, though, is whether China will change and allow the independent rule of law to take hold. Having collided with a civilisation that *does* have a rule of law, and been dragged kicking and screaming into a globalised world where contracts and courts and judicial independence are important, will the Chinese government start to allow some restraints on governmental power?

Or, more important, with all that historical and philosophical baggage, *can* it allow such restraints? I'm not sure that it can. I think restraints on government power may be contradictory to the whole concept of China and its existence as a state. I think perhaps the need for autocracy just to hold China together may make the country fundamentally unreformable, and that sooner or later the modern economic juggernaut is going to slam up against the immovable wall of Chinese history.

But I'm not sure. And if there were such a thing as a Chinese jury, I think it would still be out on that one.

Su Zhongqiu opens his laptop to show me some digital versions of his favourite modern Chinese art. He clicks on one link, and up pops a photo of the corpses of two human babies, propped together like store mannequins, on display at an exhibition in Beijing.

I shy away from it, disgusted.

He smiles. 'See. You westerners are too fragile, too delicate,' he castigates me.

Su is an avant-garde artist who also teaches art at a university in Xi'an. We meet in a tearoom in the centre of town. He is a tall man with a goofy smile, but you would not know from his unremark-able appearance about his startling taste in modern art.

I had arrived in Xi'an thinking I would take the opportunity to explore the city's cultural scene, and through a friend of a friend, I had come across a bunch of artists and photographers, including Su Zhongqiu (pronounced *soo jong-cho*).

Like so much else in the country's history, art had been a victim of Chinese orthodoxy. Sometime around the Tang dynasty of the eighth century, the official style had been set, and Chinese artists had for the next 1,200 years set about trying to emulate it. Not that it was a bad style of painting. Like the Confucian bureaucratic system of government, it was very good, and certainly far ahead of what was going on anywhere else in the world. The problem, with the art as with the government bureaucracy, is that it stayed that way for more than a millennium.

Certainly, there were periods of reinvigorating Chinese traditions through the ages, but generally speaking, there was no perception of a need for a Renaissance, because the whole of Chinese life was already one big rehash of the art, literature and teaching of the ancients.

Traditional Chinese art said much about the Chinese world view. While the person of Christ had focused so much of Western art upon the human form, Chinese art was always more about the landscape – the mountains, the rivers – with human figures often playing just bit parts in the natural drama and grandeur of the painting.

As Confucian orthodoxy crumbled, and everything traditional came under attack, modern art had enjoyed a brief flowering in the big cities in the heady days of the 1920s and 1930s. But then art, like everything else, was subjugated to the needs of the new Communist orthodoxy, and art for art's sake went out of the window.

In the 1980s, in art as in so many areas, China emerged from its Maoist shell and tried to work out where to pick up after a thirty-year assault on traditional Chinese culture. The result has been a mix of a rewind to established Chinese forms and a fast-forward to a completely postmodern style, which pushes the boundaries of art even more than Western postmodernism. If traditional Chinese art was too rooted in tradition, modern Chinese art is in danger of being completely deracinated. (This has not stopped contemporary Chinese art from becoming hugely fashionable among China's nouveaux riches, and also internationally. In November 2006, a painting by modern artist Liu Xiaodong sold at a Beijing auction for $2.7 million.)

'So who do you like?' Su asks me.

'Er . . . Jackson Pollock?' I proffer, screeching in forty years late to the postmodernism debate.

'*Yiban ba!* He's rather average!' he says. 'How about *Dai Mian He Si Te?*'

'Who?'

'*Dai Mian He Si Te.* He did that thing with the shark.'

He raises his eyebrows. *Surely* I can't be such a loser that I haven't heard of *Dai Mian He Si Te.*

'Damien Hirst!' I salvage my credibility.

'Right,' he says, 'I like him.'

'You, you westerners, brought us a new concept of art,' Su continues. 'This idea of challenging the eyes. Our art used to be all about harmony, like our society. *Shanshui.* Mountains and water. Landscapes. Balance. It used to be separated from the dirty business of real life. Then your artists said, We want to challenge Western morality with our art, and they did. And of course it caused a storm. Why? Because even though you in the West are free to be atheists and free to be offensive if you want to, not everyone is. There are still many religious believers. Here, though, there is no religion, and no sensibility about that sort of thing. Everything is possible. Now Chinese artists are saying, "*We* can do this, we're Marxists and atheists, *we* can do this." And we can! And we do!'

This sounded a little like the argument put forward by Ye Sha, the radio talk-show host in Shanghai. The idea that there is nothing any more in China that defines orthodoxy, in morality or anything else, so people just do what they want.

'We have perfected the modernism that you brought in, and do you know why?' Su lowers his head and raises his eyebrows again, talking like a man who rarely has anyone to listen to his theories. 'Because life here in China is brutal. So art is just a mirror of life. Life and death, love and hate, sex and violence. People in other countries don't have the pressure to survive that Chinese people have. In the West, you have no issues, no problems, you have free education, you have health care, you have everything. So your art is very boring. Here, the aim of modern artists is to express themselves. They want to create a kind of political freedom through their art. We can't express our views on lots of political issues, but we can do it through our art.'

'But does anyone care?' I ask.

He pauses with a smile, and sighs. 'No. That's the point. That's the problem. Art is a luxury. It can only be appreciated by people who have reached a certain standard of living. Old Hundred Names just want to make enough money to live peacefully. They have no desire to express themselves through art, or to appreciate people who do.'

Su then switches gear and seamlessly links the need for artistic and creative freedom with China's future. 'China can't become the strong and wealthy country it wants to be if it does not allow more creative thinking. Of course, art is a part of that. Art helps to develop people's imagination and creativity.'

He says that just days before, he had seen a news story on the Internet reporting that the man who helped China develop the atomic bomb, Qian Xuesen, was very sick. The prime minister of China, Wen Jiabao, had visited him in hospital and asked him what he wanted to say at the end of his life. 'We need more innovation,' Qian is reported to have told Prime Minister Wen. 'We're not producing any creative people. We are only making technicians.'

Su is triumphant at the thought that the nation's top scientist would have the same view as he does, and that the ninety-four-year-old would choose that as his one piece of advice to the nation's prime minister from his sickbed.

'This is not just about art,' he says, as we finish our tea and prepare to leave. 'We are talking about what is needed for the survival of our country. The government wants advanced education without encouraging people to think.'

There couldn't be a better summary of the Chinese dilemma today: the tension between the need to enforce orthodoxy in order to retain unity, and the need to allow freedom in order to encourage creativity. For the moment, in the cities like Xi'an at least, the government has bought off many people with economic development. If you can get people just to think about earning and spending, earning and spending, they are less likely to want to think for themselves. But what happens if the anaesthetic of prosperity wears off in the cities as it has in the countryside? And in today's globalised world, how can you become a Great Power, anyway – a country that will progress and succeed and endure – if you don't allow your people to think?

Chapter Ten

THE HERMIT OF HUA SHAN

'I'm a lost soul,' says Zheng Lianjie. 'I feel like I've lost my way.'

We're sitting in a coffee shop in Xi'an. Zheng is a youthful forty-something artist and photographer. I'm meeting him because he is heading the next day to Hua Shan (Flowery Mountain, in English), one of China's holy mountains, two hours' drive outside Xi'an. I'm heading there too.

Zheng Lianjie (pronounced *jung lyen-jyeh*) has long black hair, tied in a ponytail, and is wearing a black sleeveless T-shirt and black jeans. He grew up in Beijing and came of age as an artist in the 1980s, when, as he puts it, 'There was still idealism, there was still heroism' in China. With the crushing of the pro-democracy demonstrators by govern-ment troops in 1989, China changed, he says. Politics were out, experimenting was out, everything was out, except making money. So Zheng moved to New York, where he still spends part of the year.

We sit for a long time discussing the 'death of heroism' in China, and Zheng says he is missing something in his life, deep down.

'I've decided to escape from the modern world for a week,' he says, 'and go and live with a Daoist hermit who lives on Hua Shan.'

'There's a Daoist hermit on Hua Shan?' I raise my eyebrows.

'Yes. I met him when I visited there last year. I'm going to stay with him, in his cave, for a week.'

'Why?'

'To rediscover myself. And to reconnect with something. I don't know what.'

'Can I come? I mean, could I meet the hermit?'

'Well . . .' He pauses.

'Well, can I at least visit the hermit?' I ask. 'Briefly? I won't intrude on your own plans.'

'OK then. I don't think he'll mind.'

And with that, we arrange to meet at the Hairy Woman Cave Hostel, halfway up the mountain, the next day. Zheng gives me directions to the hostel and then tells me where the hidden path is that leads to the hermit's cave.

There were traditionally five holy Daoist mountains in China, one at each of the four points of the compass, plus one in the centre, symbolically connecting heaven and earth. Hua Shan is the Holy Mountain in the west. Its five peaks are said to resemble a five-petalled flower, hence the name Flowery Mountain.

The word *Dao* (which used to be spelt *Tao*) means 'the Way' in Chinese and refers to the way of the universe, the order behind nature, and the power within nature. While Confucianism is more of a social philosophy and Buddhism came from outside China, Daoism claims to be the one really indigenous Chinese religion. It is all about man finding his place in the great cosmic balance of things. In contrast to the monotheistic religions, with their emphasis on good fighting evil, in Daoism there is what's known as a unity of opposites. Good and evil, light and dark, strong and weak, empty and full are all part of the same whole, and each is necessary to the other. Daoism is also closely linked with the whole concept of *fengshui*, the rules of geomancy that are believed to govern cosmic harmony when people are deciding where to place buildings or graves. The *fengshui* of Hua Shan was believed to be perfectly aligned and contributed to the holiness of the site, which drew pilgrims from all over China.

It was said in ancient China that the traditional Chinese scholar was a Confucian when in office, and a Daoist when out of office. Daoism was in many ways the opposite of Confucianism, although it came to complement Confucian attributes within the Chinese character. While Confucius stressed order and duties and finding one's place in society, Daoism focused more on metaphysical questions, and on finding one's place in the universe. It had connections with folk religions. It was linked to alchemy and magic, to meditation and dietary control. Confucianism followed the rules of *li*, or 'proper behaviour according to status'. Daoism followed the concept of *wuwei* or 'nonaction'.

The two philosophies were later joined by Buddhism, which arrived from India in the first century AD. The three entwined, borrowing from each other in the minds of the people at least, and creating a bountiful pantheon of Chinese gods and beliefs. The absence of a monotheistic faith claiming to be revealed divine truth is no doubt one of the reasons Chinese people claim they have never fought a war in the name of religion. But some Chinese intellectuals lament that the lack of any firm concept of revealed truth has led to an unhealthy moral relativity in the Chinese mind. Truth has always been relative in China, while political power has not, they say, and the same is still true today.

I can see why the ancients would call Hua Shan holy. It is a magical, other-worldly place. The highest peak rises nearly 7,000 feet above the plain, its great white rock faces glowing incandescent in the sunshine. Coniferous trees cling to the sheer sheets of rock, somehow finding crevices to claw in their roots. Other green bushes and grasses find a roothold too, cascading down the rock face like strands of hair on an otherwise bald mountain.

When the Western powers arrived in the nineteenth century with their machines and their guns, they found a country still infused with the search for the balance and harmony of Daoism. But the Dao proved to be an ineffectual shield against the thrusting, forward-looking Ocean People. As China in the nineteenth and early twentieth centuries grappled with how to stave off foreign incursions, traditional belief systems came to be seen by reformers and revolutionaries alike as a major part of the problem. The Communists, as they gathered support in the 1920s and 1930s, put their faith in conquering nature, not finding harmony with it. They saw China's traditional philosophies as holding the country back. But rather than just sidelining them quietly, they launched a full-scale assault, and after 1949 many traditional Chinese beliefs were wiped out, on the surface at least.

As a result, after sixty years of Communist attacks, China can appear a strangely soulless place. There are no saddhus here, the holy men seen in every town in today's India, dressed in their flowing orange robes. There are few overtly religious ceremonies or traditions to compare, for instance, with the washing away of sins in the River Ganges. There is nothing to compare with the hajj of Muslims to Mecca, or the ritual and discipline of praying five times daily. In China, you are more likely to come across a travelling salesman hawking mobile phones than an itinerant holy man dispensing wisdom.

India and the Middle East have retained spiritualities of their own, which China has not. Although there is now a resurgence of interest in some folk religions and a growth in religious activity around the country, mainstream China feels very secular. I don't think it is a coincidence that China also has a faster economic growth rate than other areas of the world. In destroying its traditional ways of thinking, it has done away with any ethical restraints on a headlong pursuit of wealth and development.

As if to make this point, a huge power station stands belching out smoke not far from the entrance to Hua Shan, warning would-be pilgrims that the mountain is no longer the holy place it once was.

A railway has been built right along the foot of the mountain, too. There's nothing quite like the Xi'an to Beijing Express to rattle your *fengshui*.

Having been delayed in my departure, I decide with regret that I don't have time for the five-hour climb to the top of the mountain if I am to get back down to the Hairy Woman Cave Hostel by sunset. So I take the cable car halfway up and climb in the heat to the lowest of the mountain summits, the North Peak. Even here there is a stunning view over the various peaks that make up Hua Shan. All around are the great swirls of stone, like whirlpools of white rock disappearing into the mountains, rock faces that have for thousands of years whispered to travellers: 'Stay still.' 'Find balance.' 'Follow the Dao.'

Now, the cacophony of tourist voices drowns out the silence. The peasants of China may be hitting the road to find work, but the new middle classes are out travelling, exploring and trekking to the four corners of their country and beyond. I can hardly move on the mountain for excited Chinese tourists, and I sweat along the narrow mountain path with them towards the steep steps up to the next peak. A young woman, on vacation with her family from Beijing, wants to practise her English. She asks to have her photo taken with me. ('Here's me with the foreigner! Look how he sweats like a pig!') I linger for twenty minutes, my mind escaping the crowds and drifting back to the holiness of the past, and then I start the long, steep climb back down.

The Hairy Woman Cave Hostel is small, with only a few rooms plus some dormitory beds. It's not inside a cave, and there is no hairy woman (at least I don't see her), though apparently back in the mists of time there was. The inn, built in traditional Chinese style, is perched between the sheer mountain face and a bend in the winding path that leads to the summits. It centres on a traditional courtyard, which is where I throw down my daypack after a walk of several hours down from the North Peak. Zheng the Lost Artist had said he would spend the day taking photos on his way up Hua Shan. We have agreed not to use our mobile phones on the mountain. Doing so seemed sacrilegious somehow, especially since he is coming here to get away from all that. It is rather liberating to get to the hostel and have no idea when he will be arriving, and no way to find out. Perhaps he is lost on Flowery Mountain.

The innkeeper brings me a beer and a bowl of noodles, and then I just sit in the courtyard, watching the mighty mountain. The harsh golden sun sets, and the gentle milky moon rises, and a carpet of exquisite stars soon rolls out across the inky Chinese sky.

Sometimes in China, surprisingly rarely in fact, the spirit of a place, infused with those 5,000 years of continuous civilisation, catches you and transports you. Suddenly, you are connected with the magnificent Chinese past, which is perhaps why you came, and perhaps why you stayed, and certainly why you wonder if you can, or should, ever leave. I cannot remember the last instance in my life when I lost track of time, but I sit there in the courtyard of the Hairy Woman Cave Hostel for hours, looking at the moonlit mountain, running through the archive of twenty years of mental movie footage in my brain, and trying to recall those Tang dynasty poems I learned in college.

> *A cup of wine, under the flowering trees;*
> *I drink alone, for no friend is near.*
> *Raising my cup I beckon the bright moon,*
> *For he, with my shadow, will make three men.*

A steady stream of night climbers begins to pass by the hostel, whose door they cannot miss on the only footpath to the top of the mountain. Dozens of people choose to climb at night in order to reach the peaks in time for sunrise. They buy water or sit for a bowl of noodles, or just take a break from the climb. Many of them are students, taking advantage of the summer vacation to come exploring. The conversations are always the same, microcosms of the changed Chinese psyche, the young people's minds hurtling in the opposite direction to mine.

'Where are you from?' I ask.

'Hubei, but I'm studying in Beijing.'

'What are you studying?'

'Computer science.'

'Do you know what Daoism is?'

'Not really. We aren't taught about it in school.'

'Hi. Where are you from?'

'Henan, but I'm studying in Shanghai.'

'Do you know what Daoism is?'

'Something about nature, isn't it?'

'What are you studying?'

'Electronic information engineering.'

The next morning I set off early for the hermit's cave. The owner of the hostel says my friend Zheng arrived very late the night before, so I decide not to wake him. He is going to weave his way up to the hermit today, so I will either meet him on the way or when he gets there. I set off at seven, but the heat is already gathering. The entrance to the path leading to the cave is hidden, but Zheng has told me how to find it. When I reach the point I think he has described, I loiter for a moment to check that no one else has seen me. I don't want a horde of Chinese tourists following me on my pilgrimage. When it's clear no one is around, I dart up the gap between the trees and into the forest. The stone path soon becomes a simple forest path, scattered with leaves and occasional berries. There's a sudden feeling of pleasure, getting away from the crowds on a path that few people know.

It's a tough climb, and soon my shirt is soaked with sweat. I reach a turn where there is a huge boulder facing back out towards the tourist path offering a fantastic view of the creamy mountain majesty of Hua Shan itself. It feels as if I am the only person for miles around.

After a brief rest, I struggle up the path again, slipping occasionally on the moist, dark dirt. I'm supposed to be fit. I'm supposed to be training for a marathon. The heat increases and I start to puff. This had better be worth it. This hermit had better have something to say for himself. Some healthy lifestyle pointers, at least.

There is moss on Hua Shan. Moss is one of my favourite things in all the world. Deep, dank, dark, green moss. Northern China has little of it, because it never rains. Hua Shan has plenty, clinging to rocks, and to trees, and to whatever roots and bark it can find. I stop occasionally just to touch it.

After about an hour and a half of sweaty uphill climbing, a set of stone steps materialises ahead of me, some broken, most greened with time, leading to a stone arch at the top. I climb the steps and look through the arch into a tiny garden.

At the back of the garden is a huge white slab of Hua Shan rock, like some Chinese Golgotha protruding from the mountain itself. Cut into the rock are three cave doorways.

In front of the caves, up to the right, behind some large sunflowers and an overgrown vegetable plot, are steps leading to a small hut. I walk past the caves, and call out gently. '*You ren ma?* Is anyone here?'

Silence.

Then suddenly the curtain across the hut's door is lifted and out steps a small man in a pair of blue shorts and a red cotton vest.

Somehow I wasn't expecting the monk to look as though he was going for a jog.

'Are you Daoist Monk Shi?' I ask.

'I am,' he says, smiling kindly. He looks like he is perhaps in his mid-thirties, with a broad face, and a goatee that is long enough to be gently wispy at the end. His long black hair is pulled back into a bun.

I explain who I am, that I am a friend of Artist Zheng, who is arriving later in the day, and that I'm writing a book. I ask him if he would mind chatting with me for a while.

'*Mei you wenti. Huanying,*' he says. 'No problem. You are welcome.'

Although (or perhaps because) I work in one of the most worldly, plugged-in professions on the planet, wired 24/7 into what is going on around the globe, I have to confess that I have a seriously monastic streak. I love my job, the news, the travel, the writing, the intellectual engagement with the world, but at regular intervals, I feel the need just to escape from it all, to climb a mountain, and get away. When we go on vacation to rural Italy, I wander off to find monasteries, and my wife sometimes wonders if I'm coming back. A few years ago I stumbled across a magnificent old monastery in which there lived a silent order of monks. I almost joined on the spot. Talk about an antidote to rolling news.

So to me there is something completely compelling about a man withdrawing from society to live with nature on a mountainside.

My T-shirt is totally soaked, so I ask the hermit if I can hang it up to dry in the sun, and he points to a clothes line outside his cave bedroom. I sit down in just my shorts and sandals, feeling a little self-consciously back-to-nature myself.

Of course, I have questions, so I lick my pencil and start to put them to Hermit Shi (pronounced *shuh*).

First, what exactly *is* the Dao?

'The Dao is the *wanwu yuanxian de yige guilu.*'

I repeat it in Chinese and write it down, but then have to translate it slowly for myself out loud.

'*Wanwu yuanxian de yige guilu.* The law of the origin of the ten thousand things.'

Hmmm. So is Daoism a religion?

'Yes.'

So, there are gods?

'Originally, there were no gods, but when the old Daoist masters died, they became gods, and people worshipped them. And that is who the statues are, in the lower cave down there.' He points.

'So what are you trying to do here?'

'I'm trying to retreat from the *fenza shiwu*, the complex affairs of the world.'

'And what do you think of all this development all around you? This crazy development in modern China?'

'Development is good. We can't regret development. But too much development damages nature. It is a little extreme at the moment. Certainly there is too much running after money.'

'What about computer science? What about electronic information engineering?'

'Believing in science is OK. Science is the most natural thing. The only reason we have science is because, thousands of years ago, our ancestors talked about nature.'

I ask him about the massive power plant just beside Hua Shan, which to me looks like a monstrosity.

'Science is progress. Progress is good. But science cannot depart from metaphysics. If development goes against nature, it is not progress but regress. If you need electricity, then you must build electricity plants. If you don't need it, and it's excessive, then it's not right.'

Support for coal-burning power plants. That's not quite what I was expecting.

'So what about modern Chinese people, and their mind-set generally?'

'They strive for a modern lifestyle, but they have lost their roots. They should return to simplicity and truth.'

We plunge into a long discussion about the similarities and

differences between Daoism and Christianity, and especially about the knowability of the divine.

The Dao in Daoism, the Way itself, is by its nature unknowable. The first line of the classic Daoist text, the *Dao De Jing*, lays this out very clearly: 'The way that can be walked is not the True Way, the name that can be named is not the True Name.'

I always feel this single line has had more impact on the Chinese psyche than almost any other. There is no absolute spiritual truth. Truth, if it even exists, is unknowable.

Contrast this with Judaism and Christianity (or, for that matter, Islam), which claim to be revelations of divine truth.

Jesus said, 'I am the Way, the Truth and the Life. No one comes to the Father except through me.' Christianity says truth is knowable, and that assertion has shaped Western thinking. Even if not everyone believes in Christianity, the idea of an objective, existing moral truth has persisted.

When the first Western missionaries arrived in China, they managed to blend the Western and Eastern thinking rather beautifully in their translation of the opening words of John's Gospel. 'In the beginning was the Word,' it says in English. In Chinese this is translated, 'In the beginning was the Dao [the Way].'

I like Hermit Shi. He talks about things that I like talking about more than computer science and information engineering. We talk and talk, and he seems to enjoy chatting too. Finally, I say I have one last question before I must put on my now-dry T-shirt and leave him alone. He raises his eyebrows in expectation.

'So,' I ask him, 'what do you think is the meaning of life?'

I laugh as I ask it, and he laughs as he hears it.

'The meaning of life is the realisation of the Dao.'

'But how do you realise the Dao?'

'By coexisting with nature.'

I write it down, religiously.

As he walks me to the stone archway at the entrance of his

garden, I ask him if I might come back and stay with him sometime, and he agrees.

'So can I just show up?'

'Sure,' he replies, 'or you can call me.'

'Call you?'

'Yes, call my mobile. Here's the number.'

There is a gentle, wispy smoke hanging over Hua Shan as I descend the path from the hermit's cave. This would make the perfect mystical-spiritual-romantic photograph if I could just get over the suspicion that the smoke might be coming from the nearby power station.

Back at the Hairy Woman Cave Hostel, my friend Zheng is up and eating brunch. We sit for about an hour, interviewing each other about what we are doing here. He tells me more about his spiritual search, and the frustrations of living in China when all people want to do is earn money. He laments the rise of the petty bourgeoisie, as he calls them, and says that 'the economic water has submerged active thinking'. Then we say goodbye, and he sets off up the path to spend the week with the hermit, and I set off down the hill to catch the bus back to Xi'an.

At the bottom of the mountain, I walk under the railroad track as an express thunders past, elude the vendors who want to sell me Hua Shan postcards, T-shirts and sun hats, and climb aboard a minibus for the journey back to Xi'an, hoping I can just sit quietly for a while and contemplate the Dao.

The ticket collector comes around to collect my fare. He's a genial-looking guy, just this side of raffish, who could be taken a lot more seriously if he didn't have a folded wet towel on the top of his head. He occasionally takes it off to wipe his sweating face, then puts it back on his head. He asks me where I'm from, and the usual chitchat ensues, including a remarkably favourable assessment of the United Kingdom. 'Hong Kong is good, because you guys governed it,' he says.

One row in front of me, on the other side of the aisle, is a youngish-looking Chinese man with a buzz cut and very shiny shoes. He looks as though he might be an off-duty soldier, and he takes exception to what the ticket collector has said.

'So you think Britain should just govern the whole of China, do you?' he shoots at Mr Wet Towel.

'Sure. They couldn't do a worse job than this bunch,' the man with the towel replies provocatively, without mentioning Any Particular Party.

'Look, I don't love the Communist Party,' says Shiny Shoes (needing to establish his street credibility, and the fact that he's not a corrupt official), 'but you can't be that pessimistic.'

Mr Wet Towel is not to be put down by patriotism. Having collected all the fares, he sits at the front facing the passengers and, completely dismissing Shiny Shoes's argument, says, 'Of course I'm pessimistic. Living in this country. It's just too corrupt.'

The debate rages for five minutes, with no one else taking part, then the two give up and sit in silence. Finally, more passengers climb on board, and we pull out towards the main road for the two-hour journey back to Xi'an.

Chapter Eleven

ELVIS LIVES

I spend a final day in Xi'an, visiting more imperial tombs outside the city in the morning, and browsing through the city's bookshops in the afternoon. The bestsellers are all management books, guides on how to make a million, and biographies of successful Western businessmen. I flick through the history books on sale, which devote a page to the history of China since 1949, and about two hundred pages to the different periods before. I search for any remaining sign of Marxist theory, eventually finding Mao's little-read book hidden away on an upstairs floor, unmissed by the entrepreneurs devouring the business section below.

Throughout the afternoon, I also hold auditions for the role of driver in my road movie. If I'm going to spend the next two days in some guy's taxi, he had better have something to say. In each taxi I get into, I chat with the driver about everything and nothing. How much can he tell me about the local area? Will he have friends in the countryside we can stop off and see? How's his driving? They chat back, oblivious to the fact that they're auditioning for the role of a lifetime.

The minute I jump into Old Gu's car, I know he is the man. If there were Elvis Presley look-alike competitions in China, Old Gu could turn up just as he is and win first prize. He says he's nearly sixty, but he looks much younger. He has thick dark hair, slightly greased, and a slight curl to his upper lip. If he had not been contributing to the Communist reconstruction of Shaanxi province as a young man in the 1950s and '60s, I swear he would have been throwing girls in long swingy skirts over his shoulder on the dance floors of Memphis. He has a slightly laconic slant on life that makes me like him immediately. I tell him to meet me at my hotel the following day, a Sunday, at seven in the morning for an early start.

Old Gu shows up on time, and we head out of town, with me humming 'Blue Suede Shoes' in the back. His car is a well-cared-for VW Santana, with a frilly curtain across the back window and curtains on all the passenger windows too. The air-conditioning works, and we will no doubt need it later on. Before we reach the outskirts of Xi'an, he pulls over and waits by the side of the road outside an apartment block.

'Is it OK if my wife comes too?' he asks suddenly.

'Your wife?'

'Yes, she'd like to see the countryside on the way to the northwest. And it's also safer driving if there are two of us.'

As he is speaking, a slender middle-aged woman with a round face opens the front passenger door and steps in. She carries nothing but a small plastic bag. Presented with the marital fait accompli, I acquiesce, settle into the back seat, and let it go. Perhaps chitchat with two people will be more interesting than chitchat with just one. We make small talk. They both grew up in Xi'an. Their son is at university, so they have an empty nest now. They are both from China's most tragic generation. America's baby boomers were lifted up on the wings of postwar prosperity. China's baby boomers were sucked down into the whirlpool of Mao's madness. Both Elvis and Mrs Elvis had their education interrupted by political campaigns. Xi'an has many problems, they say, unemployment and corruption especially. But, after decades of turmoil they seem grateful for the relative stability a modern China.

Unless you had travelled along it all the way from Shanghai and formed a certain attachment to its shabby ways, its chaotic turn-offs and its worn tarmac, stained with oil and mud, you would probably not take Route 312 west from Xi'an. My next destination is Lanzhou, a journey of more than 300 miles, and a new motorway between the two cities provides a much more direct route. The guidebook says the trip takes fourteen hours by bus along the motorway, but it will take me two days driving with Elvis and his wife along Route 312. The old road snakes rather indirectly towards Lanzhou, forming two wiggly sides of a long, flat triangle to the north of the motorway's hypotenuse.

Elvis steers a course through the factories and new apartment blocks of the suburbs, out on to Route 312.

It is the morning of my thirty-seventh birthday, and the broad Chinese sky seems to acknowledge the special occasion by opening up into a particularly radiant blue.

Shaanxi province (of which Xi'an is the capital) has been the heartland of the Communist Party since 1935, when Mao Zedong established the town of Yan'an, about three hundred miles north of Xi'an, as the Party's base. Mao had struggled to bring the revolution to the peasants of southern China in the late 1920s. He managed to rally about 100,000 peasants at his guerrilla bases there, but they were harassed on every side by the forces of Mao's nemesis, Chiang Kaishek. Chiang was also trying to reunite the collapsed country but *without* the aid of Communism. Finally, hard-pressed by Chiang's troops, in the autumn of 1934 Mao's ragtag band of Communist Party members fled the South on what would become known in Communist legend as the Long March. They marched for nearly a year through central, western and northern China, reaching the relative safety of Yan'an in the autumn of 1935. From there, the Communists eventually launched their conquest of the whole of China in the 1940s.

More than 90,000 of the original Long Marchers deserted or perished, but the 8,000 or so who reached Shaanxi were to form the core of the Party that took over China in 1949. The barren yellow earth here proved a fertile recruiting ground for their revolutionary message of giving land to the landless peasants.

Had it not been for the Japanese invasion in 1937, which forced Chiang Kaishek to ally with the Communists against the invaders, Chiang, who was virulently anti-Communist, would probably have wiped out the nascent Communist Party. But the invasion gave the Party a breathing space. It grew stronger during the Second World War, and Old Hundred Names started to put their faith in its members, inspired by what they saw of the Communists' incorruptibility, their desire to fight for the peasants and the downtrodden, and their promises of land reform. It still took until 1949 for the Communists to conquer all of China, but no one in Shaanxi ever forgot that it was here that victory became a possibility.

Now, though, it's a different story. The Communist Party may be filling the pockets of many, but it has lost the hearts of most. Indeed, the Party lost the revolution almost as soon as the revolution was won, and Communist China unravelled into a twisted mess of famine and political struggle. By the time Mao died, in 1976, people were exhausted, glad not to have to believe in him any more. And now the spiritual vacuum that was left is being filled by something completely different.

Two hours out of Xi'an, I ask Elvis to pull his VW off the busy four-lane stretch of Route 312. A sign beside the road announces the village of Shuangzhao (pronounced *shwahng-jow*). A small red-brick church nestles beside an apple orchard, just thirty yards back from the road, sitting behind a wall daubed with a huge advertisement for fertiliser. Above the church's entrance are three large Chinese characters, which read *Fu Yin Tang*, Good News Hall.

Globalisation has not reached Shuangzhao, and foreigners are scarce in these parts, so I am greeted by curious looks as I wander over to the tiny church.

Dotted across the Shaanxi countryside are dozens and dozens of simple Protestant churches like this one, and more ornate Catholic churches too. This is the flip side of the breakdown in Communist ideology in China: the re-emergence of religion.

'*Zaoshang hao*. Good morning. *You libai ma?* Is there a service this morning?'

'*You libai*. Yes, there is.'

An old lady is standing at the entrance to the church, like a female St Peter, checking off the members of the congregation as they enter through its less-than-pearly gates. She tilts her head to one side to get a closer look at the foreigner in front of her, and her face breaks into a huge, toothless grin.

She ushers me in, arms waving, voice rising, like a parent welcoming home the prodigal and sits me down at the back of the church, next to two other old ladies. If it weren't for their beaming, toothless smiles, the triumvirate of grannies could have stepped right out of Act 1, Scene 1 of *Macbeth*. Three benevolent witches, cooking up good spiritual spells at the back of a rural Chinese church.

The inside of the church is simple. Some pictures of Jesus on the walls and just bare, low benches for pews. An altar at the front has the large Chinese character *ai*, meaning 'love', written on it in bright red. The character is the focus of the little church, like a simple manger in a Renaissance painting, radiating light out to a stable and to the world. The character attracts my attention, partly perhaps because it is written in such a striking red, jumping out from the browns and greys and greens of the rural church. But the character also seems to clang loudly against everything around it in the countryside. Chairman Mao, like Confucius before him, offered many things to the Chinese people, but love was not one of them. Perhaps that is why the churches are now full.

There are about forty people in the congregation, young and old, mostly local farmers, many looking as though they have walked in straight from the fields. They are fascinated by the white man in their midst. One of the Three Grannies, eighty-three years old, says she has never seen a westerner before.

They do not have a minister of their own and are waiting for the itinerant preacher to arrive. He preaches at several churches every Sunday, and one male member of the church, who wears very thick glasses and turns out to be the organist, says proudly that the minister has been to theological college. Many of China's rural clergy barely have a secondary education, let alone college training, so it is a source of great pride to this congregation that their minister is well educated. I ask them questions about their church and about themselves, and I hear familiar tales of persecution because of their faith in the 1950s and 1960s, and then a resurrection of the church in the 1980s and after. Christ is providing them with something other than Route 312 in which to place their hope.

Before the Communist Party came to power, in 1949, there were roughly 3 million Catholics and 750,000 Protestants in China. When the Communists kicked out western missionaries after 1949, Chinese Christians became almost immediate targets of persecution. Western Christians feared for the survival of the Chinese church.

A few official churches were allowed by the Party in the 1950s, to give the illusion of religious freedom, but most Christians were forced either to renounce their faith in favour of the Communist Caesar or be sent to jail or labour camp. Hundreds of thousands of Christians spent decades in horrific conditions as a result. Then when Mao died, in 1976, social controls were loosened a little, many Christians were released from jail, and more churches were allowed. Many still refused to join the 'official' churches, believing the ministers installed in such churches were stooges of the government. They insisted on meeting in their homes, in so-called house churches. The Communist Party would often persecute house-church Christians and try to close down their congregations, sometimes simply by demolishing their homes.

As with the early church in Rome, persecution led to the growth not the death of the Chinese church. Now, even conservative estimates put the total number of Christians at around 75 million (about 15 million Catholics and about 60 million Protestants). That is only about 6 per cent of the population, but is still more than the 70 million members of the Chinese Communist Party.

Since the 1980s, the church has gone through several decades of astonishing growth, filling the spiritual vacuum left by the demise of Communism.

The Party has now quietly accepted that it will not be able to get rid of religion. In fact, amazingly, Chinese officials will admit off the record that Chinese people *need* something to believe in. But the growth in numbers does not mean that all Christians are treated well, this again being a choice that comes down to local officials. If they don't like Christianity, they can make life difficult for believers, as they can for anyone. If they don't mind Christianity, then life is smoother, as it seems to be here in Shuangzhao. I have visited villages in eastern China where the local officials even encourage Christianity. The Christians are the only ones obeying the law and paying their taxes, they say.

Half an hour after the service is due to start, a young man with a friendly face approaches and says it looks as if the minister is not coming. Everyone looks around rather disconsolately. Granny Two mutters something under her breath. Then the younger man has an epiphany.

'The *yang ren*, the Ocean Person, can preach the sermon!'

Everyone's eyes turn to me, and there's a very slight pause as the idea sinks in, to them and to me. I protest that I'm not used to preaching sermons, and certainly not in Chinese. The man is insistent, his eyes shining at the brilliance of his suggestion. Unfortunately, the whole church is soon also converted to the idea. Everyone gathers around me, yakking away in heavily accented Mandarin that I barely understand, saying yes, I would be the one to preach. God had led me here, they say, and so I must preach. No one has even asked me if I am a Christian.

'You can't leave here until you've preached us a sermon!' Granny Three says, grabbing my arm.

'But I'm not qualified to preach sermons. I haven't been to theological college.'

There is no escaping. The smiles broaden, and the imploring becomes more insistent. I feel I can't just leave them in the lurch, so finally I agree. I grab a Chinese Bible, and remembering my conversation with the hermit just days before, I stand up and preach on John 14:6. 'Jesus said, I am the Way, the Truth and the Life. No man comes to the Father except through me.'

Heads nod politely as I preach hesitantly at the front. The Three Grannies squint through their glasses at the strange sight. A child sitting at the front whispers something inaudible in his mother's ear. When the sermon is over, I suggest we say a prayer, and I say one myself out loud, in Chinese. The congregation then starts praying out loud, one person after another, overlooking the rather poor sermon I have just preached and thanking God for this Ocean Person who has delivered the message, praying that God will bless him and them, and then saying simply, 'Thank you, God, for your love.'

There is a purity and intensity to Christian believers in China, and it overflows in their prayers. Mention Christianity to ordinary Chinese people, and they are not burdened by visions of crusading soldiers, fornicating popes or right-wing politicians. They have heard about this belief relatively late in the faith's long and winding history, and for them it is a matter of the heart. This is perhaps how it was supposed to be, I think to myself, as the final 'Amen' rises from the congregation.

They all open their eyes and look up from their prayers. A few of them seem surprised to see I'm still standing there. I suggest we sing a hymn, and the man with thick glasses sitting behind the ludicrously decrepit old organ cranks out the tune of the final hymn, which everyone joins in. The singing over, I wish them many blessings and thank them for their hospitality. The Three Grannies rise slowly in unison and ask me to stay for lunch. I explain that I must reach Pingliang by evening.

'Pingliang?' repeats Granny One, as though it's the end of the earth. 'He's going to Pingliang,' she explains loudly to Granny Two, who has taken hold of my hand and is showing no sign of letting go.

'Pingliang?' asks Granny Two. 'Well, if you've got to be in Pingliang by sundown, you'd better get on the road.' She looks deeply into my eyes and smiles a toothless smile, and we all move towards the door and walk out to the road together.

Elvis and his wife have been sitting patiently in the car all this time, unaware of the spiritual drama that has been unfolding inside the church. But they don't seem too annoyed by the wait. They're off on an expenses-paid trip to Lanzhou, so stopping for a couple of hours is no problem, although they seem bemused by my interest in the intricacies of rural life.

It's lunchtime by the time we drive away from the church, so not far down the road, Elvis pulls over at a row of rather grubby restaurants for something to eat. We choose one of the larger ones and step inside. An attractive woman emerges from behind a curtain at the back of the room. She's wearing a ridiculously fancy dress and heavy make-up, and she looks at me as though I might be wanting more than just a bowl of noodles. The door behind the curtain is ajar, and I can see a bed in it. This is clearly a one-stop shop, where truck drivers, or anyone on the road, can stop to fulfil all their bodily needs. And over it all, a picture of Chairman Mao looks down from the dirty, peeling wall. Welcome to modern China, Chairman. It's all coming round full circle.

I don't know what the woman in the flowery dress was serving up behind the curtain, but the food she cooked was delicious. We're gradually leaving Rice Territory now, and slowly entering Noodle Territory. The influence of the Muslim northwest is starting to seep into the food, the smells, the looks of the people and the music. Along with a steaming bowl of thick beef noodles, the lunch table heaves with a plate of lamb kebabs, some spicy chicken and a few dishes I don't even recognise.

One of the great things about travelling in China is that the food is so good. You can be in the middle of nowhere, show up at some little shack like this one, and be served a delicious stir-fried meal. KFC and McDonald's may be making inroads into people's tastebuds in the cities, but for the majority of Chinese people traditional Chinese food – so different region by region – provides some welcome continuity in an age of upheaval. And people now have meat to eat, not once a month, not once a week, but every day.

The most barren parts of Shaanxi, including the former Communist stronghold of Yan'an, are further north, out of reach of Route 312, but even here the black road winds its way through an increasingly yellow landscape. It's known as the loess plateau, a phrase rarely used in the West outside loamy geological circles but used all the time by English-speaking Chinese people. In Chinese, as usual, the word is much more logical: *huang tu gao yuan*, literally 'yellow earth high plain'. The loess plateau stretches between the North China Plain, where Beijing is located in the east, and the Gobi Desert in the west. Much of the land here is over 4,000 feet in altitude, with the Great Wall forming the plateau's boundary to the north. The yellow earth has always been difficult to cultivate and is prone to water erosion. It rarely rains here, but when it does, it can re-shape the landscape. A heavy rainfall can cause great chunks of the land to drop away, and the whole region is riven with ravines and loess cliffs, where the soil has collapsed like a great melting yellow iceberg.

Though not fertile on the surface, underground this region has some of the nation's richest deposits of coal, and not far to the northeast of Route 312 is a whole belt of coal-mining towns. China produces around 35 per cent of the world's coal, and mining provides many people in the hopeless small towns of Shaanxi with their only possibility of employment. China also reports around 80 per cent of global deaths in mining accidents each year. More than five thousand miners die in an average year in China's inefficient, chronically unsafe coal mines (and those deaths are just the ones that are reported). That is more than one hundred times the number killed in American mines.

It is one of modern China's most brutal economic food chains. The government needs coal to fuel the factories to keep the economy growing and thereby to prevent social discontent. Unscrupulous mine owners know they can make a lot of money selling coal to the hungry Chinese economic machine, so they maximise production, at the expense of safety. Poverty-stricken miners, with little hope beyond their next pay packet, go down the mine shafts, even though they know they are unsafe. Their lives are a commodity seemingly more expendable than the coal that they produce. The government launches occasional crackdowns on illegal mining, and tries to implement safety standards, but as everywhere in China, such crackdowns are at odds with the general need to keep the economy growing, so the local snakes of regional officialdom rarely listen to the supposedly strong dragon in Beijing.

Mr and Mrs Elvis wait patiently for me as I get out of the car every five or ten miles to talk to farmers in the field. We pull up outside some caves set just back from the road and talk to the families who live in them. The caves have proper wooden doors and windows at the front, and interiors that disappear deep into the cliffs. The farmers say they are very warm in winter and very cool in summer, and they invite me inside. We chat about the struggle to make ends meet on the edge of the loess plateau. The people are poor but hospitable, and we sit and talk and laugh together, and I wonder at their ability to endure such hardships and still welcome a stranger like a long-lost son. All of the families have children in the cities. Some have travelled to Xi'an, some westwards to Lanzhou and even Urumqi, cities along Route 312 that I will be visiting. None of them relies solely on farming any more.

There are two major problems for people living in this poverty-stricken corner of China, which expose the ecological and social fragility of China that lurks not far below the shiny surface. Each issue is causing tears in the fabric of Chinese society, and could come to have major implications for the country.

First of all, there is no water in northern China. The rivers have all dried up, the people say, and they have to trek a couple of miles to collect drinking water from a standpipe in the nearest town. This is a huge problem. The Yellow River, which flows from the Tibetan Plateau through the yellow earth of Shaanxi and should empty into the East China Sea, is so over-exploited that in eighteen of the last twenty-five years of the twentieth century there were periods when it failed to reach the sea. In one year, 1997, it failed to reach the sea for 226 days, and for much of that year it didn't even reach Shandong, the last province it is supposed to pass through before reaching the ocean. This is an extraordinary situation for what is the world's fourth longest river. The government has now launched a plan called *Nan Shui Bei Diao*, the 'South-to-North Water Diversion Project', a multi-billion dollar scheme to build three canals that will divert water north to the Yellow River from the Yangtze.

Much of the water that is available is dangerously polluted, with local officials unprepared to treat sewage or factory outflow or close down polluting factories for fear of slowing down local economic growth. If growth slows here, as everywhere in China, social unrest is likely to increase.

In addition to all this, the water table in northern China is dropping by an average of seven feet per year as city officials drain underground aquifers for the water their cities desperately need. The situation has reached crisis point.

The other big problem in this poor, poor region is that few of the sons of the farmers can find a wife. Many women aborted female foetuses in the early 1980s, when the one-child policy was introduced, because if they could have only one child, they wanted it to be a son. Now that generation of men has come to marrying age, and there are too few women available. Again, the problem is the same all over China. The government admits it will be short of 30 million brides by the year 2020. One of the mothers I meet says the only hope is that her 23-year-old son will go to the city and meet a migrant girl there. 'He will never find a wife here,' she says. 'And even if he does, the bride-price will be too high.' The market economy is working, it seems, even in mate selection.

I had the previous year met a group of North Koreans who had escaped into China and fled inland to Ningxia, quite near where I am now. They had said there were many North Korean women there who had been sold by middlemen as wives to the local Chinese peasants. Soon after I finished my trip, the Chinese press reported the detention of sixty-nine women from Burma who had been smuggled into Henan province, through which I'd just passed, and sold for about $2,500 each to Chinese farmers desperate for wives. The official gender ratio in 2005 was 118 boys to every 100 girls, but in some villages the ratio is as much as 140 to 100.

Across rural China, there are millions of stories like theirs. Lack of water, lack of women, lack of opportunities, despite the new mobility brought by the roads and the rail network. Rural China is changing, and some farmers' lives are being transformed. Many of the rhythms of rural life have been broken. The mind-set of farmers is changing too. But it's not an easy transition, and they're coming from a level of subsistence that is very low indeed. In urban China, you can see the pursuit of happiness emerging. In rural China, it is still the pursuit of survival. Think about the rural characters in the novels of a writer like George Eliot. Think Thomas Hardy. Think the end of *The Mayor of Casterbridge*: 'Happiness was but the occasional episode in a general drama of pain.' That is where China's farmers are coming from, the place from which 750 million people are trying to escape. Now, some opportunities are there, as they never have been before, and slowly a road is being made by many, out of the centuries-old poverty of the countryside. But it is a long road, and a difficult one.

Finally, as the shadows lengthen in the evening sun, Elvis, Mrs Elvis and I reach the city of Pingliang. The new motorway, with its more direct route to Lanzhou, has taken a lot of traffic away from Pingliang, but even here, there are construction sites all around. As usual, there is one big hotel in town, and I check in. It costs about twenty dollars for a reasonable room and bathroom. As usual there are many large SUVs parked outside, most of them with official licence plates. Right outside the entrance is a karaoke bar. Close your eyes and you could be in a small city anywhere along Route 312. The architecture, the construction, the karaoke bars, the feeling of modest improvement in lifestyle, the absence of any signs of abject poverty, but the feeling that it is going to take a long, long while to reach anything beyond 'moderate prosperity'.

It's been a long day's driving. After a quick meal together, we say good night and turn in early, the distant wails from the karaoke bar echoing into the warm summer evening.

The next morning, I'm up bright and breezy and ready to hit the road. I head through to the hotel dining room, knowing that, since this is a completely Chinese hotel, there will be almost nothing I want to eat. Considering the universal deliciousness of Chinese cuisine, it has always been a mystery to me how Chinese breakfasts could be so bad. You would think after five thousand years of continuous civilisation they could come up with something a little better than pickled vegetables and rice gruel. I consider berating the staff on this point, but realise I don't know how to say Rice Krispies in Chinese, so I grab a couple of sweetened bread rolls and sit down in the corner of the dining room with a pot of Chinese tea.

Elvis and his wife struggle down bleary-eyed about ten minutes later, and soon we are back on Route 312, heading northwest.

They seem very lovey-dovey this morning for a couple who have been married for so long. She starts peeling him some apples and popping the segments into his mouth with a smile as he drives. Perhaps love is not dead in China.

We have not gone far down the road, though, before the car swerves slightly, and Elvis jolts himself upright. It's only nine in the morning, and he is falling asleep at the wheel. Chinese roads are dangerous enough without a sleepy driver weaving all over the place.

'He stayed up watching television,' explains Mrs. Elvis, pushing him slightly with her elbow, as if to urge him to pull himself together.

'Right,' I murmur.

And then I realise: Mr and Mrs Elvis are not married at all. She is his lover, and they are off on a little lovers' jaunt to Lanzhou at my expense. He hasn't been up watching television. They have been up all night getting better acquainted.

'Watching television, eh?' I ask. 'What was on?'

'Oh, you know, just a good movie.' Elvis tries to continue the game.

'It must have been *really* good for you to stay up so late.' I raise my eyebrows really high, and he glances in his rearview mirror to see me looking straight at him with a faint smile on my face.

'Yes, it was,' he says, realising that he's been rumbled.

There's an awkward silence for a moment, but then everyone settles into the new reality. Without anything direct having been said, we have reached a quiet understanding, which is what Elvis and his 'wife' were expecting in the first place. China is the ultimate 'don't ask, don't tell' country. 'Mind your own business' might have been the first commandment of Confucianism (and then Communism too).

We stop three more times for Elvis to get out and stretch. Mrs Elvis is trying everything possible to keep him awake. She prods him constantly, and dabs him occasionally with her wet facecloth. We stop for a toilet break, and she massages and pummels his back and shoulders. She even tries to get him to jump and dance beside the road just to wake him up. I suggest that perhaps I should drive but he insists he is wide awake.

We weave our way across the border into Gansu province, wild, wide-open Gansu, the gateway to northwest China, where the yellow earth will soon dissolve into the desert proper. The slow wiggle that the two-lane Route 312 has become suddenly hooks up with the four-lane motorway that has shot straight out from Xi'an to Lanzhou. We pass a man whose job is to pick up tiny pieces of litter on the shoulder of the new highway, and I ask Elvis to pull over for the last time before we reach Lanzhou. I walk back to ask the man about his job, and what the new road has done to his life. He simply says he has to pick up litter along the road, and he gets paid two dollars a day to do so. More he doesn't know.

I turn away from him and back towards the taxi, sitting alone on the new black tarmac. Its red paint is the only fleck of colour in an otherwise yellow landscape. Mrs Elvis is leading her lover in a tango on the hard shoulder of the road.

Chapter Twelve

THE LAST GREAT EMPIRE

What is China? And who are the Chinese?

Such questions might seem superfluous when the answer stares out from any map or atlas you pick up. China is a country with borders like any other, and the people who live within those borders are Chinese. Right?

Well, not exactly. For a thousand miles, driving along Route 312 from Shanghai to the frontier town of Lanzhou, 'What is China?' has been a relatively easy question to answer. You can define it culturally, ethnically, geographically, or any way you like; there may be thousands of local dialects, differing almost from county to county, but any way you choose to define it up to Lanzhou, it is clearly Confucian-based China, inhabited by ethnic Chinese people (often known as Han Chinese).

But out here, as I approach the west of China, definitions become hazy.

The author Peter Fleming (whose brother Ian wrote the James Bond 007 novels) was a young correspondent with *The Times* when he attained a degree of fame in the 1930s by travelling across a disintegrated China from Peking to Kashgar in the far west of China, and on to British Kashmir. In his wonderful book *News from Tartary*, published in 1936, Fleming describes the joy of arriving in Lanzhou after an eight-day journey of 'jolting, irksome squalor' from X'ian.

There is a bazaar much nearer in atmosphere to the bazaars of Central Asia than to the markets of Peking. It is all very different from the China you see from the Treaty Ports; you have the feeling that you are on the frontiers of another land, that you have come almost to the edge of China. As indeed you have.

Lanzhou was, and is, the end of homogenous ethnic Chinese China. It is where the tectonic plates of Han China start to grate up against those of Central Asia. I still have at least another 1,500 miles to travel on my journey along Route 312 to the Kazakh border. By distance, Lanzhou (pronounced *lan-joe*) is not even halfway across the country. But the areas I am about to cross are populated by many different peoples who are not ethnically Chinese. They live within the borders of the People's Republic of China, but many of them feel no affiliation with China or Chinese culture. Their religion, their history, their language, every reference point you care to mention is different from those of the Han Chinese, yet Beijing says they are Chinese. Most of the so-called minority peoples live peacefully within the Chinese state. But many Tibetans and members of the Uighur ethnic group (pronounced *wee-gur*), who inhabit the west, believe the regions where they live should not be part of China, and there are movements inside and outside China to resist rule from Beijing.

The reasons for this resistance have their roots in the very nature of the Chinese state, and the complete transformation it has undergone in the last 150 years.

For centuries (millennia, in fact) China was defined not so much by the territory it covered but by its culture, similar to how the concept of Christendom defined Europe before the advent of the nation-state in the seventeenth century. What made you Chinese in the past was not so much where you lived (though of course that was part of if) but whether you accepted the teachings of the ancient Confucian texts, the bureaucratic system of government and Chinese imperial authority. Barbarians on the fringe of the empire could become Chinese by adopting Chinese ways, and some did, just as barbarians in ancient Europe could become Roman by adopting Roman ways, and then, during the Dark and Middle Ages, infidels could become part of 'Christendom' by accepting Christianity.

For China, though, there was also a sort of twilight zone of people who were on the fringes, who did not adopt Chinese ways but whom the emperor and mandarins in Beijing considered part of the empire, and part of the broader imperial family. This was especially true after the conquests of the eighteenth century, when the Chinese Empire invaded and incorporated Chinese Turkestan (now called Xinjiang) and Tibet. The Uighurs, Tibetans and others would send tribute to Beijing, often just to keep the emperor off their backs. Rulers in Beijing were happy to keep a fairly loose relationship with the border peoples too, not forcing them to adopt Chinese ways as long as they sent tribute and kowtowed to the emperor when they were supposed to.

That all changed in the nineteenth century, with the coming of the Ocean People. China's elite gradually realised that the West was playing by completely different rules. Here were people from beyond the Chinese world who did not accept either the traditional Chinese worldview or the superiority of Chinese culture. The Ocean People were not interested in a tributary relationship with Beijing. They came from a continent of equal nation-states, all vying for supremacy, and they had no time for the pretence of Chinese superiority. More importantly, they knew their own weapons were infinitely superior. As the Ocean People began to carve up China, it eventually became clear to China's rulers that the Chinese way of ordering the world culturally could not continue, and that if they wanted China as an entity to survive, the Chinese would have to take on the West at its own game. After much resistance and deep, deep soul-searching, many of them concluded that, to save themselves as a nation-state, they would have to destroy themselves as a culture.

So the Chinese began to ditch their culture, and their cultural way of defining who they were, and they started to think more in terms of the nation-states of Europe. The Confucian classics and thousands of years of Chinese history said that China was the centre of the world and the Chinese were the world's superior people. The military defeats and humiliating treaties forced upon them in the nineteenth century told them they were not. Europe was superior because it used modern technology and weaponry, so China would have to learn something of that if it was to avoid being carved up completely. In 1905 the Chinese abolished the all-important Confucian examination system, which had given the emperor and his mandarins their legitimacy for two thousand years, and then, in 1912, the whole imperial system itself was over-thrown.

Now, if you are defining for the first time the line on the map to show where your nation-state begins and ends, you have to decide what to do with those peoples with whom you have always held an ambiguous relationship. Are they in or out? And of course, for any ruler in Beijing, they had to be in. There could be no more fudging of who was Chinese and was not. Chinese control of Tibet and Turkestan from the eighteenth century to 1912 was in many places only nominal, and after 1912, as we have seen, China collapsed and could not enforce its control over the west at all. But soon after the Communists conquered eastern China, in 1949, they set about moving troops to Tibet and the Muslim northwest in order to draw their borders, Western-style, where it was felt they had existed under the Qing dynasty (pronounced *ching*, which ruled from 1644 to 1912). This was the ultimate sign of China's transformation from world unto itself to one nation-state among many. But the transformation has not been smooth, and the legacy for today's China is still an uneasy mix of old empire and modern nation-state.

It's a dilemma best summed up by the MIT political scientist and all-round China genius Lucian Pye, who wrote that 'China is a civilisation pretending to be a state.'

Or, to put it another way, China is the Last Great Empire. All the other empires of the nineteenth and twentieth centuries – the British and French, the Ottoman and Soviet – are gone. If we put aside for a moment the theory that the United States has become an imperial power, then only the Chinese Empire remains, wanting to go forward as a modern nation-state, but encumbered with the constraints of an empire that can only be held together by force. Few Chinese people admit this, and many who read this book are likely to disagree strongly with me, and criticise me for my anti-Chinese sentiments and my desire to split the motherland. But objective historical evidence suggests that it is true. One of the most successful myths the Chinese Communist Party has established in the minds of its people is that China has always looked the way it does today. When *The Cambridge History of China* was translated into Chinese, the map of Ming dynasty China (1368–1644) was changed from not including Tibet and Chinese Turkestan in the original English version to including them in the Chinese translation, in direct contradiction to the reality of history.

All of this history hangs in the air as you approach Lanzhou along Route 312 from the southeast.

Lanzhou holds the dubious distinction of being one of the world's most polluted cities, the deadly legacy of Chairman Mao's attempts at industrialisation in the 1950s and 1960s. The city has a population of nearly 3 million people, and it stretches along the banks of the Yellow River, squeezed on four sides by mountains. The mountains are one reason for the pollution, because the smog from the factories is unable to escape. In the 1990s, there had been plans to remedy this by blasting a huge pollution escape hole in one of the mountain ranges, but that scheme seems to have come to nothing. For local governments in China, as in most countries, there are more advantages in spending money on new industry (jobs, taxes, social stability, moderate prosperity) than there are in spending money to deal with industry's negative consequences.

The city itself, it seems to me, is too much maligned. There is a certain pleasant grittiness about it, if you like grittiness (which I do). As long as the lining of your bronchial tubes is not required to interact with the so-called air of the city for too long, you will probably enjoy Lanzhou, with its frontier town atmosphere, great noodle bars and ethnic mix. But I would imagine the respiratory wards of the city's hospitals are like war zones.

The mountains around Lanzhou are as brown as the Yellow River, which defies its name as it weaves, laden with silt, right through the heart of the city. Perhaps it's the colour of the mountains or the sight of Muslim and Tibetan faces on the streets, but when you are here, you always have a feeling in the back of your mind that there is something different out there, lurking beyond those mountains. And of course there is.

What is out there is euphemistically known in Chinese as the *xibu,* the western regions. They are made up of the whole Tibetan Plateau to the southwest, the wide-open province of Qinghai to the west, a long, narrow stretch of Gansu province (of which Lanzhou is the capital), and finally the region of Xinjiang to the northwest, where I am heading. Soon after Lanzhou, the Gobi Desert starts, and it doesn't end for a very, very long time.

It was only the night before, as I read the guidebook about Gansu province in my hotel room, that I had realised just how close I was to the Tibetan Plateau. I had not planned a diversion southwards, but as I looked at the map, it seemed too good an opportunity to miss. Xiahe, right on the edge of the Tibetan Plateau, 170 miles southwest of Lanzhou, is the leading monastery town outside the Tibetan capital, Lhasa. Several friends from

Beijing had visited Xiahe (pronounced *shyah-huh*) and told me how wonderful it is, so I changed my plans and the next morning boarded a bus south out of Lanzhou.

If you want an accurate road map of China, you have to go directly to the publishing house and rip it off the printing press. And even then it will be out of date. The speed of road building is phenomenal and the quality of the new roads amazing.

The road south is a new four-lane motorway, which neither I nor my map had anticipated, a shiny streak of black tarmac and steel barriers forging its way through the yellow semi-desert outside Lanzhou. The struggle of man against nature begins to intensify here, and many of the hillsides are terraced, allowing the local people to try to squeeze some fertility from the reluctant yellow earth.

The DVD player on the bus is pumping out patriotic songs with pictures of men and women dressed in 1950s People's Liberation Army fatigues. They seem to be teaching the minority peoples about the joys of being Chinese. There's one song about Mongolians, then one about the Tibetan Plateau. The words of the songs are helpfully written along the bottom of the screen in case anyone wants to join in.

The DVD is playing several hundred decibels above the level permissible in heavy industrial factories in the United States, though I don't at first realise this. It's only when the child in the seat behind leans over the back of the seat next to me and starts singing that I realise how, over time, I have become inoculated against Chinese noise. This is the sort of thing that used to infuriate me. 'What are you doing, kid, crooning out of tune in my ear? And what is the driver doing playing that music so loud in the first place?' Now, I astound myself by even smiling in encouragement to the boy, as though out-of-tune wailing in my ear with no sense of rhythm is just fine.

China does that to you. You go back to the United States or Europe, and people wonder why you're not jumping up and down with annoyance at some minor noise or irritation, and you look at them and think, what's your problem? We have such low thresholds of annoyance in our cosy Western world. (The danger is, though, that you also forget to fit back into Western ways of, say, road safety or table manners on returning to your homeland.)

The road flows alongside a small river for a while, then the driver turns off the super-shiny motorway on to a well-paved rural road that bends and turns down a hill before descending into the green valley of Linxia (pronounced *lin-shyah*).

Lanzhou has a mixture of ethnicities, but it is ostensibly a large Chinese city. This little valley, only a hundred miles south, is the first I have passed through that is really not Han Chinese at all. There are small Muslim communities dotted around China further east, but here, around Linxia, it is almost 100 per cent Muslim. Every village has a mosque. All the men are wearing white Islamic caps on their heads and sporting wispy beards. The women wear headscarves to cover their hair. Suddenly it doesn't feel quite like China. Many of the village mosques are a combination of architectural styles, less traditionally mosque-like than their Middle East equivalents, but not as Chinese as the main mosque in Xi'an, which was built almost like an old Chinese-style temple.

The Muslims around here are known as the Hui people (pronounced *hway*). Their ancestors were soldiers, merchants and craftsmen who came to China from Persia and Central Asia between the seventh and thirteenth centuries. After they settled in China, they intermarried with the Han Chinese and came to speak Chinese (while often retaining some Arabic too). Eventually the Hui became largely assimilated, although they retained their Islamic faith, and to this day do not eat pork. Relations are much better between the Han Chinese and the Hui than they are between the Han and other Muslim groups in northwest China, such as the Uighurs, but despite the Hui's assimilation, their faith puts a big gap between them and the Han. There are occasional flare-ups of ethnic tension, usually over some religious slur or minor issue of food or religious practice. The state always moves in quickly to break up such incidents, and all sides know that little can be achieved by more conflict, so people of all ethnicities tend to rub along side by side.

I change buses at Linxia, which also has the feel of a frontier town. Stores are full of daggers and saddles and animal furs. The bus to Xiahe is crowded and raucous and full of smoke. It is a much cheaper model than the previous one, which is good news, because the general rule when travelling in China is that the cheaper the bus, the more friendly the people. There are some seats towards the back, so I clamber over limbs and bags to reach one. Most of the people on this bus are Tibetan. The man I sit next to says, in almost unintelligible Mandarin, that he is from a minority group I had never even heard of, one of the smallest in China, called the Dongxiang.

There are fifty-six different ethnic minority groups within the borders of the People's Republic that are officially recognised and some four hundred that are not. The government in Beijing says they are all *zhong guo ren*, 'people of the Middle Kingdom', Chinese people. But if you ask them, their first allegiance is usually to their ethnic group. There are only 300,000 Dongxiang people in the whole world, and they all live around Linxia. They are Muslims, but they trace their ancestry back to the Mongols, when Genghis Khan swept through here in the thirteenth century.

'Do you have your own language? Your own script?' I ask the Dongxiang man.

'We have our own language, but it is not written down,' he replies. 'It is similar to Mongolian. But I can't read anyway, so it doesn't make any difference.'

Just before the bus departs, two rather glamorously dressed Han Chinese women get on. I had seen them on the bus from Lanzhou.

They see the seats near me and begin to squeeze their way, in a very self-consciously feminine manner, to the back of the bus. They remind me of Jack Lemmon and Tony Curtis boarding the train all dressed in drag in *Some Like It Hot*.

The two of them seem more out of place than I do, pushing their identical shocking-pink overnight bags into the overhead luggage rack between a large watermelon and a huge, coarse cloth sack full of I don't know what. Certainly these are the first shocking-pink overnight bags ever to grace this particular overhead rack. The pair clamber into the very last row of seats, diagonally behind me, brushing off the filthy cushions before they sit down.

The smaller of the two women is dressed all in white, a singularly inappropriate choice of clothing for travel in this part of China. She has short, frizzed hair that is slightly tinted and, most strikingly, bright pink-framed glasses that have thick sidebars studded with rhinestones.

Her friend is more of a femme fatale. She is dressed completely in black, like some female Gary Cooper, riding out to tame the western frontier. Her shiny black polyester top has small sequins hanging from the waist, and her matching trousers have the same sequins hanging around her ankles. She has slight streaks of brown dye in her hair. The two of them look almost comical, at the back of this filthy bus, squeezed in between the Tibetan farmers.

As they settle into their seats, chattering away in very pure Mandarin behind me, Femme Fatale pulls out a small bag of baby wipes and rather melodramatically wipes her face. She offers one to her friend, who with a regal air wipes her hands, then throws the used wipe on the already filthy floor.

'Eeeeeew. This bus is so *dirty*,' squeals Femme Fatale.

Princess Pinky nods in agreement. They set about sending text messages on their fancy mobile phones.

Outside, mud houses are zipping by, beside hoardings promoting the ubiquitous but elusive goal of *xiaokang*, moderate prosperity. Others offer the twenty-first century to the farmers of southern Gansu province:

Broadband changes your life.

If you're going to bring life-changing inventions to this part of the country, it seems to me that some kind of basic agricultural mechanisation might be a better place to start.

The road is being widened between Linxia and Xiahe, perhaps in anticipation of more tourists, and the bus frequently has to pull on to a stretch of uneven dirt track beside the road. The bumpity-bumping on the dirt track causes the large watermelon in the luggage rack to fall on to the head of a child. The child lets out a squeal but seems not to be seriously hurt. No one gets angry. No one threatens to sue. Falling water melons are just an occupational hazard of travel in China.

Finally I decide to strike up a conversation with the two princesses behind me, feeling rather sheepish at my own rather dirty state.

'We're going to Xiahe,' Princess Pinky answers my enquiry.

'How long are you staying?'

'Probably just one night, then we are heading on to Hezuo.'

'Are you on holiday?'

'Sort of holiday,' says Femme Fatale, 'but working too.'

'What sort of work do you do?'

'Cosmetics.'

It emerges that they both work for a Shanghai make-up company called Meisu, which this year has opened a branch in Lanzhou and now also has stores in both Xiahe and Hezuo, the regional capital of southern Gansu. The women are cosmetics missionaries.

'Wherever there are women, there is Meisu,' says Princess Pinky with a smile. 'That's our slogan.'

'So is there a market among the Tibetans?' I ask.

'No, it's the Han Chinese who buy cosmetics,' she says. 'The minority peoples aren't really interested in that sort of thing.'

'What do your stores sell? Just lipstick and rouge and the usual stuff?'

'Yes, but also lots of whitening cream, to make your skin paler. We hate dark skin.'

I tell her how Western women buy suntan cream to make their skin look darker. She looks repelled, not seeming to care that every face on the bus is either the dark skin of a Tibetan or Hui Muslim, or the darkened skin of a Chinese farmer who works all day in the sun. 'Dark skin is ugly. White skin is beautiful,' she says.

Then she actually asks the young Tibetan man next to her why his skin is so dark.

'I don't know,' he replies graciously in perfect Mandarin. 'We are just born that way.'

The bus crosses through a sort of wooden archway. This is Tumenguan, the entrance into southern Gansu province. Almost immediately, the countryside becomes greener and there are temples in the villages and on the hillsides, as though, in some sudden Narnia moment, we have passed through a door into a different kingdom.

I mention this, and the young Tibetan man who has just been quizzed about his dermatological details chips in. 'We're entering Gannan,' he says. 'This is a Tibetan autonomous region.'

'How's life here?' I ask him.

'It's getting better. There is more investment these days. There are now two factories here. One making medicine, the other processing milk.'

'Do people here want *xiaokang*? Moderate prosperity? As in the government slogans?'

He looks at me, bemused by my query. 'Of course we do,' he replies.

Even a foreigner who has lived a long time in China, and who knows that the Tibet question is not as simple as it is sometimes portrayed, still assumes that identity might be more important than progress.

It turns out that the young man, who says his Chinese name is Xiao Lin, is a teacher who is returning from training in Lanzhou to his hometown further south, beyond Xiahe.

'What do you teach?' I ask him.

'Chinese,' he replies.

I stare at him. 'You teach Chinese? To whom?'

'Tibetan high school kids.'

'You're a Tibetan, teaching the Chinese language to Tibetan kids?'

'That's right,' he says, smiling.

I search his face for a sign of how he feels about this. He doesn't betray much, sitting as he is beside two very Han Chinese women, but he gives me a faint smile, and he jots down his mobile phone number at my request. As he gives it to me, he raises his eyebrows as if to say, call me and I will tell you more.

Xiao Lin (pronounced *shao lin*) says he is getting off just before Xiahe to see a friend. He reiterates that I should call him. I say I will, and he jumps off, a rather modern-looking Tibetan in a sea of farmers.

There are more slogans all around, often painted on the simple brick or mud walls of houses beside the road. The Department of Family Planning here has actually quantified the financial benefit of not having too many children, though it's not clear if this is the cost of the fine for having too many or the cost of raising an extra child. Many peasants here earn only about 1,000 yuan per year from the land.

One child less will save you 3,000–5,000 RMB [$400–600]

There is other propaganda, too, encouraging and warning.

Speed up road construction. Speed up the development of the west.
There is no copper in roadside cables. Thieves will be severely punished.

But most of the road signs focus on one subject: education. The civilising mission of the Chinese in the days of old was to spread their culture, their bureaucracy, their Confucian order to the barbarians. There is still the sense of superiority towards the ethnic minorities of China's fringe, but when the Chinese threw out their own civilisation with the arrival of the Ocean People, their mission statement towards the people of Inner Asia changed too. Now, it is science and progress that they are bringing to the benighted barbarians on the fringes of civilisation.

Revive the nation through science and education.
As you work towards moderate prosperity, education is the most important thing.
Knowledge is strength.

Chapter Thirteen

MONKS AND NOMADS

The main prayer hall of Labrang Monastery is full of monks, sitting in rows, some swaying silently, some chatting, some chanting in the half dark. There must be four or five hundred of them, their shaven heads bobbing among the painted pillars. Half are facing one way, about ten rows of them in all, then in the middle of the hall, an invisible line divides them, and the other ten rows sit facing them. They sit cross-legged on cushions, some dressed simply in burgundy robes, others in larger, thicker cloaks against the surprising chill of the summer morning.

The original 300-year-old prayer hall was the centre piece of the monastery, but was tragically burned down in a huge fire in 1985, caused by an electrical fault. The hall was soon rebuilt in a way that seems to fit well with the surrounding ancient buildings. There are no windows, so the inside is very dark, illuminated only by the light that splashes in through several doorways and by the much fainter glow of dozens of butter candles that line the walls. It is an impressive space, with a high ceiling, its rows of brightly painted pillars like funky tree trunks in a coniferous forest. The butter candles, made from yaks' milk, give off the slightly rancid smell that pervades everything in Tibetan areas.

A small group of foreigners has gathered at one of the main doors, like voyeurs, peering into the darkness of some lost world. Soon, a few young monks, none of them older than ten, come to the entrance and join us. An old Tibetan woman with two long grey plaits under a Stetson-type hat prostrates herself in the space between the spectators and the monks inside. Several Chinese tourists step forward and do the same, their sensible clothing looking oddly out of step with their actions. Other Han tourists come and throw money on to the ground by the doorway. A huge monk with a frightening headdress that descends in woven metal and cloth down his back motions to the boy monks in front of us to step back. He is the *geko*, or monastic disciplinarian.

Quite by chance, I have arrived in Xiahe during an important time in the monastery's year. It is the examination period, when hundreds of young monks take their philosophical exams. This is when the monks must prove their knowledge of Buddhist teachings in an open forum, at which they are tested by the other monks. It's a tradition dating back centuries, though it was of course stopped under Mao, and has only in recent years been restarted.

'It's so spiritual,' gasps a tattooed German woman standing beside me. 'It's so wonderful that they have this to believe in. Why don't we have anything like this in the West?'

The 'exam' begins, though it takes more the form of a debate. Two young monks, probably in their early twenties, are standing in the centre of the hall, where the front rows of the two sides face each other. Suddenly up jumps an older monk several rows back; he shouts to get the attention of one of the students and then barks a question at him in Tibetan, clapping his hands with a flourish as he does so. The onlooking monks, in a sea of red, shout and hoot, as though laughing at the question or the answer or both, while the first examinee responds. The grilling goes for some time, with the two students being questioned alternately by monks on both sides of the aisle in which they stand.

The only Han Chinese are the ones at the door with the foreigners, all of us outsiders to this other-worldly scene. Our guide has disappeared. I ask some of the boy monks in front of us if they speak Chinese, so they can explain the scene to me. '*Ni hui jiang han hua ma?* Do you speak the language of the Han?'

They all just stare back at me, unable, or perhaps unwilling, to respond.

The debate goes on and on, the two students wandering up and down the rows, taking questions from any monk who wants to stand up, with more hoots and laughs going up from the other monks in chorus as answers are given. After half an hour, the foreigners and the Chinese tourists disperse. There's only so much theatre you can absorb in a language you don't understand, however compelling and unusual it is.

The prayer hall is the final stop on a guided tour of Labrang Monastery, which had begun an hour before. Xiahe has become a major tourist destination for Han Chinese people, and a Mecca (or Buddhist equivalent) for foreign backpackers. So a motley group of bearded Australians, chatty Irishmen and tattooed German women had gathered at the gates that morning to be met by an earnest Tibetan monk with high cheekbones and a cautious smile, who was to act as guide.

A Chinese tourist couple are hanging around too, looking as foreign as we do, and while we are waiting, I ask them why they have come.

'I'm interested in the minority peoples,' says the woman. 'They have such different lives.'

'Do you understand them?' I ask her.

'No, not at all,' she confesses. 'It's all very strange to us.'

Labrang Monastery itself is a sprawling complex that occupies a major part of the town. Built in 1709, it is one of the six great monasteries of the Gelugpa school of Tibetan Buddhism, sometimes known as the Yellow Hat school. Four are in Tibet proper, and one other (just near the birthplace of the current Dalai Lama) is northwest of here, in the province of Qinghai.

At its height, before the Communist Party victory in 1949, there were 4,000 monks at Labrang. That population was drastically reduced during the Cultural Revolution from 1966 to 1976 when Mao encouraged attacks on all religions. Now, though, numbers are rising again, and there are some 1,200 monks studying here.

The tour provides a fairly innocuous basic introduction, touching on nothing sensitive as far as Tibet's relationship with China is concerned. The foreign visitors ask polite questions about architecture, while gently probing to discover how frank the guide will be on the subject of the Dalai Lama. Soon the question is answered for us. We reach one hall where, on the altar next to the Buddha, is clearly displayed a picture of the exiled Tibetan leader.

'Is that allowed?' I ask our guide quietly in English, glancing over my shoulder to check there is no one official listening.

He smiles sheepishly and turns away, unwilling to answer. Beside him, though, is a bolder monk whose wind-burned cheeks illuminate his strong face. He has been listening at the fringes of our group and he leans towards me, saying, in broken Chinese, that sometimes the monks put the picture there 'because the Dalai Lama is in our hearts.'

'Sometimes the police come and take the picture away,' says the monk. 'Once they even smashed it. But someone always puts it back up.'

There was an unbelievable assault on Tibetan culture under Chairman Mao, and so much was destroyed that I came here expecting a diluted experience. But what is striking about the monastery is how Tibetan it is. Of course, as everywhere in China, there is much that is unseen. There are spies in all Tibetan monasteries, and all the monks must be careful what they say. I am sure the purists would say that, compared with, say, the 1920s or the 1720s, it is no longer genuine. But the examination and the worship and the daily rituals are clearly not just being put on for the tourists.

After the Communist victory, in 1949, Beijing drew a line on the map and defined a large part of the traditionally Tibetan areas as the Tibetan Autonomous Region, or TAR. This is sometimes known as 'political Tibet.' But large areas with Tibetan populations were not included in this political delineation, and many Tibetans still live in the provinces of Qinghai, Sichuan and Gansu, which surround the TAR. Religious freedoms in these parts, which are sometimes known as 'ethnographic Tibet', are often greater than they are in political Tibet because the Tibetans living there are not perceived by Beijing to be as likely to push for any kind of political independence. The Tibetans themselves, one imagines, recognise no such artificial boundaries and the Buddhism which still seems to flow in their veins also flows effortlessly across lines drawn on a map.

The Tibetan question is a tricky one and has become very emotive in the West. The Tibetans have been called the 'baby seals' of the international community, with the Dalai Lama's cuddly image and powerful message of non-violence gaining him and his compatriots huge waves of sympathy. Many in the West believe what most Tibetans say, that China occupied Tibet for the first time only after the Communist victory of 1949. But to understand the full picture, you have to go back a long way before that.

The Chinese government says that there have been 'brotherly relations' with Tibet since the seventh century, and that Tibet has actually been part of China since the Yuan dynasty of the thirteenth and fourteenth centuries. Certainly there were contacts back in the seventh century, and there were contacts between Tibetan leaders and the Mongols (when the Mongols ruled China) in the thirteenth century. Of course it depends how you define it, but it seems to me that they barely add up to Tibet being 'part of China'. The first real, effective consolidation of Chinese claims to Tibet did not come until 1720, when the Kangxi Emperor in Beijing ordered imperial troops into Lhasa. From that point onwards, troops and imperial officials from Beijing were stationed in the Tibetan capital, with varying degrees of involvement in Tibetan affairs. By and large, the Tibetans were allowed to continue undisturbed with their way of life. The emperor got to say Tibet was 'part of the imperial family', the trade-off for the Tibetans being that the imperial soldiers helped to keep enemies such as the Nepalese across the border at bay.

This relationship continued throughout the nineteenth century, when whatever hold the Qing dynasty had on Tibet was weakened even further by internal rebellions, and by the arrival of the Ocean People causing problems along the Chinese coastline. Tibet missed its chance at independence after China fell apart in 1912, partly because the dastardly British in India refused to champion their cause, and partly because the Buddhist monasteries, fearful that modernisation meant atheism and secularism, thwarted efforts in the 1920s to introduce social and economic reforms. So when the Japanese were finally defeated in 1945, and Chairman Mao united a disintegrated country and proclaimed the founding of the People's Republic of China in October 1949, Tibet was not in a strong position to resist demands from Beijing that Tibet come 'back' into the fold.

With no means to defend themselves, the Tibetan leaders were forced to cut a deal with Beijing and officially accept Chinese sovereignty for the first time. Chairman Mao actually tried to give them some space, not forcing the same Communist reforms on them in the 1950s that he implemented elsewhere in China. But it was no good. The Communist and Buddhist ways were diametrically opposed, and a fully-fledged uprising against Chinese rule broke out in 1959. It was ruthlessly suppressed by the Chinese and ended with the Dalai Lama's flight to India. He has not returned to Tibet since.

The propaganda war continues to this day, with Beijing highlighting the cruel and backward nature of the old theocracy from which the Tibetans had been 'liberated' and the Tibetan government in exile railing against the Chinese destruction of Tibet and its human rights abuses against Tibetans.

Between 1959 and 1976, Tibetan society was restructured along Communist lines. Nomads were organised into communes. Tibetan culture and religion were brutally attacked, and almost all of the monasteries were completely destroyed. Han Chinese officials (and more Chinese troops) were moved to Tibet, to make sure it did not rise up again and to contribute to its development and integration. In 1949 there were just hundreds of Han Chinese in what is now the Tibetan Autonomous Region, out of a population of about a million. In 2005, according to official figures, there were about 100,000, or 7 per cent of the population. This figure is far too low, especially since the influx of migrants resulting from the completion of the Tibet railway in 2006. Tibetans fear that the number of Han Chinese will slowly climb until there are nearly as many Han as there are Tibetans in the region. You can now travel by train directly from Beijing or Shanghai to the Tibetan capital, Lhasa.

When Mao died in 1976, some of the more militant Communist policies were eased, but anti-Chinese demonstrations broke out in Lhasa in the late 1980s and again were ruthlessly crushed.

The crushing of those demonstrations was seminal. It did not persuade Tibetans to love the Chinese, but it persuaded many ordinary Tibetans that opposition really was futile, just as the crushing of the Tiananmen demonstrations on 4 June 1989, persuaded the Han Chinese of the futility of any fight for democratic reform. This realisation coincided with the launch of a huge economic development programme in Tibet in the 1990s. If you can't win the people through their hearts and minds, then win them through their stomachs, was the official Chinese thinking. Along with the investment came tens of thousands of Han Chinese migrants. It was like the building of the American West, bringing with it plenty of jobs in construction, not to mention trade and prostitution.

The investment in Tibet is not all just a cynical attempt to buy off the Tibetans and make them forget any aspirations to independence. There is still a large dose of old-fashioned Chinese paternalism that wants to improve the lot of the poorest people. And certainly rural Tibet is desperately poor. (Westerners who conceive of Tibet as some kind of Shangri-la in the Himalayas have not seen the poverty and difficulty that constitutes the lives of most Tibetans.) But there is no doubt that Beijing's economic generosity also has a political side effect. When I visited Lhasa a few years before, I was amazed to find large numbers of Tibetan teenagers who wanted to head east to Shanghai to get a better job and who had little interest in politics or religion. Progress for them seemed to have become, on the surface at least, as important as identity.

'My grandmother likes the Dalai Lama,' one drunk sixteen-year-old Tibetan had told me in a Lhasa nightclub as he swigged from a bottle of Budweiser. 'I don't know much about him.'

There is one final point to make about the incorporation of Tibet into China. Although it is no excuse for the appallingly brutal way the Communist Party has treated Tibet since 1959, it is important to remember a few chapters of our own history in North America, Australia, and elsewhere. Even conservative estimates say that more than 2 million indigenous people were killed during the colonisation of North America. In Australia, the aboriginal population was reduced by disease, loss of land and direct killing by 90 per cent between 1788 and 1900. American and Australian history are full of examples of white men killing indigenous peoples just for the sake of killing them, almost for sport. And let's not even get started on the slave trade and the full onslaught of white colonialism elsewhere. Chinese atrocities in Tibet during the 1960s and 1970s, and until today, have been shocking in the extreme, but they have not yet reached anywhere near those levels. That does not excuse them in any way. All I am saying is that the white man speaks with forked tongue on these issues and you will never hear a Han Chinese person saying 'The only good Tibetan is a dead Tibetan'.

That afternoon I call Xiao Lin, the Tibetan teacher I had met on the bus to Xiahe, and we arrange to meet the following day. Then I take the afternoon just to relax and explore the town. I watch the Tibetan pilgrims, dressed in their colourful robes, trimmed with fur, gently turning the hundreds of prayer wheels that surround Labrang Monastery as though perhaps trying to turn back time. I watch the Tibetan monks in their robes in an Internet café, surfing the Web and playing online video games. I take a tiny motor rickshaw up to the beautiful grasslands a few miles above Xiahe and just ride around, breathing in the fresh mountain air. There are a few theme park style Tibetan tents for Chinese tourists to spend the night, and you get the feeling that the whole place could be on the verge of a tourism explosion. Most of the nomads from the grasslands are being settled now, and the ancient way of life is being changed. Soon, there may not be any more nomads at all.

That night I have dinner on a rooftop terrace overlooking Labrang. I sit next to a monk in flowing burgundy robes who talks in Tibetan on his Nokia mobile phone for most of my meal.

'I'm from the countryside south of Xiahe,' he says in heavily accented Chinese once we get chatting. 'Becoming a monk is the only way to get an education for many rural families like mine.'

Back at the Overseas Tibetan Hotel, groups of foreign back-packers are sitting drinking coffee. It's the first time on my journey that I have crossed paths with westerners in any numbers. The hotel is a classic backpacker joint. Computers with Internet access sit in the lobby, bearded Scandinavians hang out beside the front desk, discussing the best overland routes south to Sichuan province, and an English-speaking receptionist offers dormitory rooms for a few dollars a night.

The following day, I leave Xiahe and meet Xiao Lin in the Muslim town of Linxia, where I changed buses on my way to Xiahe two days before. I am continuing to Lanzhou that afternoon, so we go for lunch at a small noodle bar beside the bus station. He seems to know that we will be talking about sensitive issues, so he asks for a private room, which even small restaurants provide.

We sit down and order some noodles, and I tell Xiao Lin I am writing a book, and ask if he would mind if I ask him some fairly frank questions. He smiles and nods, confirming that I'm not going to use his real name, and I launch in.

'You are Tibetan. But you have been raised in the Chinese system. And now you are returning to teach the language of what many Tibetans call your "oppressors" to your own people. Doesn't that make you uncomfortable at all?'

'*Mei banfa*. I have no choice. What other choices are there open to me?'

He tells me his story, about growing up in a largely Tibetan area and finding himself always at the top of his class in the Tibetan school. So he, like all the smartest children, was transferred to the Chinese-language school, where he continued to be top of the class. This meant he would have a good shot at college, and he was duly accepted at one of the best universities in western China, one of five students in his class of one hundred to go on to tertiary education. His parents, both Tibetans with little education, forced him to speak Chinese at home so that his chances of success would be greater.

'No one blames me,' he says. 'There is no other choice. The only way to say I'm not going to take part in this is to not learn Chinese and reject the whole Chinese system. But that would condemn me to poverty. You can never get a good job and improve your living standards if you do that.'

His eyes are still bright, and his voice still soft, despite what he clearly knows is the tragedy of his people.

'Of course our culture is being diluted. The need to learn Chinese, the influx of more Chinese people. And that is sad. But it is not being completely diluted. There are some non-negotiables. For instance, I would never marry a Han Chinese girl. And my Buddhist faith is something I will never give up.'

'But what about the lifestyle? Tibetans are nomads.'

'First, there is nothing romantic about being a nomad. It's a very tough life. Second, I think nomads realise there is no future as nomads. That is simply today's world. The modern world. The globalised world. I'm not sure we can completely blame the Chinese for that.'

We slurp down our noodles in silence for a moment. It seems as though everything has been reversed. The Han Chinese have forced the settlement and the tethering of the nomadic Tibetans. Now it is the Han Chinese who have for the first time become more nomadic, untethered from their old, settled ways.

'What about politics? What about the Dalai Lama? What about Tibetan independence?'

'I don't want to talk about politics. I want to stay neutral on the subject of the Dalai Lama. I certainly would never support Tibetan independence.'

He pauses. I nod my head. We slurp our noodles. It is a tragedy, but it is a slow-burn tragedy. The killings, the destruction of the monasteries and some of the violence has eased. The main threat of destruction is now for economic and not political reasons. But even in Tibet proper there is a sense of switching gears and focusing on economic development. The number of people being arrested for political crimes (read: opposing Chinese rule) has dropped considerably. It's as though the focus of hope has shifted. It seems that many people, especially the young and the urban, have accepted that Tibet will never be independent, and that they had better just make the best of a bad situation.

In the worst-case scenario, Tibetan culture will be so diluted that it will disappear as an identity. Some elements, such as the religion and the ethnicity, might remain, but Tibet will gradually become Sinified, absorbed into the Chinese empire. Assimilation, though, won't be accomplished through the power of Chinese culture, or by the power of the Chinese gun, but by the power of the Chinese yuan, the currency that is buying off many of the Tibetan people.

A slightly more positive scenario is that Tibet (and maybe Xinjiang, the mainly Muslim region in the northwest where I am heading) might become like Scotland within the United Kingdom. The Scots have retained their identity, and they do not like the English at all, but they have been part of a country dominated by the English for so long, and the two have become so integrated in so many ways, that pro-independence parties have traditionally not received much support, even at the ballot box. But that process has taken 300 years.

Either way, it is unavoidable that Tibet and the Tibetan regions around its fringe are being transformed, not just being made more Chinese, but being made more global. Undoubtedly there will be economic benefits if the Tibetans, and not just the Han Chinese, can take advantage of the shift. But the danger is that Tibetan culture is already becoming rather like Native American culture. It has the feeling of a theme park, where the superficial elements of the indigenous culture are allowed, encouraged even, but only in as much as they fit into the culture of the conquerors. Talks between Beijing and representatives of the ageing Dalai Lama, aimed at reaching some kind of settlement that might save more Tibetan culture, seem to be going nowhere. And one day, probably quite soon, he will die, and the Chinese will supervise the selection of the new Dalai Lama, and that will be that.

So it seems likely that the process of Sinification and of

globalisation will continue. And Tibetans will have to choose between opting out, retaining identity and staying poor, and opting in, losing some identity and starting on the road to moderate prosperity. It's clear which route Xiao Lin has decided on. I thank him for being so frank, and we say goodbye at the bus station.

I'm heading back to Lanzhou, to spend a day exploring and walking the banks of the Yellow River before I head northwest into the Gobi Desert.

While I'm waiting for a bus, I notice a group of bus drivers who are sitting having their lunch. They are all Hui Muslims, and they sit laughing, joking, ribbing one another, and then ribbing me when I start chatting to them in Mandarin. Even when the conversation turns, as it inevitably does, to the US–UK invasion of Iraq and policies in the Middle East, there is no hostility towards me personally.

'Your prime minister and that evil Bush president are killing our *tongbao* in Iraq. They are killing our brothers,' says one of them, a young man with a round face and dirty shoes, who tells me his uncle is working in Baghdad, driving a truck. He gestures for me to lean forward as he pulls a laminated picture of Osama bin Laden out of his pocket under the table.

'You like Osama?' I ask him.

'Yes,' he says, smiling. 'We like Osama.'

Chapter Fourteen

NO LONGER RELYING ON HEAVEN

In the summer of 1988, as post-Mao China looked out full of hope into the big, wide-open future and wondered what kind of country it was going to become, China Central Television screened a documentary series called *He Shang*. The title is usually translated into English as *River Elegy*. The series came out at the end of my year as a language student in Beijing, and it caused a huge stir because of its negative portrayal of Chinese culture. It was a fascinating mix of images and interviews put together to support the main iconoclastic theme, which was that the idea of the Chinese being a wonderful ancient people with a wonderful ancient culture was a big sham, and that the entire culture needed to change.

River Elegy was an important film and its release was a seminal point in China's post-Mao cultural history. It represented much of what was going on in the minds of young intellectuals just before the demonstrations erupted in Tiananmen Square in the spring of 1989. The film attacked many symbols of Chinese history, from the 'cruel and violent' imperial dragon to the Great Wall, which 'can only represent an isolationist, conservative and incompetent defence' for China.

Perhaps most significant was the critique that gave the series its title, an attack on the Yellow River, which flows through Lanzhou, through the heartland of northern China, and (when it hasn't been drained completely by overuse) out to the East China Sea. Chinese civilisation grew up around the Yellow River, and the river has always symbolised China's ancient culture. There is an old Chinese saying that 'a dipperful of Yellow River water is seven-tenths mud', and *River Elegy* took the silt and sediment of the river as a symbol for the weight of Confucian tradition, clogging up the Chinese mind. The elegy of the title was an aspirational one, a hope that the traditional culture of China, which has held the country back for so long, might die and be replaced by a more progressive, western-style way of thinking.

The writers of *River Elegy* criticised everything about China's 'yellowness', from the mythical Yellow Emperor of antiquity to the barren yellow earth of the loess plateau. Yellowness symbolised the backwardness of the country and its culture, especially its political culture. This they contrasted with 'blueness', symbolised by clear ocean water, flowing from the West and bringing the much-needed science and democracy of the Ocean People to China. The film ended with the hope that the Yellow River would eventually flow out, mix with the blue ocean, and be transformed.

The fact that *River Elegy* was allowed to be shown in the first place, to hundreds of millions of people across China, says much about the freedoms that had developed by 1988, as the country's leaders allowed intellectuals to explore the best way for the country to go forward. But the series caused a storm because, although it did not openly attack the Communist Party, the script contained plenty of not-so-subtle criticisms of the Chinese imperial tradition and, by extension, of the current political system. Many conservatives objected to it.

The messages of *River Elegy* were a crucial part of the intellectual ferment in the years leading up to the demonstrations in Tiananmen Square. But when that movement was crushed by government troops, the authors of *River Elegy* were arrested or escaped into exile, the latest in a long line of soul-searching Chinese intellectuals to fail in their quest to make China into a democratic country. (In a fascinating footnote to the intellectual and spiritual searching of the 1980s, two of the main writers of *River Elegy* fled to the United States after Tiananmen, where they both became evangelical Christians.)

Independent intellectuals do not have a great track record in China. The soul-searching of the reformist elite in the late nineteenth century had led to the collapse of China in the revolution of 1912. The soul-searching of the westernised Chinese thinkers of the 1920s had resulted in the emergence of the Communist Party, which got rid of many old ways of thinking but made no progress in changing the old political model, and ultimately crushed the intellectuals who had initially supported it. And then the soul-searchers of the 1980s were suppressed in their turn.

It seems as though every time someone starts to think outside the box politically, either the state collapses or the people doing the thinking are crushed. Many people's mind-sets about science and progress have been changed, but the government will still not allow people to think about *political* change.

And this is the point. The fact that the writers of *River Elegy* were crushed or banished in June 1989 made the message I'd understood in Xi'an, 300 miles back east, even more clear. That China the concept, China the empire, China the construct of two thousand years of imperial history has never been, and *may never be,* able to allow independent thinking. The system, whether Confucian or Communist, is simply not built to permit it, because independent thinking will of course lead to questions about China's political system, and if China is to hold together, questioning like that cannot be tolerated. What Zbigniew Brzezinski, the national security adviser to Jimmy Carter, said about the Soviet Union applies to the modern Chinese empire too: that it cannot be both an empire and a democracy.

So what now? Where are the new generations of intellectuals? And could there be a new wave of intellectual soul-searching that could actually succeed? One of the most striking things about urban China these days is the near-complete depoliticisation of the younger generation (anyone under the age of about thirty-five). Most older intellectuals have, in order to survive, also shelved their thinking about political change in favour of the economic reforms that have taken place in the twenty years since Tiananmen. Perhaps with greater economic freedom and growth will come more intellectual, political freedom, goes the thinking. But will the intellectuals ever be able to speak out without being crushed, or without the country falling apart? I'm not sure they will.

There are many brave thinkers in China, some of whom are still trying to do what they can to promote political change. It is a strangely contradictory environment for them, with all the economic and social change blaring around them, yet a complete ban on the publication of any writing that is even vaguely sensitive politically. A few people who tried to set up an independent political party were jailed in the late 1990s, and there are no signs that the Communist Party will relax its stranglehold on political discussion any time soon.

This bitter reality should, I believe, cause China's suppressed intellectuals to shift their thinking a little. Many see themselves, the educated elite, as the most important agents of change. But ask them how much Old Hundred Names should be included, and most of them will say the same thing: 'You can't give the vote to the peasants.'

To my mind, this attitude of the urban intellectuals, that the peasants who make up more than two-thirds of the population are part of the problem and not part of the solution, is inherently wrong. Chairman Mao, after 1949, was wrong on just about everything, and millions of people paid the price for it. But I think his focus on the peasants was correct, and that is where today's focus should be as well, because that is what will make the difference in whether China *can* go forward as a unified country *and* possibly develop some political checks and balances.

The intellectuals are being given no space by the state, and I don't believe this is likely to change in the near future. A policy of stability *über alles* cannot allow it. If the intellectual elite were given space to explore how to develop grassroots democracy, it would be hugely significant and might begin to change the way China is governed. But in the absence of this, the whole focus for the empowerment of the people must be on the peasants: not another Maoist peasant rebellion, but the drip-drip transformation of the Industrial Revolution that enriched Europe and North America and is, however imperfectly, beginning to transform China.

As I saw back in Anhui, the situation for the peasants if they stay in the countryside is dire. But if the farmers can continue to go out and find work and then return to improve the standard of living in the countryside, it will be the rural people, and *not* the intellectuals, whose changing lives will slowly transform the country. Then one day perhaps an elegy *can* be written for the Yellow River and all that it symbolises.

The river still runs, of course, through the heart of Lanzhou, oblivious to the blame that is cast into its quiet, muddy waters. It broods, sulking almost, through the city.

I spend a lazy afternoon in the smoggy, sweltering streets around the Yellow River, eating at a noisy noodle bar, wandering through the crowded markets, and I go down to the river itself just to look at it, so symbolic, so controversial.

In ancient times, it was said that when the Yellow River runs clear will be the time of the great sage ruler. 'When the Yellow River runs clear' entered the Chinese language as an idiom of impossibility, something like 'when hell freezes over' in English. It doesn't seem as though the river is likely to run clear anytime soon. The supposed 'blueness' of Western-style industrialisation is adding man-made pollution to the silt that has caused a thousand floods. The Yellow River is now symbolic not just of the longevity of China's ancient civilisation, but also of the ecological perils of the path to modernity that the country has taken.

If half of China's problems in recent centuries have been cultural, the other half have been geographical. Geography dealt Europe an easy hand. No deserts, some mountains but plenty of coastlines too, and nowhere very far from the sea. The geography of China in its splendid continental isolation, was a different matter.

In earlier centuries, being isolated was not such a problem. China was a self-sufficient continent, but it still developed a glorious civilisation long before the West. In recent centuries, though, the explosion of invention and exploration that followed the Renaissance, the Reformation and the Enlightenment transformed European society. Chinese inventions, transmitted through the Arab world, were also a major factor in Europe's emergence, which occurred just as the glories of China were starting to stagnate. Europeans were neighbours, rivals, competitors, fighting one another too much for sure, but also progressing through competition. What China most lacked was competitors. The problems brought about by its geographical isolation were compounded by the conquest of the western regions by the Qing dynasty in the eighteenth century, which added still more difficult terrain to govern.

Lanzhou marks the start of this more difficult terrain, a stretch of land which has always been known as the Hexi Corridor. Hexi (pronounced *huh-shee*) means 'west of the river' (as in the Yellow River), and the narrow corridor of habitable land that stretches northwest from Lanzhou to the last fort of the Great Wall, at Jiayuguan, 350 miles to the northwest, has historically been known as 'the neck of China'. It was the only way for goods to flow in and out along the Silk Road from the northwest in ancient times, and the Chinese did everything possible to keep a stranglehold on it. The fort at Jiayuguan (pronounced *jah-you-gwan*), known as the 'mouth of China', was the Chinese equivalent of the Khyber Pass, which guarded entry into British India from the northwest.

Soon the Qilian (*chee-lyen*) Mountains will rise on the southern side of the road, pushed up from the Tibetan Plateau as though by two divine tectonic hands, establishing a natural southern barrier against the galloping Gobi. To the north of the road soon begins the desert proper, which stretches north for more than 500 miles.

History and progress race each other northwest along the Hexi Corridor. The Lanzhou to Urumqi railway completed in 1963, runs in places alongside the remains of the Great Wall of China. Route 312 lies to the south of the railway and the wall, a sort of live third rail, also heading northwest. The oasis towns along its path dot the road like beads, hanging loose on a necklace along the southern perimeter of the desert.

Until Lanzhou, Route 312 has been an anonymous projection of asphalt, a Communist-era road that no one outside China has ever heard of. Now there are two Routes 312 that emerge from the outskirts of Lanzhou, and two bridges that carry them across the Yellow River. There is the old ramshackle road, which has served as the main route into the northwest since the 1950s, for the few goods or people that didn't travel by rail. And then there is the new Route 312, a four-lane highway that now takes the growing volume of long-distance road traffic up into the desert.

Both roads find it hard, though, to wear the mantle that history has laid upon them. For this is now the Old Silk Road, the skein of trade routes that in ancient times stretched like golden threads across the Gobi Desert, linking China to Central Asia, Persia and eventually Europe. Historians say it starts in Xi'an, because Chang'an (as it was then known) was the capital of China at the height of the Silk Road, in the seventh and eighth centuries, and the starting point and final destination of everything that flowed along it. But in my mind, the Silk Road has always begun in Lanzhou, because it is only here that it really starts to *feel* like the Silk Road. There is desert, there are oases and there are camels.

For the first few hours out of Lanzhou, the scenery is forgettable. The desert starts with the ragged, anonymous hills that stifle the road with their yellowness. Before Lanzhou, the yellow of the loess plateau had begun to seep into everything, but there was still greenery beside the roads, and fields full of crops. Here, most efforts at cultivation have been abandoned, and the low hills rise and fall in their yellow waves as though chlorophyll had never been invented.

Apart from the colour, it is the emptiness that you notice. It's very easy to feel claustrophobic in Han China, which is so saturated with settlement and the history of settlement. There is barely a square mile of land, rural or urban, that is not crammed with thousands of people. Here, occasional villages cling to the yellow hillsides, but the land is largely uninhabited. There is a feeling of intense liberation as the road stretches its legs out into the desert. I write in my notebook: 'You are now leaving Chinese airspace.'

Three men in dirty workmen's clothes are sitting just in front of me on the bus. They are migrant workers who have been in Tibet, building the railway that will link the Tibetan capital, Lhasa, to the province of Qinghai. Originally farmers from a valley just off Route 312, they are returning home to gather in the harvest.

The Tibet railway opened in 2006, a major government-funded project linking Tibet by rail with the rest of China for the first time. It is the world's highest railway, and it runs for more than 700 miles from the city of Golmud to the Tibetan capital, Lhasa. The point where the track surges through the Tanggula Pass on its way to Lhasa is at an altitude of 16,640 feet – higher than the highest peak in the lower forty-eight states of the US (Mount Whitney), and higher than the highest peak in Western Europe (Mont Blanc). Passenger cars are pressurised like aeroplanes to prevent altitude sickness.

The government says the railway will aid Tibetan development.

Activists abroad and Tibetans in Tibet say that it will just facilitate the influx of Han Chinese into Tibet, and the extraction of natural resources. Both analyses are correct.

'How was the pay, working on the railway?' I ask my travel companions.

'Very good,' says one of them with a grin. 'About 2,000 yuan a month.'

That's $250, twice what the average farmer can earn in a year.

'But we are *nongmin*, we are farmers,' he goes on, 'and we have to come home in the summer. Once we've harvested the crops, we'll head back to Tibet to finish the railway.'

'So your lives are much better than before?'

'Of course!' says the same man, his smile revealing a couple of crooked teeth. 'It used to be *kao tian sheng huo*. Relying on heaven to survive. But now it's not.'

There's a silence as we ponder the magnitude of what he has just said. I ponder it, at any rate.

'That's a big change,' I say, eventually. He nods.

It's not an overnight change. But while the intellectuals are prevented from pushing political reform, this is what is changing China. It's the first time in history that a farmer from this, or any, valley near here has been able to say, 'We are not relying on heaven to survive.' If the rains fall, or the crops die, it will cause them problems, but they will not die. It's the first stage in the empowerment of Old Hundred Names, in their eternal struggle with heaven. It is very small, and it is strictly economic. The farmers are exploited when they get to their new industrial jobs, and the villages they return to are even poorer here in Gansu than they were back in Anhui. But the people of Gansu province are grateful for small mercies, and for these three men and their families, it is empowerment all the same.

Huge electricity pylons stand out on the hills like scarecrows, a glorious sign of progress, no doubt, to the people of these distant, poverty-stricken valleys. Soon the three men get off the bus and wave goodbye, returning temporarily from their new identities as migrant labourers to be the farmers that they once were. They and their forebears have wrestled with the land, and with heaven, for so many centuries, and frequently they have lost. Now there is another option.

It is still several hours' journey up Route 312 to the first major oasis town of the desert, Wuwei. The road is wide and straight, and the buses, blue trucks and occasional cars speed along, faster than any camel caravan ever travelled. In Wuwei, I change buses and leave Route 312 temporarily, heading two hours north, to the city of Minqin. Wuwei is already on the fringe of the Gobi. Travelling to Minqin (pronounced *min-chin*), I am plunging into the heart of the desert. This town of 300,000 is perched precariously at the end of a road that extends up from Route 312 like a green pier sticking out into an ocean of sand.

For centuries, the biggest threats to Chinese settlements here were horsemen from the north. Now the biggest threat still comes from the north, but in the form of the encroaching desert, which is creeping towards Minqin at the rate of ten to fifteen feet every year. There are still a few villages to the north and east and west, but gradually people have left them and moved either to Minqin itself or even further south. The desert is merciless in its consumption of land, a situation tragically compounded by man-made blunders, such as the damming of what rivers there are and the inefficient use of water resources. Past deforestation has not helped either, and efforts now to plant trees to reverse the process do not seem to be working. Just as China needs to be expanding cultivable land, it is losing it.

Minqin is poorer than many of the cities along Route 312. Salaries, even for the fortunate, hover well below a hundred US dollars a month. Its apartment buildings are old, and the balance has not even begun to tip from bicycles towards car ownership. But there is still an energy in Minqin, as there is in most small Chinese cities, however poor, as though the people are refusing to accept their geographical fate and are determined to push towards their own modest goal of 'moderate prosperity'.

A few months earlier, at a party in Beijing, I had met a young Chinese guy, a friend of an American friend of mine, who works in Beijing but whose hometown is Minqin. I had mentioned that I might be passing through in the summer. He said that he would be there visiting his parents and that I should give him a call. So I did, and he picks me up at the bus station and takes me to meet his family.

His brother-in-law insists on taking us out for dinner that evening with all his work buddies. It's not often that a foreigner shows up in these parts, is the general tone of the invitation, and we want to show you a good time. We embark on a delicious meal of stir-fried Chinese dishes, over which ten inquisitive, increasingly inebriated small-town Chinese men quiz me on everything under the setting Gobi sun. They are among the town's more fortunate residents, many of them minor government officials or employees of state-owned companies that still exist here. All are curious about their visitor, possibly the first foreigner many of them have ever met. What do I think of China? What do I think of Chinese universities? What do I think of Japan? Why does the United States support the Dalai Lama and the banned spiritual movement Falun Gong? Is health care in Europe really free? Why do Americans love guns?

Then it gets personal. Chinese people, brought up on a diet of Hollywood movies, political sex scandals and western rock star misbehaviour, assume that Western men, married or single, are just twenty-four-hour party animals (to put it politely). They ask me how many mistresses I have and how many mistresses most Western guys have, and are disappointed to learn that their guest is more Cliff Richard than Mick Jagger. 'No mistresses?' says one man, with a potbelly and an outrageous comb-over. 'Every man should have many mistresses before he dies.' Smiles broaden around the table and heads nod.

My hosts soon resolve that the only way for me to redeem my masculinity is to take part in some drinking games, which they now explain. All the games involve the infamous Chinese wine known as *baijiu,* which really is the most disgusting beverage ever squeezed out of a grain of rice. I had so far managed to get through the evening without actually having to drink any. Then one of the diners stands up and proposes a toast:

'I'd like to toast Journalist Qi, to welcome him, and to thank him for coming to this backward little town of China.'

'No, no,' I say. 'You are developing very fast.'

'No, no,' says he. 'You don't have to be polite. We know we are backward. We must tell the truth. But we are glad to welcome you here.'

I then proceed to do rather well at their schoolboy drinking game. Distantly related to stone-paper-scissors, but louder, it involves two participants thrusting forward a certain number of fingers of one hand while both shout out a number. If the fingers you thrust out, added to the fingers your opponent thrusts out, come to the number that you shout out, then your opponent has to drink. If he gets it right, you drink. Pretty simple, really. Somehow I keep getting it right, but not without losing a few, and grimacing as I down the requisite shots of the dreaded rice wine. I then manage to feign interest in a conversation with one of the men who is not playing the game and extricate myself from the really hard-core drinking that ensues. Even so, a few shots of *baijiu* are enough to make me wobble slightly as we leave the restaurant and I wander back to my cheap hotel.

Chapter Fifteen

'WE WANT TO LIVE!'

When it comes to reporting on China, I have always subscribed to Woody Allen's theory. You'll remember that New York's most famous pessimist once said that 80 per cent of success is simply showing up. And so it is with modern China. I defy any reporter to make China boring. Almost everything about it is surprising and interesting, in part because it is so different from what you're expecting. One of the great things about living here, quite apart from the opportunity to fill up the Q, X and Z sections of your address book, is just going with the flow, walking out in the morning with only a very vague plan and seeing where the day takes you. It's almost always somewhere you'd never have predicted.

When I told friends in Beijing that I was going to travel Route 312 from east to west, several people asked me if I was going to set up lots of interviews and meetings along the way. As it turned out, I did call ahead a few times, and I did some research to set up interviews on subjects that I definitely wanted to include. If I'd been less busy, I might have prepared more. But either way, there would have been plenty to write about. By and large, I got on board the bus, taxi or camel, and just went.

Anything can happen on the road in China, and invariably it does, but some days are better than others, and there were few twelve-hour spans on this trip that were quite as extraordinary as the long summer's day that began in a dingy hotel with no towels in the centre of Minqin.

Since I knew I was to leave early the next morning, I had left the curtains of my shabby room wide open. The room had no air-conditioning, and the night had been hot. The rice wine had contributed to a deep night's sleep. The orange fingers of the dawn wake me only slowly as they unfurl over the forgettable town outside my window. I take a cold shower (the only sort available), check out of the hotel, and head to the bus station, which is already awake, as bus stations always are.

Drivers compete for business. Others load bags on to the roofs of their buses. Passengers sit at the small portable food stalls in front of the main station building, eating fried cakes filled with bean paste or boiled dumplings as they wait for their buses to depart. Steam rises from the cauldrons and woks of the itinerant food vendors.

There is only one direction out of Minqin, and that is south, along the narrow green corridor back to Route 312. You can feel the desert, looming out there somewhere, everywhere, but unless you are crazy, or a Mongolian nomad, or a crazy Mongolian nomad, there is no reason to go north from Minqin into the Gobi Desert.

The bus is heading for the town of Jinchang, further up Route 312 to the northwest, so rather than heading down to Wuwei and turning right, it dives off across country on the hypotenuse to 312, along a narrow road lined with spindly trees, and a few mud houses, clinging to the road like iron filings to a magnet. My eeny-meeny-miny-mo seat-choosing routine has landed me next to a local man of about forty, who is doing some small-scale business, selling grain and rice in Minqin and Jinchang. It turns out that I'm the first foreigner he has ever met, and he manages to resist for all of a minute and a half before pulling the blond hairs on my arm. We go through the usual quiz of whether I like China and arrive pretty quickly at how many children I have.

'Two.'

'Will you have more?' he asks.

'Possibly.'

'So your country doesn't limit the number of children people have?'

'No, that is left up to the individual,' I tell him. 'In my country, the state cannot interfere in the personal lives of its people.' I always make this point, my contribution, however small, towards bringing on the revolution.

At this point, the woman sitting across the aisle from me interjects. She, like all the other passengers, has been listening to my conversation with my neighbour.

'It's not right to have more than two children,' she says.

'I beg your pardon?' I ask her in my most faux-polite, you-talkin'-to-me? voice.

'It's not right to have more than two children,' she repeats.

'I think you can say you don't agree with it, or you wouldn't have more than two yourself, but you can't say it is *bu dui*. You cannot say it is not right.' I smile at her.

She smiles right back, the smile that many middle-aged Chinese people smile when they are about to patronise a foreigner. She has short, dyed black hair, the greying roots of which are just visible at her centre parting. She is dressed in nondescript brown trousers and blouse, the archetypal well-meaning middle-aged Chinese woman, from the Lost Generation of the Cultural Revolution, perhaps forty-five years old, perhaps fifty-five. She is friendly but opinio-nated, and no doubt ready to give me a lecture on loose Western morality or how to bring up my children or, as in this case, how many children to have.

'Why do you say it's not right?' I ask her.

'Because I work in family planning,' she replies proudly.

'So you are a doctor?'

'Yes. I'm in charge of family planning in this county.'

'And you travel around enforcing the one-child policy?'

'Yes.'

It is dawning on me what her job involves. Travelling with her are two young nurses, probably in their late twenties or early thirties. One is seated beside her, looking very prim and proper, the other is behind her, leaning forward on the headrest of her seat to take part in the conversation.

'So . . . you travel around giving women check-ups?' I ease gently towards the questions I really want to ask.

'Yes. That's where we're going now.'

'And what happens if you find that there are women who are pregnant who shouldn't be pregnant?'

'We try to persuade them to have an abortion.'

'And if they don't agree?'

'We have to force them,' she says, pausing slightly. 'You know, *zhong guo ren tai duo le*. There are too many Chinese people.'

Every Chinese person says this. It is, of course, true, but it has been drummed into Chinese heads by so many years of propaganda that it has become a mantra. More importantly, it is not just this woman's viewpoint, it is also her job to do something about it.

'But how do you force them? What if they won't go?'

'There is a department of the police in each town or county that enforces the family-planning laws. They go to the woman's house and, if she will not come voluntarily, she is taken to the clinic by force.'

Many family-planning officials in urban areas, even in small towns, know they should not talk to westerners about such issues. They know it is a sensitive subject in the West, and one that provokes criticism of China, even though many of them do not understand why. This woman feels no such constraints.

'But what if there is a woman who is eight months pregnant, and she shouldn't be?' I ask her.

'She is . . .' The woman makes an action with her hands in front of her stomach, an action of flushing something away.

'But that's a living child, that could be born and survive.' I gasp.

The woman shrugs her shoulders and smiles faintly. '*Zhong guo ren tai duo le*. There are too many Chinese people.'

I'd often heard of these cases. Indeed, it is common knowledge that ever since the one-child policy was instituted, in the late 1970s and early 1980s, forced abortions and sterilisations have become completely routine, even into the third trimester of pregnancy. But I had never met someone involved in the process.

'So you are the person who actually has to perform that operation?'

She doesn't seem to mind my questions. 'Yes,' she says, laughing slightly.

Chinese laughs say many things, and it is not possible to tell if this is a laugh of pride in her job at keeping the Chinese population low or a laugh of embarrassment at having to do such work.

'But don't you find it . . . a bit brutal?' I can't help screwing up my face as I ask the question.

She smiles again. '*Shi biyao de*. It's necessary. *Zhong guo ren tai duo le*. There are too many Chinese people.'

I turn to the two younger women, looking for confirmation that they wouldn't be involved in such brutality. Perhaps they just stand by but don't take part.

'But how do you actually *do* it? How do you kill an eight-month-old baby?'

One of the younger nurses volunteers, rather hesitantly. 'You inject into the mother's uterus, and that kills the child.'

'But she still has to give birth to the child, doesn't she?'

'Yes. Sometimes the child doesn't die in the womb and is still alive when it is born. But, we leave it . . . and it . . .'

The nurse, who I later learn is the mother of a young child herself, has a slightly pained look on her face and she stops in mid-sentence, as though torn between the emotions of being a mother and what she has been told is her duty to her country.

I am completely aghast, and I am clearly not the only one. A small man with a mousy face sitting in the seat behind me, has been listening to the whole conversation. *'Zhong guo ren huai tou le,'* he mutters. 'Chinese people are too evil.'

'I beg your pardon.' I think I didn't hear him correctly.

He just shakes his head, not wanting direct confrontation with the doctor, and turns away, to look out of the window at the scrappy desert scrubland rushing past. His arm is cradled around a boy of about eight.

'So do you have to do this very often?' I turn back to the doctor.

'Much less than before. In the 1980s it was all the time. Now, people's thinking has been changed, and they want to have fewer children. They see the benefits.'

'But have you done one of these operations recently?' I ask.

'Not within the last two weeks or so.'

She hasn't realised that what she is saying is sensitive. To her, it is logical, and patriotic and good. When I ask her how she feels as a mother doing these things (she herself has two grown children, she'd told me, born before the one-child policy was implemented), she doesn't even understand the question. Chinese people look at the western world, with all the teenage pregnancies and their consequences, and wonder what on earth we think we're doing, allowing that to happen when it could be solved by a simple medical procedure.

Chinese friends from the countryside have told me (though I have no sure evidence of it) that family-planning officials have buckets of water in the operating room where forced abortions take place, and that children who are not killed by the injection are drowned in the buckets. I am just about to ask the doctor about this when the bus brakes suddenly and she and her two nurses stand and walk to the front, smiling their goodbyes.

For a moment I want to follow them off, but they are already descending the steps, getting out at a small village in the middle of nowhere. I would have to retrieve my backpack and persuade them to let me go into the clinic with them, which would be unlikely. Then officials would arrive and want to check my passport, with its journalist visa in it. As I hesitate, the bus sets off again, and I am left looking out of the back window at the three women beside the road, gathering up their bags.

I sit fuming, and regret my decision not to get off.

Perhaps the most shocking thing is that the doctor is just an ordinary middle-aged woman. She doesn't look evil or inhumane. She has children. Perhaps she has grandchildren. But she is faithfully implementing this brutal policy apparently as calmly as though she were designing traffic systems. How is it that the Chinese government is able to make people do these things? What is it that can make a mother of two override her humanity and think she is doing a wonderful, patriotic thing by killing eight-month-old unborn babies?

For all the changes, and the glitzy lights of Shanghai, Nanjing and Xi'an, the state is still paramount in China and will be obeyed on the issues that it cares about. Ultimately, in China, for all the changes, the rights of the individual do not count for much.

The bus rattles on across the fringes of the desert, and I continue to fume, and to hate China. It's one of those days when I am simply glad that I am leaving.

Our narrow road is running parallel to Route 312 now, about fifty miles north of it. It's too tight for two buses to pass at normal speed, and the driver slows when trucks and buses come in the opposite direction. Old Hundred Names ride their bicycles along the road, to market or a neighbouring village, wobbling in the slipstream of the buses or trucks that pass. There are few private cars except an occasional official black Volkswagen or Audi speeding through on an inspection tour, or returning from a long lunch.

The man with the mousy face sitting behind me doesn't want to talk, but another woman gets on the bus and sits herself down next to me. Her work has something to do with irrigation in the nearest town, and we chat a little about the importance of water conservation. Not surprisingly, she says the water situation here is desperate. When we reach Jinchang, another forlorn desert town, I change buses for another two-hour ride to the town of Yongchang, a few miles from a village where I've heard that locals make some extraordinary claims about their ancestry.

In ancient times, the Silk Road west of Lanzhou was all about movement. The Sons of the Yellow Emperor stayed where they were, in eastern China, while out in the west, where so-called civilisation met so-called barbarism, few Han Chinese people settled unless forced to by exile. But other ethnic groups were constantly shifting, and movement along the Silk Road has created a maelstrom of ethnicities in China's northwest. Perhaps the most tantalising claim of ethnic origin comes from a small village just off Route 312 in central Gansu province, in the shadow of the western stretches of the Great Wall. The village is called Liqian, which happens also to be the ancient Chinese word for Rome. Some historians, and now some residents, claim that the people who live there are descendants of a Roman legion that came to China two thousand years ago.

The idea that the people of Liqian (pronounced *lee-chyen*) and descended from Romans was first put forward by an Oxford professor who rejoiced in the name of Homer Hasenpflug Dubs. In 1955, in a lecture to the China Society in London, Dubs put forward his thesis, that in 53 BC, when the Romans were defeated by the Parthians at the battle of Carrhae in modern-day Turkey, a group of Roman soldiers was taken prisoner and transported to Central Asia, where they were captured by the Chinese and taken back to China.

Dubs based his whole theory on a couple of rather vague

references found in Chinese historical writings. One was a military formation used in battle in China that was similar to one used in Rome; the other was a similar type of building. And, er, that's about it.

I had read about the Lost Roman Legion some time before. It had even been written about in the official Chinese press and hailed as a sign of contact between the two great civilisations two thousand years ago. When I saw that Liqian was very close to Route 312, I had decided to pay a visit.

Liqian itself is a small, dusty village, with no paved road. I'd connected by minibus to the nearby town of Yongchang, and then a grinning taxi driver in a battered Chinese-made taxi had driven me the fifteen minutes to Liqian. There don't seem to be many people in the streets today, but on stepping out of the car, I see a man driving a blue tractor trailer towards me. It is belching out smoke into the clean rural air. I flag him down, and he pulls up beside me. His hair is slightly lighter than that of most Chinese, and his nose, while hardly aquiline, has a no-ticeably high bridge. He fixes me with a pair of uncannily green eyes.

'*Ave. Civis Romanus sum,*' is what I want to say.

'*Qing wen, ni shi Luo Ma ren ma?*' is what I actually ask. 'Excuse me, but are you a Roman, by any chance?'

'*Shenme?*' He does a double take, squinting at me against the sun. 'What?'

'You know, the Romans, green eyes and all that,' I persist.

'Oh, Romans,' he says, suddenly realising what I am asking. '*Keneng.* Possibly.'

'*Keneng,* but you're not sure?' I ask.

'Right.' He pauses, with a slightly goofy grin. '*You ren shuo.* Some people have said that.' And that's all he has to say on the matter.

I stop several other people, and everyone is equally hazy about their possible Roman roots. The only thing vaguely Roman about the dusty village is a forlorn little portico put up by the local government with pseudo-Roman pillars containing a stone tablet, on which is inscribed in Chinese characters a summary of the story of the 'Lost Roman Legion of China'.

It is becoming clear that this is all a rather hopeful effort by an Oxford professor and a few ambitious local officials to prove a link between two of the great empires of the past. The closest links I can see are the green eyes of many of Liqian's inhabitants, but there are plenty of Tajiks, Uighurs, Persians and Pashtuns who have green eyes. China clearly has plenty of rural myths, as well as urban ones. I hesitate, wondering whether to invest more time exploring the myth, worried that a column of legionaries might march out from behind a dusty wall the minute I leave. But in the end I decide not to waste any more time here. I hitch up my toga, and jump back into the car for Yongchang, where I climb aboard a minibus for the town of Zhangye.

The driver takes the old Route 312 for a while, then joins the new road. As we speed along on a motorway as good as any in the United States or Europe, a dirt rampart appears. It looks rather old and decrepit, but it goes on and on, running parallel with the road. Suddenly I realise what it is.

'*Chang Cheng!*' I exclaim like a child to the man next to me, my finger pressed against the window. 'Great Wall!'

He smiles and nods.

It's a far cry from the sections of the wall near Beijing, which are more than fifty feet high and made of solid bricks and mortar. There, you could march an army of soldiers or tourists along the top. But here, it looks like simply a mud wall, about ten to twenty feet high. Any stray Mongol horde that wandered this way would have no trouble hopping over it. The main Gobi railway line then appears behind it, the three lines running alongside one another, heading northwest.

The reason for the Great Wall's state of disrepair here was the expansion of China's boundaries. Until the last dynasty of China (the Qing, which ran from 1644 to 1912), the wall marked the outer limits of the Chinese Empire. But in the eighteenth century the Qing rulers expanded their territory and stationed garrisons to the north and west of the wall, thus making it redundant as a last defence.

A sign beside Route 312 says 2,643 kilometres. That's the distance I've come from Shanghai – about 1,600 miles. Soon after the sign, Route 312 bends slightly north and slices right through a gap in the Great Wall, so that the wall now runs to the south of the road. The desert stretches on and on. It's not the rolling, Sahara-style sand dunes we generally visualise as desert, but more of a rocky scrubland, with small villages strung along the old Route 312, still running parallel to the motorway. Some have been there for centuries. Others look as though they have only just been built.

Even here, in the barren outer reaches of the Chinese empire, government propaganda is everywhere.

Lift high the banner of science. Oppose cults.
Taking drugs harms yourself, your family and your country.
Daughters can also carry on the family line.

★

The sign on the archway as the bus enters the next town says 'GOLDEN ZHANGYE'. That may be stretching it a little, but despite its isolated situation in the middle of the Gobi Desert, Zhangye (pronounced *Jahng-yeah*, population 114,000) does not feel as though it is being left behind. It has the classic feel of a mid-sized town anywhere in China. The shops are heaving with consumer goods (though not as modern and expensive as those in the shops further east), there are cars on the streets, new apartment blocks are springing up, and the restaurants are full. There are even large posters all over town of Brad Pitt and Angelina Jolie, starring in their newly released movie *Mr & Mrs Smith*. In short, Zhangye is a pleasant, bustling, if somewhat isolated, oasis town, that is bearing witness to the Renaissance of the Silk Road.

Marco Polo wrote that he stopped in Zhangye (he called it Kan Chau), towards the end of the Silk Road's last heyday in the thirteenth century, before the faster sea routes to Asia relegated it to obscurity. He said he spent a whole year here, though I've no idea how he passed the time. I plan to stay just one night. But what a wonderful evening it turns out to be.

A motor rickshaw takes me from the bus station to what the guidebook says is one of the better hotels in Zhangye. It's a nice, airy place called, imaginatively, the Zhangye Hotel. As I check in, I ask the clerk, in my most patronising white-man tone, whether he knows what I mean when I say I need to get on to the Internet.

'There's broadband in every room, sir,' he says.

I dump my backpack and head out to find dinner.

Zhangye has probably the biggest town square I've seen outside Tiananmen. Nearby, construction is nearly finished on a huge Catholic church. Who on earth is paying for this edifice? In the shadow of the church, an old lady is burning paper money beside the road, watched by what must be her grandson. It is presumably some special day for honouring the dead.

As I watch her, two men come and stand alongside me.

'You don't do that in your America, do you?' says one, making the usual assumption about my nationality and pointing to the fake money, now ablaze on the pavement.

'No, we don't,' I reply. 'And before today, I hadn't seen many people doing it in your China.'

'Oh yes, old habits die hard,' says the other man with a smile.

They both look about thirty, a little over-dressed for a Gobi oasis town, in suit and tie. They are clearly on their way somewhere.

The older, bolder one introduces himself. 'We are the local representatives of An Li.'

'An Li?'

He lifts up his bag. It has the Chinese characters *An Li* on it, and below them, the English name of the company, Amway.

'Amway? American Amway? Direct-selling Amway?'

'Yes.' He grins. 'You know it!'

'Of course, but I wasn't expecting to bump into Amway representatives in the middle of the Gobi Desert.'

'We have only had an office here for three years,' he says. 'But already it is going very well.'

I tell them that I haven't yet eaten dinner and ask if they would join me. In true Chinese fashion, they insist that dinner is on them, and we head to a noodle bar that serves the local speciality, *sun ji chao pao*, a sort of chopped noodle dish with meat. There are no free tables, so we sit on one side of a huge round table while a family sits eating around the other side. Our noodles arrive quickly, with large pieces of thinly sliced meat on top of them.

The older man tells me that his name is Ren Wei (pronounced *run way*), that he is Han Chinese and thirty-five years old. He has a broad forehead, a shock of thick black hair, and the face of an eager schoolboy. Ren grew up in Xinjiang, further along Route 312 to the northwest, and worked for five years in a factory in his hometown, even more remote than Zhangye, where his father had been posted years before. But, like so many people in small-town China, he had bigger ambitions. 'Over there, I couldn't realise my potential,' he says.

So he headed east to Zhangye, where he set about selling fake DVDs for one yuan a shot. He enjoyed the freedom of working for himself and made some money.

He then made his first big mistake, he says, investing all his savings in a travel business, building yurts and tents for tourists to stay in outside Zhangye. The venture went bankrupt, and he returned to Zhangye to look for a job. He says he worked at many businesses, including some of the big names in the beverage industry, Wahaha, Jianlibao, even Sprite, but he says it was very unsatisfying. Even if he made money for the company, he says, he personally did not benefit.

Ren heard about Amway through a friend and came along to one of their meetings. That was just nine months ago, and he is already completely hooked. He is almost shaking with excitement as he discusses his new career – the money he can earn, the possibilities it creates. 'I will do this for the rest of my life,' he says, beaming broadly. 'I will never do anything else. I just love the freedom of this.'

He pulls out his government work licence and holds it up. '*This* is my office,' he exclaims with a smile, negating sixty years of the planned economy with one gesture. '*This* is all I need.'

His friend, Li Caijin (pronounced *lee tsai-jin*), who is only twenty-six, is thinner and quieter. He used to work in an office for a state-owned railway company. He says he'd go to work, read the paper, drink tea, and like so many employees of state-owned companies, do very little all day. He has also just started, but both of them talk about their mentor, a man they call Teacher Hu, who is now, after only three years, earning the equivalent of two to three thousand US dollars a month, a huge sum for this (or any) part of China.

'He holidays everywhere, owns a new house, and a great car. It's amazing,' says Ren as he pulls from his bag a catalogue of Amway products available in China. 'Of course, we don't have such a wide selection of products as in the US,' he says, 'but it is growing rapidly, and all the products are made in China, in a factory in Guangdong, so it is very convenient.'

He reaches into his pocket and pulls out a breath-freshener spray. 'We Chinese like to eat whole garlic, you know,' he says, as though foreigners might not have noticed this. 'Now, you can buy an

Amway breath-freshener spray, and it takes the smell away.'

He takes a little squirt, then puts the breath-freshener back in his pocket and returns to his garlic-laden noodles.

There's a brief pause while we all lean forward, put the edge of our bowls to our lips, and slurp the hot soup of our meat and noodle dish.

'So what is your dream?' I ask Ren.

'My dream is to be like you,' he says. 'I always see you young westerners, carrying your backpacks on your back. You're so young, but you're so independent, and you don't have a care in the world. You're just travelling with your backpack around China. That's what I want to do. Go backpacking in your country, and everywhere.'

Li is more earnest. He says his dream is to get Amway products out to the whole world. 'We say to each other, Amway was started in the US, developed in Japan, it matured in China's coastal cities, but its real *huihuang*, its real zenith, its real glory will be seen in the interior of China, in places like Zhangye. This is where the market is.'

He is talking in almost religious terminology, and I realise that the dream of being the one who cracks the China market, who deodorises those 2 billion armpits and freshens the breath of those 1 billion garlic eaters, is not limited to western businessmen. Chinese businessmen dream that dream too.

The three of us put our bowls to our mouths once more and slurp a final chorus. Ren asks me if I want to go to their office, which he says is nearby. They are holding a meeting, he says. Never one to turn down an invitation in China, I agree. He insists on paying the bill as we head for the door.

'By the way, what was that meat with the noodles?' I ask him.

'That was donkey meat,' he says.

We walk to the Amway office past more posters of Brad and Angelina as Mr and Mrs Smith. It's a third-floor walk-up, just around the corner. Six other Amway reps, three men and three women, all as eager as Ren Wei, are already there. The men are all dressed identically in smart shirt and tie and dark trousers. The women also, though not in uniform, all wear similar casual shirts and trousers. Chinese women seem rarely to wear skirts. Teacher Hu, the man who appears to have been responsible for bringing Amway to Zhangye, is there as well. They all shake my hand, welcome me, and offer me a seat for what turns out to be a meeting to encourage new salespeople to join. Each salesperson has brought along at least one friend, and we sit in the large office on chairs that have been laid out to face a speaker's table at the front.

It then turns into a rather extraordinary evening. One after another, the reps stand up, introduce themselves, and tell what they used to do and how it was only when they found Amway that they discovered their real purpose in life: now they take home $1,000 a month.

As the first woman speaks, people in the audience shout out 'Dui! Dui! (Yes! Yes!),' – pronounced dway – like worshippers shouting 'Amen'.

Then Ren Wei stands up to speak. In his earnest manner, he thanks Teacher Hu first of all, and thanks everyone else for coming, and then, before beginning his speech, he turns towards me and thanks Mr Smith. I do one of those movie double takes in which I turn round to see if there is another foreigner called Mr Smith behind me, but it's soon clear that I am Mr Smith. From that point onwards, every speaker who stands up thanks Teacher Hu, thanks everyone else, and then nods to me and thanks me, Mr Smith, Our Foreign Friend, for coming. Perhaps they think that all foreigners are called Mr Smith. Or perhaps, even here in the Gobi Desert, people are confusing me with Brad Pitt.

'My grandchildren will remember my name,' says Ren, getting into his oratorial stride, appearing to mean every word, 'because I am going to change our family's fortunes. And I intend not just to make money for myself, but as I am more successful with Amway, I intend to give back to the society. Perhaps I will start a school for disadvantaged children. Because we must all put back into society, right? *Dui bu dui?*'

'*Dui! Dui!*' say the audience. 'Yes! Yes! Amen!'

Finally, Teacher Hu himself stands up, whereupon Ren Wei starts a clapping pattern as though he were at a baseball game. '1,2 . . . 1,2,3 . . . 1,2,3,4 . . . clap clap.'

'You can't choose where you were born, but you can choose your future,' booms Teacher Hu, to murmurs of '*Dui, dui, dui*' from the congregation.

'Don't settle for *chabuduo*,' he says. 'Don't settle for "more or less". It's not good enough for you.'

And so about twenty Chinese people in a run-down office building in a small Gobi Desert town sit and listen to a middle-aged former teacher's exposition of the Chinese Dream.

'You too can do it. You too can succeed. You too can be empowered. You too can have the car, the apartment, the respect.'

The audience is listening, and remembering, and they will get up the next morning and go out to work in order to realise what they have heard. For those who seize the opportunity, this is part of the seismic shift that is going on. The *possibility* now exists to dream dreams that might actually be fulfilled. It is starting to change China, one person at a time, and create a new nation. A nation of slowly empowered individuals.

At the end, everyone applauds one another. Teacher Hu thanks the group for coming and says that now we will divide into groups of five, introduce ourselves and discuss the meeting. 'It's a time to share,' he says.

Two and a half thousand years of Confucianism and sixty years' Communist Party rule mean that Chinese people are not used to 'sharing' in a way that seems normal in an American context. The Chinese in this respect are more like the British, if not somewhat worse, generally reluctant to open up about their emotions at all. That may be the reason that so many Brits stay so long in China. They are just relieved to find another group of people as emotionally dysfunctional as themselves.

Four small groups of five (plus the rather incredulous Mr Smith) retreat to different corners of the room, huddle together, and share.

A woman with long black hair and large glasses says it's her first time here, and she's very interested. Another nervous-looking woman is too shy to say much. One man says he sees more clearly now his own failings, and in a very un-Chinese monologue admits that he needs to reach out and seize life for himself. I give a brief few words about what I am doing and say I hope they don't mind if I write about them in my book. They seem excited at the prospect, and I thank them all for their hospitality.

When the meeting ends, Ren Wei and Li Caijin escort me down the stairs to the front door. 'No need to see me out,' I say, but in true, supremely polite Chinese fashion, they insist.

'It's amazing what you're doing,' I tell them. I have absorbed the earnestness of the evening. I mean it completely.

'You see,' says Li, taking me by the arm a little too firmly as we descend the echoey stairs, 'we want to live. Right now we are just *shengcun*. We are just surviving. We want to *shenghuo*. We want to live! You know? We want to really live!'

Those words have stayed with me, like almost no others on my whole trip across China. There could hardly be a better summary of everything that this crazy twenty-first-century Chinese revolution is about.

'OK, I'll see you in New York then, or Paris, or London!' I smile as we shake hands. They smile back, and we part at the main entrance of the building. I wander back to my hotel in the warm evening air, asking myself why on earth I am leaving this wonderful country and pondering the Chinese Dream, and the American Dream, and wondering whether one is taking over from the other.

Chapter Sixteen

RESPECT

Somehow it feels wrong to be clean-shaven in the Gobi Desert. So the next morning I leave the razor in my wash bag, draw back the curtains and cast an unshaven glance across the courtyard outside.

Just below my second-floor window is a western woman with bright orange nail polish on her fingers. I am able to appreciate this because she is doing *taiji*, the slow-moving Chinese form of exercise (often spelled *tai chi* in the West), in the courtyard just below my window. I have no idea who she is – probably the only other foreigner in Zhangye – but very slowly she is moving her arms and body in time with some centuries-old rhythm that she has apparently tapped into, here at the Zhangye Hotel.

In the city's massive central square, not far from the hotel, several dozen middle-aged and elderly Chinese women appear to be heading in the opposite direction spiritually, or aerobically at least. They are looking up at a giant TV screen, which looms over the square, and all are trying to follow the exercise lesson being shown on it. The screen is filled with five impossibly fit-looking Chinese women doing a lively workout in time with some throbbing western music. The leader is barking out commands. The cohort of somewhat less fit-looking Gobi Desert grannies are trying to get their bodies in touch with the twenty-first century.

For me, it's another wonderful clear-blue-sky day, another grey

Gobi Desert bus station, and another bus ride along the Mother Road. For some reason, all the ticket collectors at Zhangye's small bus station, in control of every bus's movement in and out of the town, are women. All are dressed in dull grey uniforms. More strikingly, they are all wearing the brightest red lipstick imaginable. It makes a rather arresting sight, as though they have decided to make a collective statement against the tedium of their jobs, the greyness of their uniforms or the colourless expanse of the Gobi Desert. Or perhaps they all just like red lipstick.

The buses they are directing are almost all full, mostly with construction workers heading west to find work. The camels have long since ceded their role as ships of the desert to the long-distance buses that ply Route 312, and traffic has increased enormously. The cargo has also changed. It is still about trade, of course, but now it is also about construction and communications.

A massive project is under way, almost unnoticed by the world outside. China is busy constructing its western regions, just as the United States opened up its own west more than a hundred years ago. Beijing is trying to hook up its undeveloped west with the rest of the country, and as was the case for the United States, there are problems taming both the wild landscape and the local peoples.

The project is called the *xi bu da kai fa*, which literally means 'Great Opening Up and Development of the Western Regions'. (Some critics say the verb *kai fa* translates more correctly, and appropriately, not as 'development' but as 'exploitation'. In English it is often referred to simply as the 'Go West' campaign.) It was officially launched in 1999, but the campaign is the formalisation of a policy of central government investment in the western regions that had begun earlier in the 1990s. Beijing says its aim is to raise the standard of living of people who live there, especially the ethnic minorities in Xinjiang, Tibet and other remote provinces. That is no doubt true. What Beijing does not mention is the political advantage of buying off the local ethnic minorities in order to decrease the possibility of unrest. The gleaming tarmac surface of Route 312 is very much a part of that effort.

The Silk Road has somehow permeated the western conscious-ness, with its exotic images of camels lolloping along, laden down with spices, porcelain, and of course reams of raw silk in exquisite colours. The reality – grimy towns, poverty, bandits, filthy inns, endless barren desert – was rather less exotic. But many things *have* improved since Marco Polo came through nearly eight hundred years ago, and much of that change is due to Route 312. Better infrastructure and communications have been crucial in bringing development to China's far-flung provinces. Today, the larger oasis towns on the route are bustling with life, but in between, many of the smaller settlements are still grimy desert towns, which offer little and expect less.

Sitting beside me on the bus is a Muslim, a member of the Hui minority group, the descendants of Persian and Arab traders who settled in western China centuries ago. He says his name is Zhang Guoqing, but he adds proudly that his Islamic name is Mohamed Ismael, and that he speaks Arabic fluently. He has rolled up his trousers to keep cool, revealing a pair of almost transparent white socks, and a pair of black shoes with heels that seem a little too high for any man who is not actively involved in some sort of Latin dancing. He in turn glances at my grubby cargo shorts and my hairy legs and my filthy, sunburned feet, trapped in their favourite sandals. No self-respecting Chinese man would ever wear sandals without socks.

Zhang is a merchant of the New Silk Road. He is a 34-year-old mobile phone salesman who travels across the desert with a bag stuffed full of every type of mobile phone. He stops at each oasis town, does deals with the department stores or whoever else wants to do business, then moves on. Zhang has been travelling up and down Route 312 for seven years now. He says the new Route 312 has made a huge difference to his work. Travelling the old road on the old buses took for ever, he says. Now the next town can be reached in just hours.

'Over the last few years, everyone has wanted to own a mobile phone,' he says. 'It's a status symbol. But now there are too many salesmen, and there is too much competition, so business is not as good as it used to be.'

His own phone is one of the latest Nokia models, much fancier than my own, which he looks at with a glance of satisfaction, as though by the modernity of his phone he has personally avenged the Opium Wars.

It can be embarrassing these days in China for the not so technically adept or the not so fashionably inclined westerner. I win prizes in both categories. Chinese people are obsessed with new technology, and are constantly looking over the shoulders of foreigners in airport waiting rooms or on planes or now, it seems, on long-distance buses, to check out what we're doing, what we're wearing, and how advanced our technology is. I have been castigated by a Chinese businessman at an airport for having an outdated laptop (it was about a year old), by a Beijing taxi driver for how shabby my car is (not a Mercedes or Audi, just a battered old Jeep Cherokee), and by any number of digital enthusiasts for my insistence on using a camera that needs film.

So here is another live rail heading west, to join the two Routes 312 and the railway: the unseen information superhighway, sizzling along the Hexi Corridor into northwest China. Salesman Zhang and his mobile phones, the wired hotels and the Internet bars are all having a transformational effect on Chinese society, even this far west. In North America and Europe, mobile phones and the Internet have changed society, but in many ways they have just made more convenient what was already available. The impact in China has been far, far greater. At the start of 2007, there were already 137 million people online in China, accessing information that was never accessible to them before. The mobile phone has also transformed communications. In early 2007, there were 461 mobile-phone users in China, an increase of 68 million on the previous year. In some areas where there are not even land lines yet, people have leapfrogged directly to mobile phones. All the way along the New Silk Road, there is perfect mobile phone coverage.

Diagonally in front of me are two men who appear to be colleagues, one in his twenties, the other probably in his fifties. I start chatting with them, and they turn out to be seed salesmen, travelling to Jiuquan on business. Jiuquan (pronounced *jeo-chwen*) is where I'm headed too.

Sitting behind me is an older couple who used to work in the oil industry here in Gansu but have now retired back east to the coast. They've struck up a conversation with an oil worker sitting next to them, which I join in.

'How were the roads back then, when you lived here?' I ask the couple.

'There were almost no roads in the 1960s,' says the man, a youthful-looking sixty-year-old. 'We didn't need them, because we never needed to go anywhere. If we did, we would go by train.'

'This road,' says his wife, 'the old Route 312, was not even paved.' She is tall and rather elegant, in spite of being cramped into the back row of the crowded bus, which is packed full of about thirty or forty people.

The new Route 312 is straight and fast, a symbol of modernity that looks almost *too* modern for the harsh, barren environment of the Hexi Corridor. The new Route 312 has quickened the pulse of this part of China, a new artery that has improved access to the small towns here, in a way that the railway could not. The road gives flexibility to the travelling salesmen to reach the smaller villages and towns, to bring the economic revolution even there.

A slim pipeline is just visible a long way out in the desert to the right of the bus, pouring oil from the northwest in through the neck of China to feed the hungry east.

'That's for oil from the Tarim Basin, going to be refined at Lanzhou,' says the oil guy, in his deep bass voice. The Tarim Basin is one of China's biggest oil fields. 'They're building another one into China from Uzbekistan.'

All the different strands – the new Route 312 and the old one, the railway and the information superhighway, make a huge difference to the people who live here. But I think perhaps the pipeline is more important even than the tracks and tarmac it runs beside. So much in China now depends upon oil. Its importance resonates silently down through every stratum of society. The Communist Party must keep the economy growing, otherwise the unemployed and underemployed could cause social unrest. To keep the economy growing, the Party must build new factories and create new jobs. (Some economists have calculated that 24 million new jobs must be created every year in China in order to do this.) To fuel the factories and the construction, China must have more oil. And to achieve that goal it is searching for oil within its own borders and going out into the world, making deals in Africa, Central Asia and Southeast Asia.

'Has China got enough oil?' I ask the oil guy.

'Not yet,' he says, staring out into the desert.

Everyone retreats into his or her own thoughts, gazing out of the bus window, the unending yellow scrubland saying something different, no doubt, to each pair of eyes. The snow-covered Qilian Mountains still rise up to the south of the road; the desert extends beyond the horizon to the north. This is the final stretch of the Hexi Corridor, some 350 miles long, which ends at the 'mouth of China', the fort at Jiayuguan. We're still some six hundred miles from Urumqi, and nearly a thousand miles from the end of the road.

The bus rolls on, passing other larger buses, and then being passed by blue East Wind trucks and the occasional black Volkswagen. Flimsy curtains are drawn to block out the fierce desert sun.

A wire fence separates the road from the open scrubland of the desert, and beyond the fence are small groups of people, walking around looking at the ground, and occasionally stooping to pick clumps of greenery from the dry desert earth.

'What are they doing?' I ask.

'They're picking *facai*,' shouts the younger seed salesman above the noise of the warm wind rushing in through the open windows. 'It's a type of edible grass. They sell it to Hong Kong.'

'Is it tasty?'

'Not really. But the name of the plant sounds like the words for "get rich" in Cantonese, so the Hong Kongers like to eat it. They are very superstitious.'

The ticket collector comes back to collect fares. Her nails are painted with intricate twirly patterns, her face is beautifully made up, and she looks far too glamorous to be a conductor on a long-distance bus across the Gobi Desert. In a different life, she could have been in Hollywood. A younger woman with a baby sitting two rows in front is staring over her shoulder from her seat, and she smiles shyly when I catch her looking at me.

'Your baby is very fat,' I tell her.

She beams back at me with pride.

'What do you think about China?' the older seed salesman suddenly asks me. He's a balding man, with a kind face, who says his name is Zhou (pronounced *joe*).

'*Wo hen xihuan.*' I smile inanely. 'I like it.'

'What do most people in the West think about China?' asks his young colleague. I tell him that people in the West are a little confused about China because it's a country that seems very capitalist but is run by a Communist Party.

'We're all confused about China,' says Mr Zhou with a smile. 'It's a confusing time for many people. There is so much change.'

There's a brief pause. I'm tired of asking the same questions, so I try to think of something new. 'What do you want most from the West?' I ask Mr Zhou.

He doesn't hesitate. 'What we want most is respect,' he blurts out, as though he has waited all his life for a foreigner on a bus to ask him this question. 'Yes, we want respect more than anything. I want to go abroad, like you people when you come here. You come to China, and we respect you because you are wealthy and civilised. That's what I want too. I want to go to your country, and be respected, and get a good job there and not be looked down on.'

The old couple seem slightly surprised by both the passion and the eloquence of Zhou's response, but they are nodding their heads. So is everyone else.

There is another pause. The desert moves on outside. The quality of the new road, here as elsewhere along my route, has already subliminally created in me something of the respect that Zhou craves.

'And we want peace,' he adds.

'You Americans like to make money through war, don't you?' the older lady says suddenly.

I try to explain that most people in the West don't want to make money through war, that they make money through hard work. What the government wants to do by going to war is a different thing altogether, not really anything to do with the people, who also want peace. Many people in America and Europe were opposed to the Iraq War, I tell her.

She looks at me long and hard, no doubt the pictures of wounded Iraqi civilians that fill Chinese government news programmes lingering in her mind.

The younger seed salesman turns round and smiles at me. 'We Chinese invented gunpowder, but you westerners invented the gun with which you came here to kill us. We Chinese invented the compass, but you westerners used it to sail out east and occupy our land.'

People smile again. There is no animosity in his voice, or their nods. It is history. It cannot be changed.

'Do you think China is slowly getting respect?' I ask Mr Zhou.

'Yes,' he replies, 'but it will take a lot longer.'

'How long?'

'At least twenty years,' he replies.

Heads nod silently again.

'Chinese people are quite patient, aren't they?' I suggest.

'Yes, they are,' he replies.

There are few things that exemplify the Chinese desire for respect as much as the Jiuquan Space Centre. After all, only two countries had put a man in space before China did in October 2003, and they were the the superpowers of the Cold War, the US and the USSR. If you are looking for signs that China wants to be the next superpower, at a time when 100 million of its people are still living on less than a dollar a day and the rest of the world is cutting back its space programmes, launching a man into space seems pretty symbolic.

After about four hours, Route 312 arrives at Jiuquan. The town's name means Spring of Wine, which seems strange for a desert town on the edge of largely Muslim Central Asia. It was a major stop on the Old Silk Road and is clearly an increasingly important stop on the new one. Like all the Gobi oases, it is a town transformed in recent years. People are passing through, of course, but now they are settling here as well, taking advantage of the new opportunities, some no doubt linked to the huge space centre in the desert a hundred miles outside the town. Moderate prosperity is a goal here too. The outskirts of Jiuquan are a jungle of construction cranes and new apartment buildings. Its department stores are full of the mobile phones sold by salesmen such as my new friend Zhang. There are Internet bars. Everyone is talking to everyone else.

Part of the reason for China's space programme is undoubtedly concern about the so-called 'weaponisation' of space. The old paranoias learned at great cost during the Opium Wars about being militarily prepared are still there.

But equally important is the programme's prestige value. It's as though the Chinese are saying, 'You can put men in space, can you, you westerners? Well, we are the world's oldest civilisation. We invented the compass and gunpowder and the printing press, and we can put a man in space too. We can compete with you at your own game.' It helps to stir up patriotic pride in the nation, and by extension the Party, at a time when its ideological legitimacy has disappeared.

Not everyone in China is convinced of the necessity of a space programme, though. In fact, many people do not even know about this landmark achievement. When the first manned Chinese spacecraft, named *Shenzhou 5*, was launched in 2003, I did the obligatory interviews with the painfully proud young Chinese patriots at the universities in Beijing, who told me how much it showed about China's development and future. But then I drove fifty miles outside Beijing and asked some farmers who were husking a pile of bright yellow corncobs what they thought of the launch of *Shenzhou 5*.

'What's *Shenzhou 5*?' asked several of the women.

I was telling this story to a fellow journalist in Beijing, and he laughed and said, 'That's nothing.' He had driven a hundred miles outside Beijing and found a farmer couple whom he had asked about China's flight into outer space. The old man had looked at him and asked, 'What's outer space?'

I stop a taxi and ask the driver if he can take me to the space centre, but he says you need a special permit from the police to show at the checkpoints along the road, and the permit takes a while to process. He suggests it might not be that easy for foreigners to get a permit. So, reluctantly, I decide to head straight to Jiayuguan (pronounced *jah-you-gwan*), which is Jiuquan's twin, just forty minutes' drive across the desert.

In fact, with all the construction on the edges of each city, it probably won't be long before the desert between them is squeezed out and the twins become joined into one giant megalopolis. It's easier for officials to expand their cities here. They don't have to steal some peasant's land.

I check into the sprawling Jiayuguan Hotel and head out for a run. It's late afternoon, but the sun is still high. The desert heat, combined with a slothful week without training, make it hard going.

ADOPT A SCIENTIFIC DEVELOPMENT OUTLOOK, says the billboard on the edge of town. BUILD A HARMONIOUS SOCIALIST SOCIETY.

I like Jiayuguan. It has an open feel. Although there are huge factories on its outskirts, pumping acrid smoke into the permanently blue sky, they are far enough away not to impinge directly on the town. I like the wide roads, the low buildings, the big sky. It isn't hemmed in like so many other Chinese towns. Like most of Gansu province, it has space to breathe. But most of all, I like it because it is home to Jiayuguan Fort, the most westerly point of the Great Wall. It is a spectacular edifice, a massive square fortress that looks as though it has been dropped into the desert from outer space. First constructed under the Ming dynasty, around 1372, it was enlarged in 1539, and has been fully restored over the last twenty years. Its walls are over sixty feet tall, and the whole fort must be at least a mile in circumference.

In times gone by, this was the very end of civilisation. A Chinese person would stand on Jiayuguan Fort back in the fifteenth or seventeenth century and look out, rather like a Roman standing on the west bank of the Rhine, knowing that outside, beyond, over there, were the barbarians.

Chapter Seventeen

THE END OF THE WALL

In the summer of 1926, three respectable, middle-aged English ladies arrived at Jiayuguan, riding on a donkey-drawn cart. They were Mildred Cable, and Francesca and Eva French, who were sisters. The three were missionaries with the China Inland Mission, and during nearly two decades working here together, they had come to be known collectively as the Trio.

The Trio had gained quite a reputation for their journeys along the Silk Road. Three feisty girls from nice English homes, they had all been converted to Christianity as young women and felt the call to China. Eva had gone first, as a 21-year-old, and had narrowly escaped death during the anti-foreign Boxer Rebellion of 1900. She was joined by Mildred a few years later, and then Francesca made up the team. They had been based in Shanxi province, further east, for twenty years when they decided to move westwards to minister to the people of the Gobi Desert. Many times over the next thirteen years, between 1923 and 1936, the three women visited the oasis towns and villages in Gansu province that lay outside the Great Wall, preaching the gospel and administering basic medical care. There was no Route 312 in those days, or even a paved road of any sort, and they travelled everywhere by mule cart pulled by their faithful donkey, Molly.

Mildred and Francesca wrote several books that are full of

beautiful observations about the desert, its people, its flora and fauna, its difficulties and its joys. In her book *The Gobi Desert*, Mildred Cable describes reaching Jiayuguan and seeing the majesty of the fort.

> *Were this a clumsy, grotesque structure it would be a blot on northwest China, but its beauty and dignity redeem it from criticism, and since, in her unique way, China has ordained that her great western outlet should be controlled by a single door, she has made of that door such a striking portal as to be one of the impressive sights of the East.*

Despite the fact that China claimed to control Chinese Turkestan to the northwest, Jiayuguan was still in most Chinese people's minds the edge of civilisation, partly because of the Islamic 'barbarians' who lived beyond it, but also because of the ferocious desert and fear of the demons believed to live there. Zipping up and down Route 312 in long-distance buses between the oasis towns today, it's easy to forget how forbidding this region was, within living memory. There was a proverb quoted for centuries, until recent years, that 'no man would send his worst enemy across the Gobi in midwinter or at midsummer'. And here I am now, hopping on buses, jumping into taxis, admiring the new apartment blocks and the four-lane highway, choosing from an array of soft drinks in refrigerated cabinets as though I'm travelling around the South of France.

So forbidding was it, even in the 1920s, writes Mildred Cable, that if you were not actually setting off into the desert, you would never go out of the West Gate of the fort. But that was the whole aim of the Trio's mission, to preach the gospel to all the villages in Gansu *beyond* the Great Wall. So, as they were preparing to leave Jiayuguan heading westwards, Mildred decided to go out of the West Gate to take a look. 'I wished to prepare myself for the great adventure,' she writes. She was accompanied by a man from the fort:

'Demons,' he said to her. 'They are the ones who inhabit the Gobi. This place is full of them, and many have heard their voices calling . . . you do not yet know, Lady, the terrors of that journey. Must you go out into the Gobi? You have come from Suchow [present-day Jiuquan]. That is a good place with many people and plenty to eat, but out yonder . . . Must you go?'

Yes, replied Mildred, she had to go, because she had come to seek the lost, and, as she puts it, 'some of them are out there', a remark that the man took a little too literally, as though he might need to arrange a search party.

The Chinese were not completely unfamiliar with what was beyond Jiayuguan, because in imperial times it was used as a place of exile to punish officials or others who displeased the emperor. One Chinese official who knew the full implications of going beyond here was a man named Lin Zexu. At the foot of the majestic Jiayuguan Fort, apparently unnoticed by the Chinese tourists, is a small memorial garden with a statue in it and a poem inscribed on the stone wall beside it. The garden is a memorial to Lin, who was, says a plaque beneath the statue, 'the first open-minded politician of the modern age'.

Lin Zexu (pronounced *lin dzuh-shu*) was the man who was sent by the emperor in the late 1830s to deal with the Ocean People on China's southern coast, who were importing opium to pay for the tea and silk and porcelain they were buying from the Chinese.

As we have seen, the Chinese elite were slow to realise the full significance of the Ocean People's arrival. All the threats to China in the past had come on land, from the horsemen of the north, from the Central Asian steppe beyond where I'm now standing. Confronted with foreign refusal to cease their importing of opium, in 1839 Lin wrote a letter to Queen Victoria, requesting that she personally put a stop to the trade and asking her whether she would permit opium to be brought into Britain like this. The tone of the letter reveals that the Chinese view of themselves and the world had not changed much since Lord Macartney's failed mission in 1793, nearly fifty years before.

Magnificently our great Emperor soothes and pacifies China and the foreign countries, regarding all with the same kindness. If there is profit, then he shares it with the peoples of the world; if there is harm, then he removes it on behalf of the world. This is because he takes the mind of heaven and earth as his mind. The kings of your honourable country by a tradition handed down from generation to generation have always been noted for their politeness and submissiveness . . . The fact is that the wicked barbarians beguile the Chinese people into a death trap. May you, O Monarch, check your wicked, and sift your wicked people before they come to China, in order to guarantee the peace of your nation, to show further the sincerity of your politeness and submissiveness, and to let the two countries enjoy together the blessings of peace.

Lin mentioned how benevolent China was in its own exports, and included perhaps the first and only use in history of rhubarb as a tool of international diplomacy. He appealed to the British to consider the impact upon their bowel movements if Chinese exports of rhubarb, with all its famous laxative effects, were withdrawn.

Is there a single article from China which has done any harm to foreign countries? Take tea and rhubarb, for example; the foreign countries cannot get along for a single day without them. If China cuts off these benefits with no sympathy for those who are to suffer, then what can the barbarians rely upon to keep themselves alive?

With the British merchants (and their bowels) holding firm in spite of such threats, Lin took a fateful step; in May 1839, he commanded the seizure of two hundred cases of opium and ordered it dumped into the sea.

His hardline stance was just the excuse that the British were waiting for. When they retaliated by ravaging large parts of South China and launching the First Opium War, the emperor, who had personally approved Lin's tough policies, dismissed him. Lin Zexu became the scapegoat for China's defeat, and suffered the fate of many before him. He was cast out into the barbarian darkness of exile beyond Jiayuguan, to the Yili Valley, the place that is, in fact, my final destination, where Route 312 hits the Chinese border with Kazakhstan.

The memorial garden to Lin Zexu is now empty, except for me. There is not a single Chinese person here, paying tribute to a man who tried to save China by standing up to the foreigners. Just one Ocean Person, from the land that caused Lin's humiliation, looking up at his statue with a measured balance of respect and shame, reading the philosophical and mildly defiant poem he wrote as he passed through here, and wondering what he would think of the cement factories and petrochemical plants surrounding Jiayuguan now, or the high-speed Internet and mobile phones connecting Chinese people to one another and to the world.

Certainly Lin's revenge has been slow, and has come at a huge human cost. It has taken China nearly two hundred years to start to avenge the humiliations visited upon it by the West. And still that vengeance is not complete. But Lin's revenge is emerging at last: a strong China, a country where the borders are sealed firm, where the northern tribes do not threaten every year, and where the Ocean People do not import drugs or steal land. Lin's successors had to break with the Confucian ways he knew in order to achieve modernity, and they had to destroy many things he held dear, but the changes are happening even here.

Now Jiayuguan is a major tourist destination. From Lin's garden, you can brave the tourist stalls and wander through the huge open gate at the entrance to the fort itself. A guide is showing a group of Chinese tourists around the old courtyard, right in the heart of the fort. They are all clutching expensive digital cameras and wearing matching yellow hats. This is where the general in charge of the garrison lived, in a separate complex complete with wife and servants. The names of all the generals posted there since 1516 are listed on a board outside the courtyard.

'In feudal times . . .' the guide begins her tour. As I look over, heads are nodding, glad perhaps to be liberated from feudal times.

In my pocket I have the telephone number of a student who lives in Jiayuguan, and I am about to call him to see if he is free for dinner tonight. The contact was given to me by Princess Pinky, the cosmetics saleswoman I had met on the road to the Tibetan town of Xiahe. When she heard I was heading west, she said she had a friend in Jiayuguan whom I should call. As usual, I had assumed I would call him. Perhaps he would be the one who would give me that telling insight into life in a frontier town. Perhaps he would be the one who would introduce me to the amazing character who would make everything clear to me. But now that I'm here, I decide not to. Somehow, I just know what a student from Jiayuguan will say. 'China's future is bright. Life is improving. Let's all be friends.'

There are so many grounds for optimism in China, but today I've had enough of the optimists. Some days you're really up on China, and some days you're really down. And today, I'm just tired of the buses, the heat, the travelling and the optimists, too. Have these people never been to the AIDS villages of southern Henan? (Answer: No.) Have they never been arrested and detained without charge or trial for years on end? (No, again, for most people.) Have they never had to sell their bodies to pay for food for their families? (Maybe not.) I don't want to ask any more questions or have

people asking me questions about myself. I'm just craving something that you rarely find in China, and that is solitude. And silence.

So I find myself searching for the farthest, most deserted corner
of the fort, a watchtower where the tour groups don't go.

I stand for a long time, looking out at the wide-open Gobi and
the still-snowcapped mountains beyond. I bet there weren't any
optimists around here when Genghis and his pals swept down from
the steppe.

'Hello. Where are you from?'

Somehow a smiley, English-speaking youth has found me. We
go through the usual routine. He tells me how he has just been
accepted to a college in Beijing, 1,400 miles away, and how excited
he is to be going as a freshman in a few weeks. He says how much
he loves his country.

'I hope the friendship between our two countries grows stronger,' he says.

Someone shouts for him, and he calls in Chinese that he is over
here, behind the corner watchtower. A man appears. His father. A
soldier, who speaks no English and probably had no choices in life.
His son has choices, many of them. He is so full of hope for himself
and for his country. He wants to make China great. He is courteous
and friendly, and eager and idealistic, and overflowing with
optimism. It is impossible not to like him.

Whoever said it is better to travel than to arrive never took the
night bus from Jiayuguan to Dunhuang. Like the intrepid Trio, and
many others before and since, I decide to travel overnight. It should
take me just eight hours, but instead it takes sixteen. Route 312 is
being widened. The project is scheduled to be finished by 2007, so
by the time you read this, it will probably not be a problem, but for
sixteen bone-shaking hours it's a problem for me.

Further east, before Route 312 reaches Jiayuguan, where there are towns and villages beside the road, the new four-lane motorway has been built *alongside* the old 312 – two straight black lines flowing west beside each other. But it is not without reason that Jiayuguan is known as 'the mouth' of China, for outside the mouth, there really are very few villages at all. So there is no reason to retain the old road. It has been dug up and is being relaid as a four-lane motorway. While this road is being built, both lanes of traffic have been diverted to the actual surface of the desert, parallel to the road.

If the music of the Old Silk Road was the sound of camel caravans, the theme tune of the New Silk Road is the kung-fu movie on the long-distance bus. We've barely pulled out of Jiayuguan bus station when the driver slips in a pirate DVD of *Fists of Fury*, or is it *Lethal Ninja*, or perhaps *Warriors from the Magic Mountain*? I lose track. True to form, none of the Chinese passengers seem to notice the kicking, punching, and shouting that explodes from the small television set mounted at the front of the bus.

My sleep is governed by the bumps in the road and the mobile phone of the man next to me. It plays Beethoven loudly whenever it rings, which is often. No matter where I sit on a bus, I always seem to end up next to the guy with the orchestra in his underpants.

I wake with a stiff neck around daybreak, expecting to be almost at Dunhuang. But the driver says we are nowhere near. We haven't even reached Anxi, a town about 130 miles west of Jiayuguan. Dunhuang itself lies about seventy miles off Route 312 to the south. After we turn off 312, the traffic works end, and the driver is able to accelerate along the tarmac to try to make up some time. Fluffy white clouds dot the bright blue sky overhead. Old beacon towers made of mud can be seen by the road, towers on which fires were once lit to help people navigate towards the oases. Mobile phone towers now stand beside them. I receive a text message from a friend who is sitting beside the swimming pool of a luxury hotel in Bangkok.

The bus seems to be half full of construction workers, heading west in pursuit of work and a better salary, perhaps a hundred dollars a month, not ninety (and that makes a big difference), benefiting from the central government's recent campaign to develop the western regions. They are mostly Han or Hui people (the Islamicised Chinese). A journey like this, taking them far 'outside the mouth' of traditional China proper, now seems as natural as anything. There are no demons in the Gobi any more.

I sit next to an older man, over fifty, who seems a little out of place among all the young migrants.

'Life is *so* much better now,' he says to me. 'There are so many more opportunities. We used to have to scavenge simply to get food during the fifties and sixties. Now, every dustman has a mobile phone. Are you telling me that isn't progress?'

It's easy to lose sight of how much things have improved in China when you travel the length of Route 312 and spend so long in poor rural areas. For people like this man, who experienced the famines of the late 1950s and the chaos of the Cultural Revolution in the 1960s, modern China, for all its many problems, is a million times better. There are no crazy political campaigns, no lunatic economic campaigns, no forced denunciations of neighbours. It's your perspective that makes all the difference. For me, the mere *possibility* of government intrusion in my life is unacceptable. For him, the fact that those possibilities have receded, even if they are still there in the background, means modern China is paradise. 'Compared to what?' is always the question you have to ask in China. This man has probably seen and suffered things that few westerners have ever had to bear. Now he can choose what he does. And that, for him, is progress.

The bus struggles on, a lonely speck inching across a sea of sand. The Mongolians to the north of here have a saying about the raw beauty of the Gobi Desert. They say, sometimes you must go down to the Gobi to stretch your soul. As you travel across it for hours and hours, you start to understand what those Mongolians mean. After the teeming towns and villages, and the hills and valleys of eastern China, the land and the sky here open up and embrace each other, and make you want to stop, get out and embrace them too. But be careful what you wish for.

We have turned off Route 312 but are still about sixty miles out from Dunhuang when suddenly we hear a rather ominous grinding noise from the engine. The bus loses power and pulls over to the side of the road. It would have been hard to pick more forbidding territory for this to happen. There is literally nothing but desert for miles around. No truck stops, no villages, nothing.

The driver lifts the cover over the gearbox beside the steering wheel, then gets out to take a look under the bus. After a while, it becomes clear that we are going nowhere, so I make him open up the luggage compartment. I grab my backpack and walk a hundred yards up the road from our stricken bus, trying to flag down another one. A few don't stop, but finally one pulls over, and I have to run up the road in the heat with my heavy pack on my back to where it has stopped. The driver opens up his luggage compartment, and I throw in my rucksack and jump on board. It's full of Japanese tourists, who must be driving from the nearest rail link, at Liuyuan, just beside Route 312. The bus is beautifully air-conditioned and is not playing loud kung-fu movies.

Finally, oh so very finally, we approach the city. The desert slowly starts to recede and is replaced by purple gorse bushes, then poplar trees and some cornfields, and finally the road is lined by the full dazzling green of the oasis. This is Dunhuang, the legendary Silk Road oasis and home of the 1,600-year-old Mogao Caves, where travellers would stop to pray for safe passage across the worst of the desert, as it opens up towards Central Asia.

Chapter Eighteen

THE CAVES OF
A THOUSAND BUDDHAS

On the rooftop of the four-star Silk Road Dunhuang Hotel, a group of wealthy Greek tourists are standing looking out at the rolling dunes known as the Singing Sands and dreaming of a time gone by. Behind them are some Spaniards, who also seem in a kind of reverie. Beside them are two Americans, staring straight up into the star-studded night sky. A stray Englishman sits sipping his beer, knowing better than to be taken in by all that fake Silk Road tourist schlock, but all the same, he looks up at the sky and breathes deeply, as though the crescent moon might be exuding some tangible smell of the Orient. It is hard, in Dunhuang (pronounced *doon-hwang*), not to be sucked into the sheer romance of the whole thing. For westerners, the town is a place to dream all your exotic Arabian Nights dreams of the East.

A few miles away, a roomful of young Chinese men sit fulfilling their fantasies of the West. There are no Arabian Nights here, and their only thoughts of the Silk Road are probably how to get as far away from it as possible. The gaggle of Chinese youths is sitting in a twenty-four-hour Internet café in the centre of Dunhuang, their eyes glued to their computer screens as they do battle in online video games. On the pavements outside, aspirational young couples window-shop at stores awash with choices, electronics and

227

cosmetics, clothing and real estate, relishing the new prosperity of their town and perhaps thinking about the possibilities of travel outside it.

Not since the Bund in Shanghai has the contrast between East and West been so stark. Foreigners try to re-create some intangible, romantic Chinese past, while Chinese people try to escape the past and build a tangible, very unromantic future.

The Silk Road Dunhuang Hotel has been designed to fit into the Western image of the Silk Road. With its faux adobe walls and its cool, high-ceiled lobby, it is built in a style that seems, to the foreign eye, to be Central Asian. I have no idea if it is, but the fact that it fits into my preconceived idea of Silk Road architecture makes me feel good about staying here, even though it is the most expensive hotel in town, and they charge westerners extra for breakfast. It doesn't hurt that it has a wonderful rooftop bar, from where you can see the dunes of the desert and the bright, bright stars splashed across the sky at night.

The name Dunhuang in Chinese means 'Blazing Beacon,' which gives you a good visual idea of the town's geographical situation. It has always been a crucial oasis town, though its population has increased greatly in the last century, to over 100,000. The Silk Road from the ancient capital at present-day Xi'an to Central Asia and Europe ran almost directly to Dunhuang, roughly along the path now taken by Route 312. Just north of the town, the Silk Road branched into two main routes: the Northern Silk Road, which I will be following, snakes northwest to Hami and Turpan and Korla, skirting the northern side of the fearsome Taklimakan Desert. The Southern Silk Road wove, and still weaves, its way southwest, through the ancient, less-visited towns of Miran, Khotan and Yarkand along the southern rim of the Taklimakan. The Blazing Beacon of Dunhuang was the last big oasis before the huge stretches of desert, and it signalled to the traveller that here was food, water and shelter.

It was, and is, though, much more than just a watering hole. For

Dunhuang is the home of some of the oldest and best-preserved Buddhist cave paintings in the world, where travellers would gather to pray for protection in crossing the desert, or to give thanks for safe passage. And, what's more, events that took place in this obscure oasis town in the early twentieth century played a significant role in spurring on a weak, defeated China to reinvent itself and to become the increasingly strong and respected country it is today.

On 12 March 1907, a Hungarian-born archaeologist working for the British government in India stumbled into Dunhuang from the southwest after a three-week trek across the desert. He and his team of local helpers, camels and horses had travelled 260 miles from the ruins of a forgotten desert city called Loulan to the west, and they were exhausted, filthy and hungry. Dunhuang in 1907 was a poor, grimy, isolated town, but it was like the Promised Land for the archaeologist and his weary caravan.

The man was Aurel Stein, and what was to take place over the next few months would ensure his name endured in lights in the annals of Western archaeology but lived in infamy in China.

The Middle Kingdom was still five years away from the over-throw of the imperial system, but the country was already in a state of near-collapse. The colonial powers had carved out their spheres of influence and were milking China dry. The imperial elite had hung on desperately to their delusions of cultural grandeur, unable to accept their weakness and unwilling to give up their power. Several waves of reform from below had been stifled by pressure from above, especially from the ultra-conservative empress dow-ager. But after the Western powers suppressed the anti-foreign Boxer Rebellion in 1900, and forced humiliating financial repara-tions upon the court, even the empress dowager and her die-hard conservative allies realised that they had to change. But it was all too late, and soon the country collapsed.

In the western regions in 1907, Chinese control was extremely shaky, even though the lands outside the mouth of Jiayuguan Fort had supposedly been part of the great Qing dynasty empire since the conquests of the mid-eighteenth century. The Qing dynasty had made one last effort to pacify the west in the 1880s but had not won any local hearts and minds in the process, and a weak central government plus poor communications throughout the country meant that Beijing exercised very little direct control on remote regions such as Gansu, Xinjiang and Tibet. The feeble remains of the imperial court in Beijing were focused on trying to defend China against the Ocean People coming from the east. Little did they suspect that some cunning Ocean People would sneak in from the west with archaeological, not military, objectives.

The British and the Russians had begun their geo-strategic chess game, immortalised as 'the Great Game' by Rudyard Kipling in his book of the British Empire, *Kim*. A large part of their respective interest in Gansu, Chinese Turkestan (now Xinjiang) and Tibet was strategic. The Russians had expanded into Central Asia and were scouting the periphery of their new empire. The British were concerned about Russian incursions into imperial India, so efforts began in earnest to map the regions surrounding the subcontinent. The British sent spies, often undercover, to survey the adjacent territories, primarily to learn if a Russian approach to India from the north was possible or planned.

The other, secondary interest – of the British, Russians and many others – was archaeological. There had been rumours for some time during the mid-nineteenth century that there were Buddhist cities hidden beneath the shifting sands of Chinese Turkestan, and perhaps an entire forgotten Buddhist civilisation. Covert forays by British intelligence officers resulted in a number of interesting finds, which persuaded archaeologists in British India that there were indeed fantastic artefacts under the desert, and a race began among the European powers to find them.

The man who emerged as the grandfather of large-scale European exploration there was an obstreperous Swede named Sven Hedin, who made four expeditions to Central Asia between 1893 and 1935. Hedin was known for his eccentricities, such as playing Bizet's *Carmen* on his music box in the middle of the desert. But he was an intrepid explorer who braved atrocious conditions in summer and winter, and drank his fair share of camel's urine when his water supplies ran out in the desert. On his second expedition in 1899, Hedin discovered the long-lost city of Loulan, a formerly prosperous outpost on the Silk Road that had disappeared under the sand when the Tarim River changed course in the sixth century.

Sven Hedin, and the famed Russian Nicolay Przhevalski, who also roamed all over Chinese Turkestan and Tibet, were first and foremost explorers, but they dabbled in archaeology. (Hedin was also a geographer and cartographer.) Aurel Stein, by contrast, was a top archaeological scholar, an Orientalist, whom the great Asia scholar Owen Lattimore later called 'the most prodigious combination of scholar, explorer, archaeologist and geographer of his generation.'

During his first expedition in 1900, accompanied by a whole caravan of camels and local guides, and his intrepid terrier Dash, Aurel Stein travelled up from India and along the Southern Silk Road, where he began to excavate the ancient cities of Dandan-uilik and Niya. There he found not only evidence of Chinese presence from the eighth century but also clay seals on wooden tablets depicting Greek deities, showing that Western artistic images had travelled east along the Silk Road. Up to that time, no one knew that European influences had ever reached that far.

On his second expedition, in the winter of 1906–7, Stein had visited Loulan, the desert city that Hedin had discovered seven years before. He had carried out a thorough archaeological dig in sub-zero temperatures (it was considered easier to work in freezing cold than in baking heat) and discovered more fascinating documents which revealed much about the former Chinese outpost in the west.

So, on that cold March morning in 1907 when he finally arrived in Dunhuang, Aurel Stein was flush with success. His memoirs of the trip, a fascinating book called *The Ruins of Desert Cathay*, suggest that he was not expecting to do anything more than visit the Caves of a Thousand Buddhas, a series of man-made caves that had long been known to travellers who stopped at Dunhuang. But soon after his arrival, he heard from an Urumqi trader that a Daoist monk named Wang Yuanlu, who had appointed himself guardian and abbot of the caves, had discovered a secret grotto that had been sealed for centuries. The word in the bazaar was that the cave had been full of ancient manuscripts.

With Jiang, his faithful Chinese amanuensis, close at hand, Stein went to visit the abbot and set about building a friendship with him, with one purpose only in mind: to persuade the monk to let him see, and then possibly *take*, some of the precious manuscripts.

Stein sought common ground with Abbot Wang in their mutual admiration of Xuan Zang, the Chinese monk well known throughout China for his travels to India in search of Buddhist scriptures in the seventh century. Abbot Wang was indeed thrilled that Stein was a fan of Xuan Zang (pronounced *shwen dzang*) and in the end agreed to let Stein read some of the ancient documents, and then to go inside the library cave itself. Stein's understated description of the experience belies the importance of the discovery.

The sight the small room disclosed was one to make my eyes open. Heaped up in layers, but without any order, there appeared in the dim light of the priest's little lamp a solid mass of manuscript bundles rising to a height of nearly ten feet, and filling, as subsequent measurement showed, close on 500 cubic feet.

It was a treasure trove of manuscripts in many languages, including Chinese, Sanskrit, Tibetan and Uighur, some 40,000 in all. After weeks of tiptoeing gently around Wang and the abbot's fears of losing his influence over the caves, Stein's Chinese helper Jiang managed to persuade Wang to part with some of the manuscripts. By increasing the sum, he gradually acquired more, until he had paid £130 for twenty-nine crates full of manuscripts, paintings, embroideries and other relics, which were then shipped back to the British Museum.

When he returned to England, Stein and other experts analysed the documents and concluded that the library cave had been sealed up around AD 1000, the dry desert air helping to preserve the manuscripts. One of the documents turned out to be the world's oldest known printed book, the Diamond Sutra, a scroll made of seven panels of paper on which carved wooden blocks were used to print. (It is now housed in the British Library, which, along with the British Museum, has said it is not giving any manuscripts back to China.)

When word of what Stein had discovered got out, the race was on. He was followed by a brilliant French archaeologist and linguist named Paul Pelliot, who also talked his way into the library cave at Dunhuang and managed to cart off hundreds more of the manuscripts back to Paris. Then came Albert von Le Coq, a German sent by the Ethnographic Museum of Berlin. Russians and even Japanese started getting in on the act. Finally, in 1923, Professor Langdon Warner was sent to Dunhuang by the Fogg Museum at Harvard. He had developed an ingenious way to strip frescoes off walls and set about doing just that in some of the caves at Dunhuang, shipping the frescoes back to Boston. All of the archaeologists plundered what they could, not just at Dunhuang but at many sites in Gansu province and Chinese Turkestan. And China was powerless to stop them.

News reached Beijing and Shanghai of the Ocean People raiding the Caves of a Thousand Buddhas, and it further fuelled the anger of China's increasingly nationalistic urban youth. By that time, China had collapsed completely, after the failure of the 1912 Revolution, and then suffered the humiliation of the Treaty of Versailles in 1919 which, in ending the First World War, handed all Germany's concessions in China to the Japanese. The inability of the Chinese government to stop the pillaging of its precious artistic heritage played a major role in motivating China's youth to reinvent, reinvigorate and restrengthen the country. A huge wave of nationalism was emerging in the cities of the east, and by 1925, when Langdon Warner returned to pay a second visit to the caves, he could gain no access. The door had closed on twenty years of robbery, which had a fundamental impact on the Chinese psyche.

What then unfolded, though, was a double tragedy (as Chinese tragedies so often are), because what the earnest patriotic youth of China finally settled upon for salvation was the Chinese Communist Party under Chairman Mao. And Mao did not save China's past, he destroyed it. During the Cultural Revolution, anything old or religious became a target, and many of the treasures along the Silk Road, including some of the caves at Dunhuang, were damaged.

Now, a hundred years after Stein took the scrolls, and forty years after the Red Guards came calling with their sledgehammers, the caves at Dunhuang are open to the public, and the tourist trade is bringing in large amounts of cash for the region. The Caves of a Thousand Buddhas, and Dunhuang itself, are gradually avenging the humiliations of the past and making sure they never happen again. The town's new-found confidence is being flashed out by three neon Chinese characters on top of the Communist Party headquarters in the centre of Dunhuang.

'*Beng xiaokang,*' it reads. 'Rush towards moderate prosperity.'

★

The Mogao Caves lie about twelve miles from Dunhuang. Aurel Stein reached them by camel across the short stretch of desert from the town. Nowadays, tour buses and taxis zip back and forth all day. It's a short drive, past the city's small but busy airport, into the wide-open desert again just briefly, before you see the low yellow cliff face ahead to your right, dotted with a honeycomb of caves. A mobile phone tower stands nearby.

I wonder aloud to my chubby taxi driver about the layers of religion in this place. 'It's amazing how this area was such a centre of Buddhism 1,600 years ago, and then along came Islam and replaced it all.'

He grunts.

'And now it's a layer of atheism,' I say after a pause. He grunts again.

'*Ni xin jiao ma?*' Do you believe in anything?' I ask him.

'*Bu xin*. No, I don't believe,' he replies.

'Do you think it's all superstition?'

'Yes.' He nods, not really paying attention. Then he points to the first caves, cut into the rock face coming up on our right. 'These are the caves where the monks used to live. The painted caves are up ahead.'

Stein's photos of the caves show their entrances fifty feet up, reachable only with a ladder. In the 1960s, however, before the madness of the Cultural Revolution, with the caves in bad shape after decades of neglect, concrete walkways were built outside the three rows of caves, so that all you have to do is climb up some stairs to get to them. A sort of pebble-dash concrete finish was added to the cliff face as well, presumably to prevent it from crumbling, and sturdy doors have been added to each cave to control access. All of these renovations may well have been necessary, but together they give the cliff face with its walkways the air of a badly built urban housing estate. This is my first visit to the caves, and as I purchase my ticket, enter through the gate and walk towards them, I am honestly not sure if these are the famed 1,600-year-old Caves of a Thousand Buddhas or some closets used for storage.

Once you get used to the rather strange modernisation of the outside, though, you can start to sink into that whole 'wow, these have been here 1,600 years' state of mind that is evident on the faces of many visitors as they tour the site.

Buddhism entered China in the first century AD, but the Han dynasty was avowedly Confucian, and it was not until the fall of the Han, and the period of disunity from AD 220 to 589, that Buddhism made real inroads into China. That period is sometimes compared with Edward Gibbon's characterisation of Europe after the Fall of Rome in AD 476 as the 'triumph of barbarism and religion'.

The caves are all man-made, the first one dating from AD 366, when local legend has it that a Buddhist monk named Lezun had a vision of a thousand Buddhas here and convinced a wealthy Silk Road pilgrim to fund the first cave temple. Over the centuries nearly 500 of them were carved out of the rock. Some of the caves are tiny; others reach more than fifty feet high to house huge sculptures of the Buddha. As pilgrims came along the Silk Road, they carved out more caves, and many, like the famous monk Xuan Zang, brought new scriptures. Traders would sponsor a cave as a place to pray for safety when travelling the Silk Road. They were abandoned around the fourteenth century, with the advent of Islam, and rediscovered only 500 years later.

The caves are impressive. I tag along at the back of a tour group made up of mainland Chinese and Taiwanese tourists together. The guide is telling how the earliest artwork is from the Wei dynasty of the fourth century AD, when Buddhism was starting to take root. The art of this period still retains its Indian influence, evident in the slim statues with fine hands and large heads. During the sixth and seventh centuries, as trade along the Silk Road grew and Chinese influence increased, the paintings and sculptures began to include more female figures, with the growing influence of the female Chinese deity Guanyin.

No artificial lights are allowed in the caves, so the guide uses a flashlight to boost the weak rays of sunshine that struggle in through the narrow entrances. Many of the grottoes are decorated with paintings of Buddhist figures and stories from the past as well as coloured friezes, in the original bright orange, green and blue paints.

Soon we come to the most famous one in the whole complex, cave number 17. It is set into the rock halfway along a corridor that leads to another cave.

'This,' says the guide, 'is the Library Cave. In 1900, the self-appointed abbot of Dunhuang, Wang Yuanlu, by chance came upon this cave, which had been completely sealed up. Inside it, he discovered a treasure trove of ancient documents, nearly 1,000 years old, that had been preserved in the dry desert air.'

He describes some of the documents, including the Diamond Sutra.

'But then, the *daobaozhe*, the robbers, arrived.'

The robbers were Stein, Pelliot, Le Coq, Warner and the others. The guide betrays no emotion as he relates the story of how the foreigners robbed the Library Cave, carting the contents back to European museums. He says the word *robbers* without any real animosity, a matter-of-fact description about something that happened a hundred years ago.

I follow the group for an hour or so, then peel off and head to the small museum, which catalogues the whole history of the 'robbers' and what they took, complete with photos of Stein, Pelliot and the others. On the way out, I get chatting to the woman standing behind the counter.

'Have you forgiven us for doing all this?'

In a typical, polite Chinese way, she lowers her head but doesn't reply immediately.

'You haven't really, have you?' I press her.

'No. You're right. We haven't really.'

Trying to lighten the mood a little, I tell her that I am about to go to London, and perhaps I can have a word with the people at the British Museum and ask them to return the treasured manuscripts.

'Good. You should do that,' she says, her face brightening. 'Please do that.'

I end the day at Dunhuang's other main attraction, the Singing Sands, a series of sand dunes named after the eerie sounds they are supposed to give out when the wind blows. For those who have oohed and aahed their way through the high culture of the Mogao Caves, the Singing Sands offer a chance to ooh and aah in a slightly more relaxed atmosphere, for the two main attractions here are camel riding and sand surfing.

A steaming herd of tourists, Chinese and foreign, is nervously eyeing a steaming herd of camels at the entrance to the sands. Occasional pairs of humans break from their group and head for as friendly a member of the camel fraternity as they can find, clambering on to a saddle on the animal's back with the help of the camel's owner, then being led out across the sand. Nothing quite says 'Old Silk Road' like a two-ton, two-hump Bactrian camel, and they are in huge demand wherever there are tourists who want to relive the thrill of trekking across the dunes.

I stand trying to resist being sucked into such a shabby show of wanton tourism. But the urge for my own little Lawrence of Arabia moment gets the better of me. I sidle up to one of the camel drivers with the pathetic approach of someone trying desperately not to look like a tourist and eventually climb on to a particularly noisy, smelly beast. It's only a half-mile walk in the shadow of the lunar dunes to the tiny Lake of the Crescent Moon, hidden away among the mountains of sand. The lake has attracted pilgrims for centuries.

I trail two women from Hong Kong, who squeal and chatter and shout at their camels in Cantonese all the way to the lake.

The camel driver waits with my mount at the lake as I sweat my way up a very long wooden staircase that has been cut into the sand to the top of the dunes. From there, it's a stunning view out over the teardrop lake, the dunes and the city beyond. There's a crowd at the top, all sitting to gather their breath and enjoy the view with a gentle desert breeze blowing and the sunset exploding in front of us.

The way down is somewhat easier. It involves sitting on a small toboggan that looks more like a tea tray and pushing off, sand flying everywhere as you speed, shrieking, to the bottom of the dune.

Mildred Cable and the French sisters came to Dunhuang many times during the 1920s and 1930s, and there is a wonderful description in one of their books of the three middle-aged English missionaries sand surfing. You can still almost hear the squeals.

Chapter Nineteen

ENDURANCE

Two hours out of Dunhuang, and I've just rejoined Route 312, heading west. The road is only one lane in each direction, with a narrow hard shoulder in case, heaven forbid, you should break down out here. A rather sad white line at the edge tries to separate the asphalt from the desert, but mostly the two just merge. We're approaching the border with the region called Xinjiang, formerly known as Chinese Turkestan. A few buses and small blue trucks whizz past, plus the occasional massive articulated truck, three times as long as their blue cousins, almost pulling our modest red VW taxi into its slipstream as it accelerates past. Up ahead, one of these behemoths has tipped on its side down a slight bank, and lies like a beached whale in a sea of sand.

'The driver must have fallen asleep,' says my taxi driver. The two truck drivers are squatting in the shadow of the stricken truck, presumably waiting for assistance.

'Shouldn't we stop and see if they need help?' I ask.

'No. They probably have someone coming already to rescue them.'

'Don't get involved' is still the first rule of life in China.

The colours all around are muted today. The desert is a scrappy, scrubby yellow, stretching for ever on either side of the road. There are coarse, dirty green clumps along the roadside of what I think is known as camel grass, though frankly, if I were a camel I would turn my nose up at them. Even the sky today looks rubbed down with smudges of grey-white clouds. There are no settlements here. Humans are strictly just passing through. The only spark of colour is the yellow paint of the dashed lines down the middle of the black strip of tarmac, pointing towards the western horizon.

Suddenly, up ahead are several more bright yellow dots on the road. As we draw closer, it becomes clear they are cyclists, five in total, three wearing the yellow shirts of the Brazil soccer team. This is *real* desert, and I can't believe anyone would be cycling out here. I tell the driver to pull over just beyond them, where I jump out and flag them down.

'Hey! *Ting yi xia!* Stop! Can you stop? Where are you going?'

'Yining,' says the front cyclist, pulling to a halt in front of me. His friends pull up behind him. Yining is the town right beside the Kazakh border, where I'm heading too.

'Where are you coming from?'

'Lanzhou.'

'Why are you biking?'

'We just wanted to get out and explore our own country a little. It's an adventure.'

The five of them are typical smiling, friendly Chinese students, eager to answer my questions, even though it would be over a hundred degrees in the shade if there were any. They are all members of Muslim ethnic minorities of the northwest and are studying at the Arabic school in Lanzhou.

We chat for a few more minutes, and then I climb back into the car, feeling slightly embarrassed to be driving as they climb back on their bikes behind me under the merciless Gobi sun.

I had set off early from Dunhuang that morning, driven two hours north, and then turned left, westwards, back on to Route

312. A huge tollgate marked the entrance to the next section of the desert. A mile or so after the toll, just before we had met the cyclists, a massive articulated truck had pulled on to the road from the open desert. It was not even pulling off a side road – there are no side roads – but was literally driving in off the Gobi.

'He's avoiding the toll,' said my driver. 'He just pulled out into the desert a few miles before the tollgate, looped around and rejoined the road a few miles after it.'

The desert here is neither the fine Sahara-type grains of the Singing Sands nor the hard beige scrubland surface of the previous sections of the Gobi. It has a layer of black across the surface. The driver says it is known as *heisha*, which means 'black sand'. 'It's iron ore,' he tells me. 'It isn't good enough quality to mine, but there are some mines out there.'

He points, northwards, to the vast emptiness beyond. 'Tin, aluminium, copper, iron ore, gold.' Huge deposits of mineral resources lie beneath the desert sands. Oil and gas are already pumped east to fuel China's economic boom, and the possibility of finding more out here could prove very important as China's quest for energy intensifies.

Xinjiang (pronounced *shin-jahng*, meaning 'New Frontier') is the size of California, Texas, Montana and Colorado combined (or if you prefer, Britain, France, Germany and Spain). If it were a country, it would be the sixteenth largest in the world, but it has a population of just 20 million people. Strictly speaking, Xinjiang cannot be called a province. Its official title is the Xinjiang Uighur Autonomous Region. The Uighurs (pronounced *wee-gurs*) are the dominant ethnic group out here, and the one that causes Beijing the most problems.

The government propaganda has not changed, but the language has. For 2,000 miles, Chinese characters have dominated the road signs. Now they have to jostle for space with the place names written in the Uighur language, which uses Arabic script.

Push forward Hami's economic development.
Protect China's underground cables.
Love your girl children.

My mobile phone vibrates, as all Chinese mobile phones do on entering any new province or region. A message says, 'Welcome to Xinjiang.' Then comes another one: 'Looking for a gift? Khotan jade is perfect for any occasion. Call this number now.'

Soon we arrive in the tiny town of Xingxingxia (pronounced *shing-shing-shyah*), or Starry Gorge, the small scrap of human habitation that has always marked the traveller's entry into Xinjiang. It is the site of one of the Old Silk Road's best known fresh water wells. After passing through the gorge that gives the town its name, I stop for lunch at a small roadside café. The town barely qualifies as an oasis, it seems so barren.

The owner of the small café is called Lao Zhang. He looks older than his forty-five years and has already been running his little truck stop here in Starry Gorge for ten years. He is Han Chinese, originally from the city of Turpan, further west on Route 312. Lao Zhang (pronounced *lao jahng*) is a cheerful kind of guy. It doesn't take much to make his slightly pursed mouth break into a huge smile, and then a laugh explodes from within him.

When I enter his tiny café, he is in the kitchen, stir-frying some food for two truck drivers who sit waiting to eat lunch. He comes through and smiles, and I decide to go and chat to him while he cooks. Despite a wide-open window, the kitchen is a furnace, the gas flame leaping up the side of the grimy black wok as he cooks.

I stand beside the open window and simply ask him how life is. My question opens a floodgate.

'How is life? How is life? Life is not good. Do you know why? Because the officials have sealed up our well. The well that has given water to Xingxingxia for centuries has been sealed up with concrete.'

He looks up from his blackened wok, then splashes soy sauce into the stir-fry, which sizzles as he tosses it. 'The officials here are so evil, so incredibly immoral, it almost defies belief.'

'But why on earth would they want to do that?' I ask him.

'Because . . .' He pauses again and steps back from the stove, wok in hand, to look at me. 'Because they run the local water company, and they want to force everyone to buy their water.'

Even when you think you know something of the venality of Chinese officials, stories like this can still take your breath away. Lao Zhang says that he remonstrated with them, but they would not listen. He says they used the classic post-9/11 argument of government officials in Xinjiang, a region with a high population of Muslims. 'They said that if I kept on protesting, they would arrest me as a terrorist.' And when you are arrested as a terrorist in China, you have no recourse, no lawyer, no protection. So Lao Zhang had to shut up. But he refuses to buy their water.

The food is ready. He swirls it into a dish and disappears behind the dirty curtain to deliver it to the two truck drivers. He comes back, wipes his hands on an even dirtier towel, and stands looking at me, as though really sizing me up for the first time.

He makes me a bowl of noodles, then comes out and sits with me in the shabby little dining area.

Lao Zhang has a fire in his eyes that you seldom see in China. He doesn't seem like a normal café owner. In a different era, I imagine he could have been a revolutionary. But here he is, in the middle of the desert, trying to make a living for himself and his wife and child. 'My daughter wants to be a policewoman when she grows up,' he says, 'so she can control the corrupt officials.'

The two truck drivers finish their lunch and leave. Lao Zhang and I talk for half an hour. The little café is baking hot. Lao Zhang is hotter. He has more stories of official corruption, more anger at the local officials, more tales of abuse of power, tales that you will hear in every truck stop, in every vilage, in every town across China. He waves his arms and fumes, seeming glad to get it all off his chest.

'So is there nothing you can do about it?' I ask him finally.

He stares at me intensely, beads of sweat rolling slowly down his temples. Then he holds up two fingers. 'There is only one thing to do, and I can tell you what it is in two characters.'

From the fire in his eyes, and the barely restrained fury in his voice, I honestly think that he is going to say '*Ge ming.*' Revolution.

But he doesn't.

'*Ren shou,*' he says, spitting the words out between his teeth. 'Endure. That is all we can do. *Ren shou*. We can and must endure. That is all we have ever been able to do.'

I stare at him and slowly shake my head. He has just summed up thousands of years of Chinese history. Endure *is* all that Old Hundred Names have ever been able to do. For all the progress in the wealthier parts of China, endure is all that hundreds of millions of common people in the poorer countryside and the western regions ever see themselves doing in future.

At certain crisis points in history, the endurance has become too much, the pressure has built up, and the volcano has erupted. Revolutions have started and have overthrown the ruling dynasty. But they have not led to a change in the system. They have simply replaced one emperor with another, and with a new dynasty that ends up being just as corrupt as the last. There has never been any separation of powers, any linear narrative of change, any Magna Carta. Just power concentrated in the hands of a few officials, trapped in an unending cycle of history.

Months later, I found a passage in Mildred Cable and Francesca French's book *Through Jade Gate and Central Asia*. It is written as the missionary trio are delayed at Starry Gorge in the 1920s on their way to Urumqi. The soldiers garrisoned there are preventing everyone from passing through, and several youths are being detained at the same inn as the Trio. These young men had been press-ganged into the military, and half a dozen of them had been flogged, apparently for desertion. 'A spirit of blank hopelessness dominated the place,' wrote Cable and French. They then stepped back and looked at the big picture of China, based on thirty years of experience.

The Chinese are a long-suffering people; they bear the tyrannies of their oppressors, and the dominion of rapacious officialdom, with a pathetic resignation, but the hour is at hand when they will rise and avenge the wrongs of generations. In such an hour, no violence is regarded as an excess, and they will deal with their oppressors in their own way.

That was in 1926. Their prophecy was fulfilled in the first years of Communist Party rule in the 1950s, when landlords and 'ruling classes' were mercilessly put to death by the new peasant leaders.

Is there a new uprising coming? People like Lao Zhang are getting by, just about. Everyone can put up with corruption if his own lot is improving each year, however slightly. But if the economy stalls, there are plenty of very angry people now, right across China, ready to avenge the wrongs of rapacious officialdom. Mao's words from 1927 keep coming back to me: 'A single spark can light a prairie fire.' The grass on this and many parts of the prairie is very, very dry.

The fire in Lao Zhang's eyes has blazed until this moment. Now that he has exploded, he shakes his head, his eyes seem to glaze over a little, and I wonder how much longer that fire will be there.

I pay him for my bowl of noodles and ask if can see the well. He leads me outside to a little culvert down a slope underneath Route 312 as it rolls into town. It has a massive cap of concrete sealed over the top. I look at it, shaking my head in disbelief. He scoffs through his teeth and turns away. Then I say goodbye and wander up to the road, to look for a ride onwards to the next big town of Hami.

And that is how I come to be standing in Starry Gorge, talking to the truck drivers at the petrol station. We chat while we wait for the police car to move from its position just up the road. They tell me about the game of cat and mouse that they play with the police all the way along Route 312. Several of them have come from Shanghai; some from Guangzhou, in the very south of China; one from Beijing.

There is an official sign beside the petrol station that says, CLAMP DOWN ON THE THREE RANDOMS.

'What are the Three Randoms?' I ask.

'*Bu yao luan shou fei, luan she gang, luan fa kuan*. No random tolls, no random roadblocks, no random fines,' one of them replies, saying that it's a campaign against corrupt police and local officials, who impose all three.

'That's rather ironic,' I reply, 'that the police car would be sitting waiting to randomly fine you a few hundred yards from an official government sign that says he shouldn't.'

The trucker smiles the weary smile of every Chinese person. The smile that says simply, 'You are a foreigner, and this is China.'

Then the word comes through that the police car has moved on, the drivers scatter to their vehicles, and Liu Qiang offers me a ride in his big blue East Wind truck, with the huge industrial filter on the back.

'We need a multi-party system,' Liu says, picking up the conversation about local corruption. 'We need checks and balances on the government. It's just too corrupt.'

His words of hatred for local officials echo those of Lao Zhang at the café. Liu tells me more stories of corrupt police along the road in every province across China, a litany of official abuse of power that, to be fair, goes on in most developing countries. But in contrast to much of the developing world, Liu and many Chinese retain an age-old Confucian belief that the central government leaders are good, and it is just the local officials who are corrupt. The respect of the central government and mistrust of the local officials seems to be the exact opposite of the American mind-set.

Driver Liu is not only frank about politics but very open about his private life. I ask him if he visits the prostitutes who are available at every truck stop, and he says he does.

'Of course, this isn't a very good phenomenon,' he says, making it sound as though he's talking about someone else. 'But I'm a guy, so it's in my nature, right?'

When you hit the desert driving west in the United States, you know at least there is the shining sea of the Pacific Ocean the other side. Here in Xinjiang, the desert never seems to end. Nor, it seems, does Route 312. We travel for hours through the middle of the emptiness, talking about everything and nothing, becoming firm friends even though we'll never meet again. We stop briefly at a small, dusty village named Luotuo Quanzi, which means 'Camel Corral'. You can tell you are in the wild west by the names of the towns and villages. Camel Corral is like Starry Gorge, lined with grimy little cafés, but here there is more choice of food. Each truck stop specialises in food from a particular province. The signs outside proclaim HENAN FOOD, SHAANXI FOOD, ANHUI FOOD and so on. Every driver wants food from his own province, Liu explains, and here they can catch up on news from home over their favourite dish.

After another hour of open desert, we approach the exit off Route 312 for Hami, and I prepare to get out. Over years of living in China, I have spoken to dozens of Chinese professors and experts, intellectuals and urbanites who give the impression of having their finger on the pulse of the nation and an ability to interpret it for foreigners. Sometimes they do it very well, but if you really want to know about China, *real* China, there are few better ways to find out than a long conversation with an ordinary long-distance truck driver, barrelling across the Gobi Desert.

Chapter Twenty

THE GREAT WALL OF THE MIND

There are few more wonderfully artistic nor mesmerically beautiful writing systems in the world than the characters of the Chinese language. Chinese has no alphabet, but is made up of 214 different 'radicals' which are combined to make characters. The radicals are not the characters we are all used to seeing on Chinese restaurant signs; they are the constituent parts of those characters. There is a radical for 'water', which is just three little lines; there is a radical for 'man', which looks like a man with two legs; there is a radical for 'animal'; and so on. Every character is made up of a mixture of radicals, with some radicals being used to hint at the meaning of the character and some radicals used to give clues to the character's phonetic pronunciation. So any character to do with water (river, sea, canal) contains the 'water' radical, plus another radical or two. Most characters that have something to do with wood (tree, forest, table, chair) contain the 'wood' radical, plus others. And so on.

Some Chinese characters are made up of interesting combinations of radicals. A 'pig' radical underneath a 'roof' radical is the character for 'home'. A 'woman' radical together with a 'son' radical is the character for 'good'.

Once characters have been formed, you can put different characters together to make more complex words. In general, new characters cannot be created (though a famous Chinese linguist named Zhao Yuanren did once translate Lewis Carroll's nonsense poem 'Jabberwocky' into Chinese, using invented characters to capture the slithy toves that 'did gyre and gimble in the wabe' of Carroll's original). So if a new concept appears, it is described by putting existing characters together.

The system is very logical. For instance, when the Chinese first came across the giraffe, they did not reach back into the roots of some ancient mother language such as Latin or Greek to create a new word, they used characters that already existed. The Chinese word for a giraffe is *chang jing lu*, which literally means 'long neck deer'. The word for computer is *dian nao*, which means 'electric brain'. Even words that are not new are often wonderful combinations of existing characters. A lobster is *long xia*, which means 'dragon shrimp', and my own particular favourite, the word for 'womb', is *zi gong*, which translates literally as 'child palace'.

All of this made the introduction of the typewriter into China rather difficult, the introduction of Scrabble even more so. To write on a computer in Chinese, you must write the character's transliteration in the Western alphabet (*qiu, xia, zhao, meng,* or whatever − all of which have multiple characters that make the same sound), hit Return, and a choice of the characters romanised that way comes up. You then choose the one you want. Learning their ABC has become a crucial part of Chinese children's learning their characters and pronunciations.

The Chinese language, in many ways like Chinese civilisation itself, has always been self-contained and difficult to get into. That is still true for the outsider. In addition to the radicals and then the characters, there are the arpeggios of the language's four tones (the flat first tone, the rising second tone, the falling-then-rising third tone and the falling fourth tone). Characters that are spelled exactly the same way in our alphabet have completely different meanings depending on their tone, the most famous being *mai*, which when used with the third tone means 'to buy' and when used with the fourth tone means 'to sell'. (This may explain why the Chinese stock market is in such turmoil.) How you write the characters is important too. A man with poor calligraphy is seen by educated Chinese in the same way that educated westerners might view a man wearing a cheap suit.

However, getting into the language (learning how to read, write and pronounce characters) is by far the most difficult part of learning Chinese. Once you are inside, it is much simpler than English and most Western languages. Grammar is extremely simple. There are no tenses, no declensions, no plurals, because Chinese characters cannot change. They simply are.

The simplicity of the language has a flip side, though. The fact that characters cannot change gives the whole language an inflexibility that even Chinese scholars admit can stunt originality. Chinese schoolchildren still learn characters by rote, and critics say the way they learn is bound to affect the way they think.

I'm not sure if it is quantifiable, but I have long wondered how close the link is between the unassailable fortress of the written Chinese character and the unassailable fortress of the imperial (and then Communist Party) state. Words in alphabetical languages are fluid and malleable. They are able to change and evolve, and it doesn't seem entirely coincidental to me that the political systems of their countries can too.

The great Chinese iconoclast of the early twentieth century, Lu Xun, whose grave I had visited in Shanghai, thought deeply about this. He said that China could never become a great country if it did not ditch its way of writing completely: 'If we are to go on living, Chinese characters cannot . . . The characters are a precious legacy handed down by our ancestors, I know. But we can sacrifice our inheritance or ourselves: which is it to be?'

My reason for raising all this here is not to debate whether the Chinese character system needs to be scrapped – that doesn't look likely at present – but to discuss a specific linguistic twist that says much about the part of China I am now travelling through. It also says a lot about the historic relations between Chinese rulers in Beijing and the Muslims of what is now Xinjiang.

Until the eighteenth century, the Chinese character *hui* (pronounced *hway*) was used in imperial edicts to describe the Muslims of northwest China. One of the constituent radicals of the character was the 'dog' radical. China, the fount of all civilisation, stretched as far as the last fort of the Great Wall at Jiayuguan. Beyond that were the barbarians, who were no better than dogs, and the character used to describe them reflected that. (This attitude towards non-Chinese was true not just with regard to the Muslims of the northwest, but also to the Ocean People. In the nineteenth century, one of the early British interpreters, Thomas Taylor Meadows, wrote that the Chinese 'were always surprised, not to say astonished, to learn that we have surnames, and understand the family distinctions of father, brother, wife, sister, etc.; in short that we live otherwise than as a herd of cattle.')

Then, in 1760, something fascinating happened. The Qianlong Emperor (who more than thirty years later would humiliate and send home the British envoy Lord Macartney) had just conquered Chinese Turkestan, the huge swathe of territory that I'm travelling through, which begins at Starry Gorge and is now called Xinjiang. The 'mouth' of China at Jiayuguan Fort was no longer the mouth. The Chinese Empire had been expanded, taking away the necessity of the Great Wall – indeed, from that time on, the Great Wall fell into disrepair because the empire now extended beyond it. The Qianlong Emperor thus, for the first time in a thousand years, territorially if not culturally, claimed to have brought the Muslims of Turkestan *into* the Chinese Empire.

As if to mark this change, the imperial court issued an edict in February 1760. It said that official documents should no longer employ the 'dog' radical in the Chinese character used to describe the Muslims of Turkestan. It was to be done away with altogether, and starting that spring, scholars of the imperial archives note that none of the imperial documents use the 'dog' radical when writing the character 'hui' to refer to the people of the region.

Never before can a few strokes of a brush on a page have symbolised such a hoped-for psychological shift. The change indicated that the emperor in Beijing no longer saw these barbarians as barbarians, that they were being brought into the imperial family, being made part of the Chinese Empire, and that they had consequently been elevated above the status of animals. In short, they were no longer 'them'. They could now be considered part of 'us'.

There was just one slight problem with this. 'They' were happy being 'them'. 'They' didn't want to become part of 'us'. And the same is true today.

The Chinese have ventured into Turkestan three times in their history.

The initial instance was in the second century BC during the Han dynasty, and lasted on and off for more than three hundred years. The period was characterised by a tug-of-war between the Han Chinese and the 'barbarian' Xiongnu tribes to the northwest. When the Han dynasty collapsed, though, in AD 220, so did China, and along with it Chinese influence in Central Asia.

The second foray westwards came in the seventh century, when China was finally united again, under the Tang dynasty. But by that time, a new power had appeared in Central Asia. The Arabs were pushing east and bringing with them the new religion of Islam. They defeated the Chinese at the battle of Talas (in modern-day Kyrgyzstan) in AD 751, and again the Chinese retreated. (An interesting footnote to this defeat: it was at Talas that captured Chinese soldiers first gave the secret of making paper to the Arabs. From the Middle East it found its way to Europe in the twelfth century.)

It was not until the Qianlong Emperor's conquest, 1,000 years later, that the Chinese intervened successfully again in Turkestan, and they haven't left since. Yet if you go to the website of the Chinese government or to Chinese history books, they say that Xinjiang has been a part of China since 60 BC.

The Qianlong Emperor's expansion into the northwest was largely for strategic reasons, to create a buffer zone against anyone who wanted to invade, and that is still part of Chinese thinking today. The initial takeover of both Xinjiang and Tibet was military, but the subsequent governing of the regions was not aimed at colonisation. The local Muslims (and Tibetans in Tibet) were allowed to continue with their day-to-day life and, crucially, with their religion. The Qing dynasty rulers were not at that stage trying to turn 'them' into 'us', but were taking the relatively soft line of simply bringing 'them' into 'our' big multi-ethnic imperial Chinese family.

The fact that they even expanded into Xinjiang is largely because the Qing rulers were not Han Chinese, they were Manchus. The Manchus had invaded China from Manchuria (now northeast China) in 1644 and, in order to rule such a huge empire, had adopted many Chinese ways. But they had retained some Manchu ways as well. They were originally hunters and horsemen, with a pan-Asian view more similar to that of Genghis Khan and the Mongols than to that of the Han Chinese, and they set out to build a bigger empire than the traditional Chinese one, which stopped at the last fort of Jiayuguan

This is a crucial point because what modern China today has inherited is essentially a Manchu empire. If the Qing dynasty of 1644 to 1912 had been ruled by *ethnic Chinese*, I doubt if they would have expanded into Turkestan and Tibet. (You will recall that the ethnic Chinese Ming dynasty, from 1368 to 1644, had burned every ship in its navy, hardly the act of a country bent on expansion.) But once that Manchu empire had been enlarged, it became a point of honour and pride for subsequent Chinese rulers to retain it, even after the Manchus were overthrown in 1912.

In the late nineteenth century, the Muslims of the northwest became more unruly, chafing at Beijing's control, and rebellions broke out. Conquering Xinjiang had been one thing for the Manchus; governing it proved something else altogether. And it was then that Beijing's policy changed from one of letting 'them' be 'them' in the family of 'us' to one of actively trying to change 'them' *into* 'us'.

The first attempts were rather brutal and not very successful. In 1877, after a Muslim uprising in the region, a Chinese general called Zuo Zongtang, with a huge army in tow, swept through Xinjiang. He forced local Muslims to change their customs to Chinese customs, and forcing the teaching of Chinese in schools.

Then, Chinese influence in Xinjiang waned as the country collapsed after the failure of the 1912 Revolution. Following a brief period of trying to maintain a sensitive line with the Muslims in the 1950s, the Communist Party embarked on the second Chinese attempt at turning 'them' into 'us', this time through enforcing Communist policies and through the forced immigration of Han Chinese to the region. In 1949 there were about 300,000 Han Chinese out of a population of 4 or 5 million in Xinjiang. That was roughly 6 per cent of the population. In 2000 a census showed the figure to be 7.5 million Han Chinese out of a population of 19.25 million. If you include the armed forces, that makes the Han Chinese now just under 50 per cent of the population of Xinjiang. And the numbers of Han are growing all the time, as more migrants arrive, attracted by the opportunity of jobs in the booming west.

Despite all this, though, the Uighurs and other indigenous people of Xinjiang have *still* clung to their own identity. The Chinese too keep themselves separate from the Uighurs. The Great

Wall, built to keep the Chinese separate from the barbarians, may be crumbling in these far western outposts, but the Great Wall in people's minds, the divisions between different peoples, is harder to destroy, for both the Muslims and the Han Chinese.

So now, Beijing is trying a third policy (while retaining the other two). It is pouring money into western China and trying to buy off the Muslim peoples with economic opportunities. At the same time, it is using an increasingly integrated education system, and an improved transportation system, to start earlier in Uighur children's lives the process of trying to turn 'them' into 'us'.

This policy is being played out in real time in the parking lot of Hami bus station, in the life of fourteen-year-old Rebiya. She is a small girl, dressed in a plain blue shirt, jeans and trainers, looking like a Han Chinese teenager except for the fine Turkic features of her face. She is embracing – or rather being embraced by – her mother, who is dressed like a traditional Uighur woman, in a long voluminous dress, headscarf and gold earrings. Her mother is weeping. Her father, a handsome man with a bushy moustache, is standing stoically, gently patting Rebiya on the back.

I have come across Rebiya quite by chance. After a couple of hours wandering around the pleasant but unspectacular town of Hami, I had bought a ticket on the overnight sleeper bus for Turpan, 250 miles to the northwest. Rebiya is one of a group of forty ethnic minority students in Hami, and thousands from all over Xinjiang, who are taking the overnight bus this bright summer evening to the regional capital of Urumqi. All forty of them are milling around at the bus station, and an extra bus has been laid on to accommodate the overflow for the twelve-hour journey.

In Urumqi they will take part in an orientation programme with local education officials before they all board a train and head east, to high schools in Shanghai, Xiamen, Tianjin and other cities near China's Pacific coast.

Rebiya is one of the top high school students in Hami, and this is a reward for her hard work. She already speaks accentless Mandarin Chinese, unlike her parents, whose Mandarin is coated with a very thick Central Asian accent. The government chooses the best students from the ethnic minorities in all the schools in Xinjiang and Tibet, and offers them expenses-paid places at schools in eastern China. Travel, fees, books, everything is paid for. It's an offer that most families find impossible to turn down.

The Chinese government says its policy provides a great opportunity for these children to get an even better education, and that is true. Rebiya is excited to be going. But the by-product of the policy is that the cream of Uighur youth have their ethnic identity diluted and become, in their formative years, much more Chinese. For the Chinese government, it is a very efficient way of making sure a generation of ethnic minority high achievers in Xinjiang becomes more like the new generation of young Han Chinese in the east of the country.

Some observers believe that China is likely to follow the route of Taiwan and South Korea and other Asian tigers, and will, with economic growth and the emergence of civil society, evolve slowly towards democracy.

There are several main reasons to fear that political change in China will be different from that in Taiwan or South Korea. One is simply China's size. South Korea, with some 48 million people, and Taiwan, with 22 million, are smaller than most Chinese provinces. It took them only a couple of decades to industrialise and urbanise, creating a middle class that then demanded political reform. China's population is sixty times that of Taiwan, and so far the Chinese government has been very savvy about making sure the new middle class are stakeholders in the political status quo.

Another reason to fear that China will not take the same relatively smooth path to democracy is the so-called Ethnic Issue. The influx of Han Chinese into the west of China is rapidly changing the demographics there. But if Chinese troops were moved out of Xinjiang and Tibet today, I think it likely that there would be uprisings there tomorrow. And Chinese leaders must be even more concerned about giving the vote to Uighurs and Tibetans than they are about giving it to the Han Chinese. That's why Beijing is pedalling so fast to try to make Uighurs and Tibetans more 'Chinese', so that if the crunch comes (or even if it doesn't) they will be too well integrated into China to want to opt out.

As well as the Uighur children and their families gathering to board the bus, there are plenty of Han Chinese. I stand for a while chatting to people in both groups as we all wait, and it's clear how much Rebiya's generation has already been changed. The older generation of Uighurs and Han are really two completely different peoples.

The older ladies in their flowing dresses and their headscarves would fit in anywhere from Istanbul to Tashkent, while Uighur men dress more similarly to the Han Chinese. Their main difference comes down to facial hair. Chinese men can be macho, but they manage to do so without the assistance of stubble. This looks strange to visiting westerners, since in the Western mind every mean son of a gun who ever moseyed up to a saloon bar this side of Dodge City would of course have skipped the grooming pages in his *Gentlemen's Quarterly*.

Uighur men are hairy like westerners. In fact, a Uighur man can grow more stubble in half an hour than a Chinese man can grow in a lifetime, and almost all the Uighurs here have either moustaches or beards. To the Uighurs, facial hair is the sign of masculinity, and that in itself is enough to form a closer bond between westerners and Uighurs than between westerners and Chinese. Put simply, they look more like we do.

Today, though, the disparate groups, regardless of beardedness, are jumbled together like jelly beans on a pair of shiny gold buses heading west to the regional capital. Our bus finally pulls out of the dusty car park, and Rebiya's weeping mother puts her hand to her mouth to stifle a sob, as she waves her daughter goodbye.

The journey to Turpan takes nearly eight hours. It's a sleeper bus, with the bunks arranged in three narrow lines along the length of the vehicle, separated by two narrow corridors. Mine is an upper bunk right at the back, and I have to climb up, stepping on the bunk of the passenger underneath. He nods a greeting as I heave my pack up and climb on to the tiny bed.

It's a wonderful sunset over the Gobi, and I watch it, full of Silk Road reverie, as the bus head west along Route 312. The glow of the orange sun grows richer as it sets, pouring brightness and warmth into a landscape drained of colour. I would have taken more of these sleeper buses back east, if I had not wanted to jump out so often and talk to the people beside the road. Here, there are very few people living along the road, which is just one lane in each direction, so there is no real reason to stop, and travelling by sleeper means I don't have to use up a whole day travelling across the open desert.

As the sun sinks, I climb down and sit with the two Han Chinese men on the bunks below, who say they work for a heavy machinery company. They are visiting the places where their machinery has been sold and offering service to the companies who have bought it. On this trip alone, they are travelling all over Xinjiang and down into Qinghai, where they have supplied equipment for the construction of the Tibet Railway.

'You guys are literally building the country,' I tell them, and they laugh.

The senior of the two, named Li, has a crew cut and a deep voice. He is very macho but also very courteous. Just the kind of man you want touring your facilities in western China, or policing your ethnic minorities for that matter. He looks me in the eye and sizes me up carefully, but he has a quick laugh and a generous manner.

His friend, who doesn't tell me his name, is chubby and smiley, and clearly plays second fiddle to Li. I ask them what they think of Xinjiang. Li looks out at the sun setting over the desert as Hami disappears behind us. 'It's epic, it's magnificent, it's mysterious, it's . . . unbelievable. I think every Chinese man should see this place. It was here hundreds, thousands of years ago, and will still be here in thousands of years. It makes me feel like a blade of grass.'

I have seldom heard a Chinese person talk that way about anything. Li looks out of the window at the barren landscape flashing past in the half-light.

Both he and his friend are extremely optimistic about the future. They are both in good jobs, and they are doing something for their country. China is becoming wealthier, they say. China is becoming a better place to live.

We talk for a while as the sun sets, then I wish them good night and climb back on to my bunk. I can't take my eyes off the orange moon that is rising, travelling alongside as we accelerate into the night. Mildred Cable, once again, wrote some of the best descriptions of crossing this part of the desert. The Trio travelled at three miles per hour on their donkey-drawn cart, but Mildred's sense of the spirit of the desert can still be felt today, even when viewed from the bunk of a large, noisy, Chinese-made bus, travelling twenty times as fast.

Silence settles on the whole party. The mules know their business, the carters . . . tramp in the starlight, with sure feet. The traveller, if his line of communications with God be open, sits in a rapt sense of the Divine which checks self-expression, and commands the tense stillness of utmost reverence. The spirit takes control of the self-expressive soul . . . The desert has caught you, and you, the so-called teacher of men, shall be taught . . . Man-made constructions never again look imposing.

Chapter Twenty-one

'CHINA IS A COLONIAL POWER'

'What's your name?' asks the young, unshaven Uighur man as he sits down at the table next to me in a small but bright café in Turpan.

'Robert,' I tell him. (Many people in Asia have trouble with the shortened version of my name.)

'Like Robert the Bruce?' he asks in English, raising his eyebrows.

'Yes!' I reply. 'How on earth do you know about Robert the Bruce?' My namesake was a king of Scotland in the fourteenth century. After initial defeats by the English, he took refuge in a cave and, as every British schoolchild knows, while living in that cave, he saw a spider trying to make its web but failing, over and over again. Eventually, the spider succeeded in swinging itself far enough to complete its web, and this perseverance persuaded him that he too must persevere until he defeated the English, which he duly did, at the Battle of Bannockburn in 1314, confirming Scottish independence.

'I read about him in a book,' says my new friend.

I compliment him on his knowledge of British history and tell him of my theory that Xinjiang and Tibet are like Scotland. They could end up like England's northern neighbour within the United Kingdom, contained within a country they don't want to be part of

262

but, after a few centuries, unable or unwilling to make the effort to secede. He listens carefully.

'Do the Scots still speak their own language? Do they still have their own customs?' he asks.

'They have not retained their language, though they do still have some of their customs. And their kilts, of course.'

'What?'

'Kilts. Like skirts. Scottish men wear skirts.'

'See,' he says. 'So we are better off than the Scots. We still have our own language. And our men do not wear skirts.'

I like him immediately. He says his name is Murat. He is in his twenties, his Central Asian looks – high-bridged nose and high cheekbones – set him completely apart from the many Chinese who are visible on the streets of Turpan.

We dive straight into an intense and very frank conversation about relations between Uighurs and Han Chinese, and about the future of his people.

'Things are getting worse here,' he admits, taking a calculated but fairly safe gamble that I'm not going to sell him out to any passing Chinese policemen.

'What is getting worse?' I ask, thinking he may be talking about direct, physical oppression of the Uighurs by the Han Chinese. But he's not talking about that at all.

'More Uighurs are choosing to send their children to Han Chinese schools. They don't have to, but they are doing it, because they know that is where the future lies. In the Uighur schools too, children are learning Chinese in the first year. It used to be third year. In twenty, thirty, fifty years, perhaps no one will be able to speak or read or write Uighur. Just like the Scots. We'll lose our language. Even now, many children can speak it but not write it.'

Some other people sit down at a table near us, and he lowers his voice.

My bus had arrived at 3.30 a.m. I'd checked into my hotel and slept late. Consequently, I had missed the group tour of the places of interest around Turpan. Instead I had bumped into Murat.

There is a general assumption among Uighurs that westerners are sympathetic to their plight. The same is true among Tibetans, and they are usually correct. Part of it is just a western tendency to support the underdog, plus general opposition to Communist Party oppression of anyone, whether Han Chinese or Uighur or Tibetan. Maybe it's also a stubble thing. I surreptitiously compare Murat's beard with my own, and I suspect he may be doing the same.

We chat for half an hour about Xinjiang, America and Europe, then I tell him what I am hoping to do in Turpan. 'I have always wanted to sleep out in the desert. Where's a good place to go?'

He smiles at the idea and looks at his watch. 'I will talk to my brother.' We exchange mobile phone numbers and agree to talk later in the day.

The Turpan Depression is the lowest place in China, and the second lowest in the world (after the Dead Sea), at 426 feet below sea level. It is also the hottest place in China, with a highest recorded temperature of 121 degrees Fahrenheit (49 degrees centigrade). The depression is a desert basin that covers nearly 20,000 square miles and has a population of 170,000, of which about three-quarters are Uighurs and the rest Han Chinese.

The main crop here is grapes, and at the time of my visit, the harvest is just beginning. Trucks laden with fresh green grapes can be seen in the streets, and baskets of them are being sorted beside the roads. Some pavements are covered by vine trellises, providing wonderful shady walkways, protecting pedestrians from the vicious heat of the summer sun.

Apart from the vines, the city itself is not particularly beautiful. There are attractive older parts, but like all cities in the western regions, it has a modern Chinese section that could be anywhere in the country. The town has a mellow feel to it, though, and many foreigners, especially backpackers, like to kick back here for a few days and do nothing. At the hotel that morning, I bumped into two bearded Swedes who had ridden all the way from Europe, with tiny panniers on their bikes that can't have held more than a change of clothes and a water bottle.

Considering the fact that we are in the middle of the desert, Turpan has a surprising number of places of interest to visitors. The first is an ancient irrigation system known as *karez*, which means 'well' in Uighur. The system was designed more than two thousand years ago, and Turpan owes its existence to it. It is made up of dozens of long subterranean tunnels, which connect the head well in the mountains north of Turpan with the city and farmland below. No pumps are needed, or any form of modern technology, or building materials. The water flows entirely by gravity. Evaporation is reduced by keeping the channels underground.

The strained relations between Han Chinese and Uighurs are evident in the small tourist venue that houses the *karez*. The whole complex feels like a theme park, like a North American Indian village, where you can 'experience' Native American culture. Welcome to Uighur World! Have your photo taken with a real Uighur dancing girl! Have her hold grapes over your mouth!

After you've walked down to view the underground streams that flow from the mountains to the city, you exit into an artificial bazaar, where small groups of Uighur women are positioned at regular intervals among the stalls. The women are all attractive, and heavily made up, dressed to the nines in bright traditional Uighur clothes. As each group of Han Chinese tourists comes along, the women strike a pose, rather like performing animals. One balances a bowl of grapes on her head as though sitting for a Renaissance painting. Another three sit at a table as if for a Roman banquet, again with grapes at the ready. Another pair of women loll around listening to Uighur music, ready to jump up and dance at the arrival of the next group of Chinese tourists.

China's ethnic minorities do a lot of dancing. Or at least, in the minds of the Han Chinese, they do. There is almost as much stereotyped thinking in the Chinese mind about Muslim peoples as there once was (and perhaps still is) in the Western mind. When you see programmes about the ethnic minorities on Chinese television, all they ever do is dance, dance, dance. And hold grapes while they dance. And talk about how China is one big happy family.

The stallholders hustle visitors like stallholders do everywhere. When I stop to look at some beautiful pashmina scarves, I am surrounded by other sellers quoting me ridiculously inflated prices. Then I realise that all the stallholders are Han Chinese, and in a fit of pique and solidarity with the Uighurs, I decide not to buy anything. If I'm going to be ripped off in Xinjiang, I want at least to be ripped off by a Uighur.

Murat calls me and says we can drive out to the dunes tonight. We arrange to meet later that afternoon, and he is accompanied by his friend-brother-cousin (the description varies), who is driving an old Volkswagen. His friend-brother-cousin speaks little Chinese and less English, and does all the driving, with Murat sitting next to him, leaning back to chat with me. 'We will do a tour of Turpan's famous sights, and then we will sleep in the desert,' he says.

'Great. Do we need to take anything with us?' I ask him.

'I have some rugs for us to sleep on,' he says. 'Maybe we could buy some food and a bottle of wine.'

'Wine? Aren't you a Muslim?'

'I only drink perhaps once a month.' He grins. 'In fact, I had some last night, but I'll make an exception today for you.'

We stop off at a supermarket and pick up some provisions, including a bottle of local red wine, produced by a company set up in Xinjiang as a joint venture between a Chinese vineyard and French advisers. Then we head out east of the city, back along Route 312.

The road passes the Flaming Mountains, which I'd missed in the dark on the way in. They are a reddish colour, with small ravines flowing down them. Especially in the glow of early evening, the mini-ravines look from a distance like tongues of fire climbing up the side of the hills.

We stop briefly at some of the other archaeological sites just east of Turpan, such as the wonderful Bezeklik Caves, carved into a cliff face on a ledge above a small river just north of the highway. These, like the Caves of a Thousand Buddhas at Dunhuang, once housed fantastic murals, many of which were stolen by foreign archae-ologists at the start of the twentieth century. They were literally hacked off the walls. We also stop at Karakhoja, the sprawling ruins of a garrison city that the Chinese established as one of their bases on their occasional forays into Xinjiang.

As we drive eastwards, Murat tells me the story his father told him of how the Chinese first came to Turkestan. He blames it all on a horse. In 138 BC, before the first Chinese military conquest of the region, the Chinese emperor sent a man called Zhang Qian (pronounced *jang chyen*) through the territory of the dreaded Xiongnu tribe to reach another tribe, the Yuezhi, with whom the Chinese wanted to ally against the Xiongnu. On the way there, Zhang Qian was captured by the Xiongnu and held for ten years. But he managed to escape and continue his journey, and eventually he reached the Fergana Valley (in modern-day Uzbekistan), where he discovered the people possessed the strongest and swiftest type of horse in the known world, which came to be known in the Uighur language as the 'blood-sweating horse' because of the way its reddish skin glistened with sweat when it galloped.

In 125 BC, thirteen years after he set out, Zhang Qian made it back to the imperial Chinese court at Chang'an, (though, rather carelessly, he allowed himself to be captured and held by the Xiongnu on the way back as well). Zhang was showered with praise by the emperor, who gave him the title Great Traveller. The emperor decided that 'blood-sweating horses' were exactly what he needed in the continuing struggle against the very mobile tribes of the steppeland, and he determined to get hold of some, thus initiating the first Chinese foray into Turkestan. The Chinese speak of this as being the start of the Silk Road, and the start of Turkestan's incorporation into China, even though, as we've seen, the Chinese hold over what is now Xinjiang was sporadic at best until the 1750s.

'You see these?' Murat shouts angrily back to me against the wind that rushes in through the wide-open windows. He is pointing at dozens of nodding oil pumps beside the road, in the shadow of the Flaming Mountains. 'These oil wells are nearly two miles deep. They pump ten tons of oil a day. Where does it all go? I'll tell you where. East, for the Han Chinese to use. How much do we get to use of our own oil? None. How many Uighurs do the oil companies employ? Not a single one. This is *our* land they are exploiting, but it doesn't make us a penny.'

He tells me about a natural gas pipeline that has been built from southern Xinjiang to Shanghai, transporting the gas of the west to the east. Then he says it. He uses the phrase I've had in mind all along but haven't said.

'China is a colonial power,' he says. 'It has occupied us and is simply extracting our resources.'

No one can say that sort of thing in public, though no doubt Uighurs say it to one another all the time. For the Beijing government, so critical of Western imperialism and colonialism, it is anathema that a Chinese citizen might suggest China itself is guilty of such a crime. But speeding along in a car with an old Uighur buddy and a stray inquisitive westerner, heard only by the wind, Murat doesn't care about uttering such forbidden words.

After an hour's drive, with daylight slipping away, we park the car, take off our shoes, and wander barefoot across a dry riverbed. Then we literally clamber up the dunes. Much of the desert up to now has been gravelly scrubland with a hard yellow carapace. These are the first real sand dunes I've seen since Dunhuang.

The sun is setting gloriously, and I suggest we pause, otherwise we will miss it. So we sit down halfway up the dune, and I pull the bottle of Loulan wine, the corkscrew and three plastic cups from my bag. It feels surreal to be sitting in the Gobi Desert with a couple of Muslims drinking a bottle of red wine. I propose a toast to Uighurs everywhere. They smile, and the three of us just sit in silence and watch the sun sink in an extravagant blur of orange.

Murat's friend-brother-cousin then heads back to the car, where he will spend the night, and the two of us continue to struggle up the dune. The wind becomes stronger the higher we climb. So we dive into a small protected valley between two dunes, stretch out our rugs a few feet apart, and lie down.

The moon is rising as beautifully as it always does over the desert, whiter, bigger, rounder than ever. And as we lie there, looking up at it, I ask Murat all the most sensitive questions about the Uighurs, and the struggle, if only psychological now, against the Chinese.

'It's not 100 per cent tragedy,' he says. 'There is no law forcing us to do this. We are willing participants in our own destruction.'

'But you have no choice, do you?'

'We have no choice. The only way to oppose assimilation is not to go to a Chinese school. But if you don't go to a Chinese school, you can't succeed, you can't get a good job. Look at me. I cannot read or speak Chinese very well. I can understand maybe 60 per cent of what I read in a newspaper. If I could read and write, I would get a much better job.'

It sounds just like what the Tibetan teacher had told me several weeks before. Murat pauses, and a minute passes, maybe five, as we just lie there, looking up at the expanding universe and the stars stretched across it.

'The world is developing, and we have to participate,' he says.

There's another pause, weighed down by a silent sadness.

'It's a slow death,' he says finally, 'and it's tragic, but what else can we do? The way I am dealing with it is by forcing my little brother to stay in school, to get the education I didn't get, to go to a good university, but to use it to help the Uighur people, not the Chinese. We can't opt out, we have to engage, with the world and with the Han Chinese, and that inevitably leads to a dilution of our culture. But we can use it to our own benefit, as much as possible.'

'So what do you want your brother to do?'

'Perhaps study medicine, so that he can come back and help to improve the health of the Uighur people.'

Murat is clearly a major influence on his brother and also on his younger cousins and friends, like the driver of our car, encouraging their engagement with the system to serve their own ends. But he draws the line at certain things. He despises the dancing attractions that serve the Chinese tourist trade at major hotels and other destinations, and he will not let anyone in his family take part in them, even though they pay relatively well. 'Why should we dance to make the Chinese tourists happy, to fulfill some stereotype of what they think we are?' he asks. 'I would rather be a poor farmer than let anyone in my family do that.'

After every statement, there is silence. There is no rush. There is time to absorb what is being said. How rarely I have that feeling.

'What do you think of the separatists who actually take up arms and fight the Chinese state?' The number of such incidents has decreased in recent years, but there are still occasional flare-ups.

'Well, I am not bold enough to be one of them. I have parents. I have a younger brother to support. But I do think they are brave, and I admire their bravery.'

'Brave, but hopeless, right?'

He pauses in the gloaming. The air is still beautifully warm, but I can feel the coldness of the sand through the thin rug on which I am lying, sand that was baking hot just a few hours before.

'Yes, brave but hopeless,' he says finally. 'We need to recognise that reality. There is no more hope for an independent Xinjiang. And that is what I've been saying. Let's move on, and get on with recognising that reality, and make the most of it.'

The wind blows some sand into our protected little gully.

'And what about America?' I ask him.

'We are Muslims. We don't want to see Muslims killed. But we are also opposed to extremist Islam, like the Taliban. If Islam rules like that, then everyone will be poor and backward. And if Saddam had been a better ruler, the US wouldn't have attacked. And in fact, we have no reason to hate America. There is another people we hate more.'

The wind creeps again into our little valley, but it is a soft welcome wind. Soon I hear Murat breathing more heavily, asleep on his rug a few feet away from me. I lie there for a while, happier than I have been at any other time on my journey. Perhaps the Chinese monk Xuan Zang slept here in the seventh century, the Buddhist scriptures he had brought back from India tucked under his saddlebag. Perhaps Aurel Stein slept here too, having pillaged the same Buddhist scriptures from the Library Cave at Dunhuang. Perhaps there is too much romance written into this crazy Silk Road. And with that, I fall asleep on the shifting sands of the desert, under a Uighur moon.

The earth duly rotates on its axis while I sleep, and I awake to a late sunrise, whose beauty mirrors perfectly the sunset of the night before. The wind has deposited a fine patina of freshly blown sand over me, and there are grains on my lips and in my nose and ears.

We drive back to Turpan, stopping at a small store to buy some naan bread and yogurt for breakfast. Not far from town, we stop again at a raisin market, where grape farmers from all around have brought their produce. Huge piles of grapes, some green, some red, are piled upon the ground, and buyers are walking around, tasting, testing and bargaining with the farmers. All the buyers seem to be Han Chinese. All the farmers are Uighurs.

On the outskirts of Turpan, I change cars. Murat has arranged for another friend-brother-cousin to drive me to Urumqi, the regional capital, a hundred miles to the northwest. I embrace him, and say goodbye.

Route 312 between Turpan and Urumqi is possibly the most impressive stretch of the road that I have travelled on the whole length of my journey. It's made up two completely straight black strips of tarmac stretching across the desert, two lanes in each direction, separated by a ten-yard strip of scrubland. In the front passenger seat is a rather glamorously dressed Uighur woman, who is also catching a ride with Murat's friend to Urumqi. Her daughter had travelled there two days previously, on the same day as Rebiya, the girl I had met at the bus station in Hami. After three days' orientation with the other 3,000 students, she too will be heading for high school in eastern China, near Shanghai. Her mother is going to see her once more before the girl leaves.

'Everyone wants to go east,' the mother says. 'Even students who weren't good enough to be chosen for free places want to pay money for the opportunity to go to a high school in eastern China.'

Despite her enthusiasm for the school programme, she complains about how the Han Chinese dominate every profession in Turpan. But she is pragmatic about where the future lies and takes the same line as Murat. '*Fenlie meiyou qiantu.* Separatism has no future. This is the only way.'

Like Murat, and like the Tibetan teacher I had met on the road to Xiahe, she will not allow her family to relinquish its identity.

'If you met my daughter, you'd hardly be able to tell the

difference from a Han Chinese fourteen-year-old. But I tell her that she is a Uighur, and she should be proud to be a Uighur. I have told her she cannot marry a Han Chinese boy, and she cannot marry a non-Muslim. She is getting a better education, and then she must come back and help her people.'

The woman, who is married to a local businessman, asks me if I am travelling the Southern Silk Road, towards Khotan and Kashgar. I tell her that, alas, this time I am not, that I am following Route 312 northwest from Urumqi to the border with Kazakhstan. She says she has just returned from a vacation along the Southern Silk Road, driving with her husband and some friends to Kashgar, and then back across the Taklimakan Desert.

The Swedish explorer Sven Hedin called the Taklimakan 'the worst and most dangerous desert in the world'. Aurel Stein said the deserts of Arabia were tame compared with the Taklimakan. Today, a hundred years later, middle-aged Uighur women, wearing big earrings and layers of thick make-up, are crossing the Taklimakan for fun.

Chapter Twenty-two

FROM SEA TO SHINING SEA

The first time I arrived in Urumqi was on a train from Xi'an in the summer of 1988. After days crossing the remote, dusty Gobi, I had been grateful to arrive, even though at that time, Urumqi (pronounced *oo-room-chee*) was a depressing, underdeveloped city in the middle of nowhere.

I didn't return until 2002, while reporting on the Chinese Muslim response to the 9/11 attacks on the US. It was, of course, still in the middle of nowhere, but in those intervening fourteen years, Urumqi had turned into Los Angeles. And now, just a few years later, it has changed even more.

The English missionary Mildred Cable wrote about what an awful place Urumqi was, though she noted that in 1926 the postal commissioner here (who for some bizarre reason was an Italian) had organised the mail system so that a letter could reach Beijing in forty-five days. She called this 'a truly marvellous accomplishment'. A letter in the opposite direction, through the Soviet Union, went slightly faster, reaching London in twenty-eight days.

Now, the people of Urumqi are connected instantaneously to Beijing and London and Moscow by broadband Internet Service. All over the city are advertisements promoting wider, better, faster connections.

Live a broadband life: this is the year of information broadband.

The city has sprawled, and now has a population of more than 1.5 million. The rhythms of eastern China have begun to infiltrate. In the past, saying there was no city in the world further from the ocean than Urumqi was confirmation of its irrelevance. Now that doesn't seem to matter. Urumqi has become a regional hub for western China, and also for Chinese influence surging over the border into Central Asia. Five hundred years after sea travel relegated the Old Silk Road to insignificance, the New Silk Road is re-emerging and becoming increasingly important, to Xinjiang and the whole of Central Asia. In the first half of 2006, Xinjiang was the fastest growing of any of China's provinces and regions in terms of foreign trade.

I check into one of Urumqi's best hotels. With my room key I am handed a voucher offering me a free massage at the 'sauna massage' facility on the fifth floor. (The voucher says 'Ladies requiring massage should call in advance.') If this is the same as every other 'sauna massage' in China, that means that, in effect, this fancy hotel, which caters to the growing army of visiting business-men from eastern China and abroad, is offering free sex to every man who checks in.

I've been researching who I want to talk to while I'm in Urumqi, and discover that the US networking company, Cisco Systems, has an office not far away. I wander over, hoping that someone might want to talk to me, and am greeted by a smartly dressed Han Chinese manager, who looks and talks as though he must have an MBA. He is about to dash out the door to the airport, to fly to Beijing and on to the US on business. He gives me five minutes of his time.

'It used to be that Xinjiang was known just for black and white. Oil and cotton. Then it was black, white and red. Tomatoes and tomato ketchup. Did you know that Xinjiang produces 31 per cent of the world's tomato ketchup?' he raises his eyebrows and smiles. 'Now look at us. Cisco is here. IBM is just across the hall. We're not making ketchup.'

He says Cisco is merely leading the way in a huge new market. 'Xinjiang is now not backward at all. It is all very connected. And people's thinking here is all very *kaifang*. It is very open. Do you know why? It is because everyone here is an immigrant. They have an open, immigrant mentality.'

I don't have the chance to ask him how he thinks the Uighurs feel about this, for he excuses himself and dashes out of the door. What we didn't get round to talking about was what Cisco is actually doing in Xinjiang. A whole range of projects, no doubt, assisting companies to get networked, but it is also accused by human rights groups of assisting the Chinese government to monitor the Internet for any signs of dissent. Cisco has sold several thousand routers to Beijing, equipment that human rights groups in the US say was programmed with the help of Cisco engineers and is integral to the Great Firewall of China, which Beijing maintains around the Internet in order to control the flow of information inside the country. Cisco denies that it has supplied China with equipment and technology to control what Chinese web-surfers view. It says the equipment it sells to China is the same as it sells elsewhere in the world, and that it cannot stop China from adapting the equipment to its own needs.

Either way, the fact that I am even having this conversation here says much about the changes in the city and its aspirations. Urumqi, like so many cities along Route 312, has become another mini-Promised Land.

The next morning I head for the Uighur bazaar at Erdaoqiao, which means 'Bridge of Two Roads'. I go looking for the old maze of stalls at the main bazaar that I'd visited in 2002. At that time, I was searching for local Muslims to speak frankly about Osama bin Laden, the attacks on America and the subsequent Chinese clampdown on the Uighurs. I had simply gone from stall to stall in the dirty, labyrinthine market, quietly asking the shopkeepers if they would talk to me.

In about the fourth shop I went into on that visit, a wonderful old stall heaving with every type of dried fruit and nuts, the Uighur owner looked cautiously around, then told me in bad Chinese to wait one moment. He disappeared and came back shortly after with a Uighur man, no more than twenty-two or twenty-three years of age, who spoke perfect Mandarin. This young man, who never told me his real name, became my guide for a week. He took me first down a maze of alleyways, towards the house of a brother or cousin or friend. We wove our way left and right through the bazaar, to try to lose anyone who might be following us, and eventually ended up at a safe house, where he sat and spoke very openly about how much the Uighurs hate the Han Chinese and how much they love Americans.

Soon afterwards, though, the US shifted its policy. The majority of Uighur Muslims are from the moderate, mystical branch of Islam called Sufism, and during the 1990s the US government had championed their freedom of religion as part of its criticism of China's human rights record. But after 11 September 2001 a handful of Uighur extremists had been captured by the US, fighting with the Taliban in northern Afghanistan, and Washington needed Beijing's help at the UN in the 'war on terror'. So in the summer of 2002, the administration of George W. Bush agreed to put a previously unknown Uighur group called the East Turkestan Islamic Movement on its list of terrorist organisations.

Few people had even heard of this group, but the US move provided, and still provides, carte blanche for Beijing to do what it wants in suppressing any kind of dissent in Xinjiang, under the guise of combating terrorism, without fear of any criticism from Washington. For the Chinese leaders, 9/11 was a dream come true. Not only was the pressure off them as the next US enemy, but President Bush was calling China a partner in the 'war on terror', and Beijing was able to extract its own price in Xinjiang for cooperating with the Bush administration. Human rights groups accuse the US government of selling the Uighur people up the Yellow River.

When I get to Erdaoqiao, I think the taxi driver must have brought me to the wrong place, because I can't find the old bazaar anywhere. When I ask a man in a carpet store, he says in bad Mandarin that the old bazaar has been knocked down. In its place stands a shiny, generic Chinese-style modern building, also calling itself Erdaoqiao. Outside the new market is a bridge over a small pool and some bronze sculptures of generic Uighur people, doing things that Han Chinese people imagine Uighur people do: one making naan bread, one playing a Uighur instrument. In other words, the thriving, very Uighur, very Muslim bazaar of Urumqi has been turned into a sort of Uighur-themed Chinese shopping centre, another branch of the Uighur World theme park I'd seen in Turpan.

To be fair to the Chinese, as my friend Murat had pointed out, it is not just Sinification that is going on, it is globalisation, of a sort that is happening everywhere. Some of the Chinese motivations for developing Xinjiang are very genuine, wanting people there to have a better life. But because, for the Uighurs, the Chinese are the agents of this modernisation, there is a particular bitterness to it.

From a security point of view, you can see why the Chinese are knocking down the old parts of the city and putting up new shopping malls. The warren of houses and shops of the old bazaar was a perfect place for me to duck and dive, whisper and plot when I had been looking for disaffected Uighurs. Today, I spend several hours walking around the new, shiny Erdaoqiao Market, trying to find someone to talk to me frankly about relations between the Han Chinese and the Uighurs, and no one will. The bright neon striplighting and the open shopfronts make conspiracy of any sort more difficult. And that is, of course, part of the Chinese plan.

Most of the Han people who live in eastern China have never been to Xinjiang or Tibet and have no idea that the Uighurs and the Tibetans are angry. They have always been told that, since time immemorial, Xinjiang and Tibet have been part of China, and that all China's ethnic minorities are happily integrated. They are also aware of the beneficial treatment that ethnic minorities receive, a kind of affirmative action Beijing employs to try to keep the minorities happy. And, of course, they read a lot of news reports about all those wonderful new shopping centres being built for the lucky Uighur people. So when they visit Xinjiang or Tibet, they are often mystified by the cool reception, and sometimes active hostility, they receive from the Tibetans or the Uighurs. Aren't we giving you everything? they ask. Aren't you getting beneficial policies? Aren't you allowed to have two children rather than one, and get into university with lower test scores?

There is a famous story from the eighteenth century told by both the Han and the Uighurs that perfectly illustrates the interaction between the two sides, even today.

The Qianlong Emperor had, during the conquest of Xinjiang in the 1750s, heard about a beautiful Uighur girl called Iparhan. Her body was said to give off a fragrance all its own, and the emperor ordered that she be brought to Beijing to become part of the royal harem. Iparhan became known as the Fragrant Concubine, or Xiang Fei in Chinese.

The emperor gave her a splendid room and a beautiful garden, but she spent her days crying for her homeland. The emperor then built her a miniature oasis to remind her of her home village, but she was still inconsolable. He built her a mosque and a bazaar and a pavilion she could climb and look west, and still she was not happy. Finally, he asked her what would make her happy, and she said she longed for the fragrance of the tree whose leaves are silver and whose fruit is gold. So Qianlong sent to Kashgar for the plant, known as the oleaster or silver-leaved sand jujube, and as the Chinese tell the story, at last the Fragrant Concubine was content.

The Uighurs tell the same story, but with a very different ending. In their version, Iparhan paces her apartment in the Forbidden City in Beijing with little daggers hidden up her sleeves in case the emperor calls her to the imperial bed chamber. In the end she commits suicide rather than face such a dishonour.

For the Chinese, the Fragrant Concubine symbolises how the wild Turkic people of the west finally became reconciled to being part of the civilised and infinitely superior world of China. To the Uighurs, she symbolises how they and other Turkic peoples have never accepted Chinese rule, and never will.

Even if you were to knock down all the Uighur buildings, though, there are two parts of life in Urumqi that would still linger. The first is the smell, of flatbread, roasted lamb and spices. The second is the music, not the measured, ordered notes of Han China, but the wilder, hypnotic rhythms of the bazaar. Both are swirling in the air on the main street beside Erdaoqiao. Unshaven Uighur men are grilling lamb kebabs doused in bright red spices on open charcoal fires, and if you are not already thinking about the road west towards Central Asia from Urumqi, just a whiff of the air here will transport you there. A little further down the road, four Uighur musicians are sprawling lazily on a bench, making a noise that seems disproportionate to the energy they are expending. All four musicians wear colourful Uighur caps; three are blowing on some kind of Uighur wind instrument, one is banging a pair of small drums. Suddenly, in front of them, a middle-aged Uighur man dressed in a suit and tie begins to dance crazily in the heat. It looks as though he has just stepped out of one of the surrounding office blocks in his lunch hour. Perhaps he's drunk. Perhaps he's just letting off steam. As you look around the streets near the Bridge of Two Roads, you feel there are a lot of Uighurs who need to let off some steam. A crowd gathers, and I stand among them, watching the man whirling like an office dervish on the pavement.

And so, finally, to a place of sublime beauty. China is a beautiful country, but I suppose Route 312 does not really witness the best of it. The east and the middle are just flat, flat, flat; Flowery Mountain, near Xi'an, is impressive; skirting the Tibetan Plateau at Xiahe had been beautiful in a wild kind of way; the Loess Plateau is earthy and real; the Gobi, of course, has its own raw, wide-open beauty. But if you want drop-dead-gorgeous, stand-back-and-stare natural beauty within a few hours of Route 312, there are few places to compare with the Lake of Heaven.

There are three mountain ranges that stretch across Xinjiang like outstretched fingers from the west. Between the three ranges are two basins. The Altai Mountains run along Xinjiang's northern border. The Pamir and then the Kunlun Mountains run along Xinjiang's southern border with India and Tibet, and the Mountains of Heaven cut a swathe through the middle. The Lake of Heaven sits on the north side of the Mountains of Heaven, two and a half hours' drive northeast of Urumqi.

I had been out exploring the city with a Han Chinese taxi driver called Wen, who had shown me one of Urumqi's transportation hubs, a huge car park where trucks are loaded with produce to head east towards Shanghai and west towards Central Asia. The signs are in Chinese, Uighur and Cyrillic.

Wen tells me his parents first came to the region as members of the Xinjiang Production and Construction Corps (or XPCC), known in Chinese as the *bingtuan*, a sort of paramilitary development agency formed in the 1950s and made up of Han Chinese from the east who were both soldiers and farmers. They have been compared to the homesteaders of nineteenth-century America, or are sometimes described as

281

'settlers', sent to protect the newly fixed borders of the People's Republic and to turn the desert green.

The XPCC still exists and is a mini-state unto itself, Xinjiang's biggest employer and landowner. Organised like a military unit, it has fourteen divisions, each with its own regiments and companies, and runs many of the labour camps around Xinjiang. During the Maoist years, the camps housed Chinese political prisoners from the east, but as their numbers have declined, the camps have come to contain mainly common criminals and a few Uighur separatists. As China has changed, the *bingtuan* has changed too, and like all Chinese state-owned enterprises, it has diversified into all kinds of business as the country has plunged into the market economy.

The hundreds of thousands of Han Chinese who came west with the XPCC were deeply indoctrinated with Communist teaching about sacrificing for the motherland. My taxi driver talks about how his parents 'ate bitterness' for two decades, in the 1950s and 1960s, as they tried to build socialism in Xinjiang.

There are now hundreds of thousands of second-generation Han Chinese people like Wen, and plenty of third-generation too for whom Xinjiang is home, and indeed the *bingtuan* do not need to encourage settlers to come anymore. The economic enticements from the investment of government money here are bringing enough Han migrants without the need for more forced immigration. In fact, Urumqi has become almost as much of a magnet for migrants as Shanghai. The centre of the city is a jungle of new office buildings, roads and hotels, and enough construction to rival major cities 2,000 miles to the east. 'All this used to be fields,' says Wen, parroting the words of every taxi driver in every city I have ever visited across China as we head through the outskirts of town towards the road for the Lake of Heaven.

Wen's wife is employed by a large Urumqi company that has just built an iron and steel works in Tajikistan, supplying steel for the reconstruction of Afghanistan. She has been working near the Tajik capital Dushanbe as an accountant for nearly a year and is making good money, he says.

We climb up into the lush, green mountains, and at the end of the road is a huge car park and the entrance to a mini-cable car system, which takes tourists, two at a time, up to the lake. The area is heaving with Han Chinese tourists.

I take the cable car to the top, and there suddenly is the most beautiful little lake I have ever seen. It feels as though a chunk of the Montana Rockies has just been plonked down in the middle of northwest China. Surrounded on three sides by beautiful pine-clad hills, the lake stretches for about a mile, and looming above it at the far end is Bogda Feng, the Mountain of God, still covered in snow in August, scraping the sky at nearly 18,000 feet.

The throngs of Chinese tourists are all gathered at one spot, beside a large rock on which have been carved the two Chinese characters for the Lake of Heaven, *tian chi*. There is a long line of people waiting to stand next to the characters and have their photo taken. Motor-boats are roaring out across the water, the buzz of their engines echoing around the otherwise peaceful lake. The need to escape the crowd overwhelms me. So I set off on the small road that leads up the east side of the lake, and within about five minutes there is nobody.

The road becomes a path and, after walking for an hour, I come across a large sign which reads RASHIT'S YURT. Rashit, it turns out, is an entrepreneurial Kazakh who speaks good English (and Chinese) and rents out spaces in his traditional Kazakh tents, known as yurts, mainly to foreign backpackers. I dump my daypack and head off further along the lake shore as the afternoon sun disappears behind the mountains.

The dappled hills rise from each side of the lake, a patchwork of contrasting greens. The coniferous trees are arranged in long, broad stripes down the mountainside. The deciduous trees seem to grow in clusters, small knots of brighter green that are just starting to think about turning yellow.

Someone has laid out the skin of a freshly slaughtered sheep to dry on the rocks by the lake. Mushrooms sprout from rotting logs. There is moss everywhere, and clean air to be breathed, and silence. An occasional goat skips up the hillside above the lakeside path. An eagle circles overhead, then flaps towards the top of a tall fir tree. I find a patch of grass among the goat droppings between the path and the lake, and sit motionless for what must be at least half an hour, watching the great bird.

Eventually, the eagle flies off, and I get up to return to Rashit's yurt for dinner. It's a simple but delicious bowl of noodles and meat, eaten with a couple of other backpackers who are also taking refuge in the mountains, resting from their journeys through China. Nothing at all happens that evening, which is wonderful in its way. As night falls, I wander down to the lake alone and stand in the dark, looking up at the stars, as I always do. We sleep with our feet pointing towards the middle of the circular tent, under thick Kazakh blankets provided by Rashit against the chill of the summer night.

The light has not yet slipped away completely as the bus pulls out of Urumqi station to start its sixteen-hour journey to the border. A kung-fu movie is already blaring, and an old Uighur man with a wispy beard sits upright with his legs crossed on the bunk behind me, his hands held upwards as he intones his evening prayers. The passengers are almost exclusively Uighurs, and when I interact with them I feel slightly embarrassed forcing them to speak Chinese. Huge harvests of tomatoes are visible in the evening light, loaded on to trucks beside the road, perhaps bound for the ketchup bottles of America.

The great American scholar of Central Asia, Owen Lattimore – who would in the 1950s be accused by Senator Joseph McCarthy of being the number one Soviet spy in the United States – in 1927 made this same journey with his wife and a Chinese servant named Moses. They were on horseback, heading west, before cutting down south through southern Xinjiang into British Kashmir. Lattimore describes in his book of the journey, *High Tartary*, how as they were riding out from Urumqi, they were passed by the Soviet consul general, driving the only car in Xinjiang.

Lattimore describes the Wild West towns along the road outside Urumqi in those days: 'The numbers of carters, pedlars, cheap-Jacks, cattle-dealers, horse-copers, occasional caravan men, touts, thieves, bullies, and plain vagabonds are swelled by tribesmen, both Mongol and Qazaq, of the kind lured to such a town: the spendthrifts and the drunkards . . . The general atmosphere is one of bullying, swaggering, sly tripping, and outrageous imposture.' Survival, concluded Lattimore, required 'a ready tongue, a front of brass, and preferably a pair of eyes in the back of one's head.'

He was one of the last foreigners to travel the old caravan routes by camel or horse. *The Times* correspondent Peter Fleming came through Xinjiang a few years later, but after that, the Japanese invaded China and the war came, and then in 1949 the Communists took power and transformed everything, with their railways and their roads. The political reforms of Mao and the economic reforms of Deng Xiapoing changed China for ever, and the four-lane highway that blasts westwards out of Urumqi is scarily modern and efficient, even though it is not (yet) humming with traffic. Soon Route 312 will be a four-lane highway all the way to the border.

What would Owen Lattimore make of this road heading west eighty years later? It took him six days to ride to Xihu, 140 miles west of Urumqi. The Soviet consul general in his motorcar made it in two. My sleek blue sleeper bus, with the words VACATION COMFORTABLE written in large English letters along its side, reaches the town of Kuitun, very near Xihu, in four hours along the motorway. It is all so safe and efficient. The Communist Party has tamed many of the deserts and mountains of Xinjiang even if it has not yet won over the hearts and minds of the region's people.

After a few hours, the four lanes narrow to two, small villages

285

hugging the tarmac; as the road nudges slowly westwards in the dark. Behind and between the narrow bands of habitation, there is little but the wide-open desert. All those hundreds of millions of people crammed into the eastern half of China, and this half is almost empty. The darkening sky squeezes out the last glimmers of the day's resistance, as I fall asleep on my bunk for the last time.

The desert has evaporated by the time I awake, and there is a large green lake beside the road. Route 312 has finally pulled up out of the desert and into a range of beautiful hills, just before the border. It's not quite like seeing the Pacific Ocean beyond Santa Monica at the end of Route 66, but it's a welcome change from the desert of the last 1,500 miles. The expanse of water is called Sayram Lake, and there is a beautiful backdrop of mountains behind it.

Just as I'm admiring the view from my bunk, the bus slows and suddenly shudders to a halt. We've broken down again, right beside the lake. Big blue East Wind trucks pass our wounded bus, blasting their horns as they go. Now, I just want to get to the border, so while our two drivers confer about the best course of action, I decide to proceed with my usual Plan B, and get out and hitch the last few hours.

A truck driver picks me up. He's Han Chinese, almost a carbon copy of Trucker Liu, who had given me a ride from Starry Gorge. His name is Mu, and he has come all the way from Shanghai too. He is the son of Han Chinese immigrants who came with the *bingtuan* in the 1950s to help to develop the west, though he as a truck driver is probably doing more to develop the west than his parents ever did.

We chat as the road winds steeply down from the hills, hemmed in on one side by a steel barrier to prevent vehicles from disappearing off the edge. Forests of deep green pine trees line the route, surprising the traveller, whose eyes have grown accustomed to the glare of the desert.

Finally, we reach Korgaz, a forlorn little town with an empty feel, which really only exists for its border crossing into Kazakhstan. It's still early, and the streets are quiet. I walk with my heavy backpack the mile or so from the bus station to the crossing, past the army garrison, along a street appropriately named Ya Ou Lu: Eurasia Road.

Beside the road, just before the border crossing, is a wide-open expanse of land and a sign announcing that something called the Korgaz International Trade Centre is about to rise from the rubble. The sign hints at the town's ambitions.

The convenient way for Chinese goods to successfully enter Central Asia.

The crossing itself is rather underwhelming: a large old metal gate, painted red and white, in front of a low-rise, white-tiled building, on which is written in large gold letters the Chinese characters for 'Korgaz Border Crossing'. Two Chinese men in green uniforms with red epaulettes are standing inside the gate, letting through only those who are going to cross the border. There's a small market to the right of the gate. Traders are selling jewellery and trinkets, swords and furs, Russian foods and Chinese toys. Even here there is an energy, a hope of improvement that I imagine, perhaps unfairly, might not exist over the border in Kazakhstan.

When I reach the red and white gate, I turn around and realise . . . this is it. This is the end of Route 312, and the end of my journey. A white marker stone beside the road reads 4,824 kilometres. I've travelled almost 3,000 miles from Shanghai, and what a long, strange trip it's been.

The road has witnessed everything: the poverty of the country-side, the growing wealth of the cities, and of course the people who travel along the road itself. It's a conveyor of hope and despair, bringing escape and choice to places that have known little of either.

Route 312 has been transformational for me, too, and helped me see so much that I didn't know. But it's not the same for me. It's very different. I've come to love Route 312 in all its schizophrenic ways, but I'm an outsider. I can leave. I *am* leaving. It's not quite so romantic for the people who have to stay.

A few Chinese people are taking photos of each other in front of the red and white gate. 'Did you come all the way from Shanghai?' I want to ask them. I hand my camera to one of them and ask him to take a photo of me, standing in front of the border crossing. A final memento.

Somehow I was expecting it to be more dramatic, that some theme music might surge up in the background as the credits rolled. But the only music is the barking of the traders in the market, and the whispered offers of the money-changers: '*Huan qian, huan qian* (change money, change money).'

A sudden wave of emotion sweeps over me, as I have reached the end of the road, and effectively the end of my time in China. I stand there, thinking back on my journey and all the people I've met, and scarcely believing that it's over. Perhaps this is what it felt like to travel west in the United States in the 1890s. Not knowing what the future held for the great country that you'd just seen, but feeling the sheer privilege of having witnessed the churn of history, the transformation of a nation, the emergence of a new power, that only takes place once every three or four generations. And whatever happens to China in the future, if I live long enough to have grandchildren and they ask me, 'Were you really there, Grandpa? Did you really see China rise?' I'll tell them, 'Yes. I saw it. I was there.'

And then I realise that I don't want to stay a single minute longer. I want to get out of here, to get on a plane, to go and see my family. I heave my backpack into a waiting taxi, owned by a pushy migrant from Henan province 2,000 miles to the east, and he drives me the fifty miles or so to Yining airport, for the long flight back to the Emerald City of Shanghai.

Chapter Twenty-three

A ROAD IS MADE

When you see China from the air, you realise the magnitude of what the government in Beijing is trying to do. It is not building a country, it is building a continent. A billion and a half people live in Europe and North and South America, divided up into more than fifty sovereign states. Nearly a billion and a half Chinese people live in one single sovereign state. To speak about building China the nation in the same breath as building Malaysia the nation or even Mexico the nation is, with all due respect to Malaysians and Mexicans, absurd.

I see it all laid out below me on the short flight from Yining to Urumqi, and then as the sun sets, on the four-hour flight from Urumqi to Shanghai. Though I've become attached to Route 312 as I've travelled westwards along it, I'm very glad not to be returning to Shanghai by road. Finally, I arrive late that night at Shanghai's smaller, older Hongqiao airport, so I don't get to ride the maglev into town again. I do, however, take a high-speed cab ride along the *Blade Runner* elevated motorway of Yan'an Road as it slices through the city, fifty feet above the ground.

This time I stay at the Peace Hotel, on the Bund. The hucksters are still there, past midnight, offering watches, women and golf clubs. The jazz band has finished playing by the time I check in, and I don't even have the energy for a late-night walk along the Bund.

The next day I sleep late, glad not to be taking a bus ride somewhere. I have a lazy Shanghai day, which involves a final daytime run along the Bund and several tall low-fat lattes. In the evening I go up to New Heights restaurant once again and look out across the Huangpu River, and think about how far from the Gobi Desert this all is.

The barges transporting coal along the Huangpu River are still plying up and down, and the neon signs illuminating the banks of the river appear to have multiplied in just my two months away. Blink, and you'll miss plenty in the new China. An Amway sign flashes out its message, and I think of the salesmen I met weeks before in Zhangye. (Donkey meat noodles are not yet on the menu at New Heights.) There is movement everywhere, and pursuit of wealth and pursuit of happiness, as Shanghai hurtles through the time tunnel into the future. I write in my notebook 'Shanghai is America' and just stand there, breathing in the bittersweet air.

It's impossible to be neutral about China. Some foreigners hate it from the moment they set foot here. Others love it so much they put down roots and never go home. I wonder if other countries divide people so intensely in their emotions. For myself, I have always tried to retain my own unity of opposites, attempting to keep love and hate in balance. But it's difficult, especially as a journalist. I'm supposed not to care. I'm supposed just to observe. But how can I not care, when a fifth of humanity is being convulsed before my eyes, and thousands are making millions, and millions are being crushed? And if I seem a little confused about China, it's because I am. And if *you're* not confused, then you simply haven't been paying attention.

But where is it all leading? The once-hated westernised city of Shanghai is now the much-loved national model that every city along Route 312 is trying to emulate. The bastard child has become the patriarch. In many ways, China *is* transformed. It *is* gradually reclaiming its position in the world. It has woken up from the Iron House of Confucianism, destroyed itself in order to save itself.

But what now? What will China become?

When I arrived in China as a correspondent, I began making timelines in my head about when China would become a full market economy, and how long before it became a democracy. And then, as every reporter here finds sooner or later, the longer you stay, the less inclined you are to make predictions. Though I had set off in search of answers, by the time I'd finished the journey I was wondering whether it would be better just to let the readers draw their own conclusions. However, my editor pointed out that if you, dear reader, have schlepped with me right across China, the least I owe you is a few suggestions as to how things *might* develop there in future. So here goes.

The previous year, when I told NPR's foreign editor that I might want to leave China sometime soon, he asked me if I would be interested in becoming Jerusalem correspondent. I said I would have to think about it. I would be very interested in learning Arabic and covering the Muslim world at some point. It is, of course, a huge story. But in the end, that did not seem what the Israel job would be about. In Jerusalem you cover Israel and the Palestinians, and that is a story that just goes round in circles. China, I said to my editor when I called him with my decision, is a linear story, on its way to somewhere, no one knows where. Never mind the bloody violence of the Middle East itself, or taking my young family to live in the midst of it, or the fact that I was really weary after six years on the road in China and Asia. I told my editor I wasn't sure if, intellectually, I wanted just to follow the endless futile cycle of events, a story that never really goes anywhere.

After that conversation, and as I was travelling across China on Route 312, I began to think about what I had said, and I realised I was wrong, and that China is a cyclical story too. It's just that the Chinese cycles are so much bigger. They are measured in centuries, decades at the least, not years or months. And it feels as though that cycle is coming round again.

This for me is really the big question facing China now, at the start of the twenty-first century, and perhaps the one that will decide whether the country goes on to greatness. Will it just follow the same cycle as every dynasty in Chinese history, or will it, *can* it, break that cycle and take a different path?

It seems sometimes as though Chinese history has never had any narrative, just a succession of dynasties, all walled off from one another. Each dynasty came into power with a new agenda, opposing the corruption of the previous one. It was welcomed; it undertook reforms. It expanded, it ruled, it revelled in its cultural golden age, and then it descended into the same corruption and incompetence as the previous dynasty. Sometimes it took a hundred years, sometimes two or three hundred. China's history has only ever been about uniting and then collapsing, reuniting and then being invaded, overthrow, collapse, reuniting and collapsing again. Why should the future be any different?

In some ways, China *is* the same as it has always been. It is still the same kind of imperial one-party government that the first emperor from 2,000 years ago would recognise. And that means there are no effective checks and balances, and there is terrible corruption, as there always has been. Confucius was wrong on one point. Human beings are not able to police themselves.

The fact that there are tens of thousands of cases of rural unrest every year is no doubt ringing some alarm bells in the leadership compound in Beijing, just as it is ringing some alarm bells in the heads of China historians. If it wasn't foreign invasions, it was peasant rebellions that heralded the demise of every dynasty. Now, in abandoning the farmers, the Communist Party has become every bit as venal and corrupt as the Nationalist Party it rose up to overthrow in the 1930s and 1940s. So far, so cyclical.

But there are several very important ways in which today's

China is different from the past and which suggest that it *may*, just *may*, be able to avoid going the way of former dynasties and perhaps for the first time form an ongoing, progressive, linear narrative to Chinese history.

First of all, the state is much stronger. Route 312 is a part of that. In the 1950s, the Communist Party set about consolidating the roads and railways that had been built in the late Qing dynasty and the Republican era. In the 1990s and since 2000, infrastructure construction has expanded at an unbelievable rate. The Qing dynasty, a hundred years ago, never mind any dynasties before that, could not control all its far-flung regions. The Communist Party can, and this means peasant rebellions are less likely to succeed.

The second difference is that today's leaders are Chinese, not Manchu or Mongol or any other ethnic group. They can therefore embody the nationalistic aspirations of the country (and the people) in a way that, for instance, the Manchu Qing dynasty rulers, overthrown in 1912, could not. For all the many problems in modern China, there is a certain amount of pride in the country's raised status in the world, especially among the urban populace.

The third reason that the situation is different is economic, and this is probably the most important. There is still massive corruption, the wealth gap is growing, and many people are being crushed, unable to cope with the convulsive economic change. But there is no doubt that the Chinese economy in many areas is booming, and there are many more options available for people with some ambition to succeed.

Route 312 is a part of this too, and the trickle-down effect is huge. Peasants are taking to the road in large numbers in the belief that somewhere over the Chinese rainbow is a job in a factory that can lift them out of poverty. Many of them have found that those jobs exist: difficult, dangerous jobs in dirty,

Dickensian factories, but jobs all the same, which enable farmers to earn more in a month than they did in a whole year of farming. Route 312, and all the roads in China, have become the steam-release valve on the pressure cooker that could previously be released only by rebellion.

With this economic transformation has come a whole new middle class, a more informed, more mature, more conscious, more rights-aware urban general public that has never before existed on such a scale in Chinese history. They have choices and social space in which to live, where the government doesn't interfere. It's not as much space as in the Western world, of course, but people have significant choices and significantly increased freedom nonetheless. They are not just listening to the voice of government, they are listening to one another and listening to themselves. But so far, they have been compliant, co-opted by the state with promises of greater wealth. Whether this alliance continues, and whether the government can keep the new middle class happy, will be a deciding factor in China's future.

Fourth and finally, China is different now because there has been a psychological revolution. Huge parts of the Chinese mind-set have been changed. It is no longer looking inwards and backwards, it is looking outwards and forwards. It has put science above belief (sometimes too much), and jettisoned centuries of tradition in order to achieve modernity. (Westerners should try to imagine having to throw out everything of value in their heritage – Greek philosophy, Roman law, Judaeo-Christian teachings of any sort, not to mention classical music and other art forms. That is what China has done to its own traditions.)

Attitudes towards the family have been revolutionised too. The family used to be the state in miniature, with the father–son bond mirroring the ruler–subject relationship. Now, though, the vertical relationship in the family is coming second to the horizontal conjugal relationship between man and wife. Youth is triumphing over age in the cities, the individual is becoming more important than the group. Again, the change is imperfect and the fallout is huge, straining the fabric of society to the limit. But compared to many developing countries, China has become a fount of modern, scientific thinking and go-getting individualism. Chinese people can now dream dreams like they never have before, and have more power in their hands to fulfil them.

So all in all, it seems to me that China is in a different situation now than in most of the other transition periods in its history. The question is, are the Chinese leaders approaching this completely different situation in the completely different way that it requires? And I have to say, the answer to *that* is no. What we have in China is a mobile twenty-first-century society shackled to a sclerotic 1950s Leninist-style political system. The economy is changing, the society is changing, but the politics are not, and that is starting to cause sufficient problems in governance, and even in the economy, to call China's rise to potential greatness into question. China is more fragile and brittle than it appears.

In order to stay in power, the Party knows it has to make some political changes, and it has done so, allowing capitalists and entrepreneurs to became party members, for a start. It has also made some administrative reforms. There are experiments with more than one candidate for posts within the party hierarchy. There are programmes to train legal officials, such as judges, by sending them abroad. The government is trying to show it is listening to the people, and becoming more responsive, to allow more alternatives for people within the one-party system so that Old Hundred Names will not seek change through demonstrations on the streets. There has been a limited introduction of elections in the villages, the lowest level of China's political system, and Chinese leaders have been looking to places such as Singapore as examples of how to govern more efficiently without introducing a full Western-style political system.

But these changes are all *within* the current system. The process has been termed 'consultative Leninism' by China watchers such as Richard Baum of UCLA, who says that the Party is attempting 'to facilitate the emergence of controlled societal *feedback* without incurring the considerable risk of spontaneous political *blowback* or, even more dangerous, organised anti-regime *pushback*.' But in the end, Baum and many other China scholars see such minimal attempts at reform as a blind alley. Singapore (population 3 million) would rank as a small- to medium-sized city in China, and reforming a medium-sized city, or making it wealthy enough that its citizens didn't care much about political reform, is a lot easier than reforming a continent (never mind China's lack of the transparent, British-style legal system and civil service that Singapore possesses).

The elephant in the room that no Chinese leader wants to talk about is, of course, democratic reform itself. China has come a long, long way in one hundred years. The path has been a winding and difficult one, but the country now has to a large extent fulfilled two of the Three Principles of the People laid out by the architect of the 1912 Revolution, Sun Yat-sen. China has international respect (the first principle), and although it still has poverty, by and large, it can feed its people (the second principle). But the revolution is still unfinished. Sun Yat-sen's third principle, of giving political rights to the people, has not been realised, and it is not at all clear that it will be realised any time soon.

There are two reasons why not: first, most Party leaders still believe in the Communist Party's almost divine right to rule alone. Second, any who believe in political reform are frightened, because of the failure of the 1912 Revolution and the simple fact that China has never succeeded in going down the democratic road before.

They were also frightened, in more recent years, by the collapse of the Soviet Union and the realisation that, while not reforming may be dangerous, starting to reform may be even more so. They could be right. Just ask Mikhail Gorbachev, or indeed look at the last rulers of the Qing dynasty between 1900 and 1912. They initiated changes and created new institutions in an effort to reform and save the imperial state, but in doing so they unleashed forces that destroyed it.

In taking the steady-as-she-goes, stability-at-all-costs approach, though, the Communist Party leaders, in their eternal fear of *luan* (chaos), are storing up a lot of problems for themselves. They are planning the new roads, the shiny new buildings, the new airports, and the actual pillars to hold it all up. But they are ignoring the need to construct the pillars of any new *political* house that will need to be built in advance, so that the collapse of the country in 1912 does not repeat itself. This means building the pillars of strong institutions and an independent judiciary, and taking power out of the hands of men and putting it into actual institutions of governance. The problem is that doing *that* would, of course, be tantamount to the party signing its own death warrant.

The situation is getting too serious to ignore. There comes a point when insisting on stability actually creates more instability, and it feels as though that point may soon be reached in China. Nero is fiddling while Rome burns, and what the country needs is a blueprint for gradual, political change.

In fact, a document was written back in the late 1980s that almost matches that description. It was drafted by the reformist Communist Party chief Zhao Ziyang (with the backing of paramount leader Deng Xiaoping) and presented to the Thirteenth Communist Party Congress in the autumn of 1987. That was a time, before the demonstrations of 1989, when China's political leaders were looking at all possibilities for political reform. Zhao's paper was not a revolutionary document espousing full democratisation, but it was nevertheless significant in laying out the first suggestions of a shift towards what Richard Baum calls 'soft authoritarian pluralism'.

At that congress, two years before the killing of the students in Tiananmen Square, Zhao (who for my money was one of the greatest Chinese officials of recent millennia) proposed a number of political reforms. He suggested, among other things, a separation of the Communist Party from the functions of state administration and a reform of the state personnel system – the notorious Nomenklatura – to minimise political patronage and ensure reliance on merit in government appointments and promotions; he encouraged an increase in the voice and legislative autonomy of the rubber-stamp parliament, the National People's Congress and the people's congresses at all levels; he suggested augmenting the watchdog role of the other so-called democratic parties, which currently exist just to provide the Communist Party with a fig leaf for their claims to be a multi-party state. He proposed strengthening the rule of law.

Zhao's proposals were never implemented. He had already been criticised by hard-liners as too liberal when the demonstrations of spring 1989 broke out, and his downfall was sealed by 19 May, when he went to Tiananmen Square to plead with the students to leave. Zhao was detained under house arrest in Beijing until his death in 2005. The Party, spooked by the fall of Communism in the Soviet bloc, continues to this day to clamp down on any meaningful political reform of the type that Zhao suggested.

But the problems are still the same; in fact they are much worse than they were in 1987. And scholar Richard Baum says, 'It can be argued that the road to the CCP's survival must inevitably run through Zhao's 1987 reform blueprint.'

The fact that the government does not seem willing to consider this, however, raises the possibility of a third outcome for China. This scenario is that China neither implodes nor becomes the next superpower, but just muddles through, remaining largely as it is. This argument has been put most forcefully by the US based scholar Pei Minxin in his book *China's Trapped Transition*. Pei suggests that China's so-called transition may not be a transition at all, and that the Chinese Communist Party's unwillingness to change its political system means that China's economy could start to fizzle out. 'Having seized political power through the gun, a former revolutionary party, such as the CCP, will unlikely seek its own demise through voluntary reform,' he writes, adding that the Party is fully able to keep a lid on rural unrest. If no major shock occurs to bring about a political meltdown, writes Pei, China could enter a period of prolonged stagnation.

Since so much of the world's economic growth and stability depends on China these days, such a downturn could have major consequences for the global economy.

The crucial part of this analysis is the phrase 'if no major shock occurs'. I think, if everything continues to run relatively smoothly, if the economy continues to grow (or even slows down a little), the Chinese government may be able to carry on as it is for a while, without too much political reform. It has already proven itself an adept ideological chameleon, able to transform itself to fit the changing environment. It may well be able to continue to bankroll its inefficiencies and keep a lid on the dissent that is bubbling up more and more from the grass roots.

However, such an analysis does not take into account the possibility of a sudden shock to the system. My concern is that something could come out of left field, something that no one is expecting, in the same way that the Asian financial crisis hit South-East Asia (though not China) in 1997–8. China is very different from Thailand and Indonesia, but the Chinese economic miracle has major faultlines running through it, and is certainly more fragile than it looks. A really huge outbreak of avian flu, for instance, or a worldwide oil shortage, or a large tariff increase on Chinese exports into the US, or a run on the Chinese banks – any of these scenarios could put huge pressure on the Chinese system. Anything that might spark a downturn in economic growth, on which the Party relies so much for its legitimacy, would be very dangerous for the CCP. Then, the angry farmers and angry laid-off workers could start to cause Beijing some real problems.

Beijing is pedalling fast to try to deal with all of these issues so that if something happened out of the blue it would not have a seismic impact on Chinese society. But the brittleness of Chinese society is very worrying, and there is only so much reform that can take place within the current system.

By a pure twist of calendrical fate, the date that may be looked back on as crucial in deciding what happens in China falls exactly one hundred years after the overthrow of China's last emperor and the failed 1912 Revolution. In 2012, if all goes to plan (and there's no guarantee of that), President Hu Jintao and his risk-averse generation will step down from their leadership roles in the Communist Party at the Eighteenth Party Congress, making way for the so-called fifth generation of leaders. Members of the fifth generation (Mao Zedong represented the first generation, Deng Xiaoping the second, Jiang Zemin the third, Hu Jintao the fourth) were born in the late 1950s or the 1960s and so came of age and began their careers in government after the reform era began in 1978. Many of them have lived and studied abroad, and are familiar with western political systems. It is generally believed that they are a different type of political animal from the fourth generation, more international, less dogmatic, more flexible. They will need to be, because I think the decade after 2012 will be when the problems, especially those of rural China, will become too widespread and dangerous to ignore or simply suppress.

It could well be the most important decade in China's long, illustrious and sometimes tortured history, when the government leaders must decide whether they want the country to go on to a different, better future, or whether they are prepared to risk consigning 1.3 billion people to the tragic cycle of Chinese history once again.

This is unknown territory. We don't know if they can do it. We don't know if they will accept the *need* to do it. And if they don't do it, there is, as Pei Minxin suggests, no guarantee that the only alternative is collapse. Even if there is no big crunch, though, nothing coming out of left field, I don't think the current system can continue as it is for ever, and the growing number of mini-crunches is likely to weaken it and lead to serious problems. In the years following the Party Congress of 2012, the combination of rising rural discontent and a new generation of leaders, hopefully more receptive to political change, could mean, *should* mean that some political reforms will be instituted.

For now, though, the Chinese leaders are working hard to keep the economy growing while simultaneously launching a big campaign to encourage people towards a 'harmonious society', especially focusing on improving the lives of the peasants. The problem is that economic growth is creating as much disharmony now as it is creating harmony.

In addition to the economic problems, there are simply too many contradictions in Chinese society. The Party wants to create a modern society, but it doesn't want to allow too strong a civil society of churches, unions, associations and other social organisations needed to build a modern nation. It does not want people using the Internet to access sensitive information, but it needs technology to become the modern country it wants to be. The Party needs to promote knowledge in order to compete, but knowledge is dangerous. It needs empowered people in order to become strong, but it can't let the people be too empowered.

Despite all the very real economic progress, these contradictions could start to cause some very real problems as Chinese society becomes even more mobile, and the political system struggles even more to keep up. The Party needs some visionary leaders to lay out a plan for the future, a blueprint for some kind of political transition. But in a country that still values stability above all else, that kind of vision does not seem to be forthcoming.

I spend my final morning in Shanghai at the city's Urban Planning Exhibition Hall. A sign outside, in Chinese and English, sets the tone: BLAZE NEW TRAILS IN A PIONEERING SPIRIT. The main exhibit is a scale model of the city, demonstrating how Shanghai will become a twenty-first-century metropolis. The exhibit is extra-ordinary. There are details of the new Yangshan deepwater port, which will soon be the world's busiest, built on three islands, twenty miles offshore, joined to the mainland just south of Shanghai by the world's longest sea bridge. Then there's the transformation of Chongming Island – more than three hundred square miles of prime real estate in the middle of the Yangtze River – into a high-tech, green research and development zone and residential area, linked to Shanghai by an eleven-mile tunnel under the river. There are yet more exhibits about the 'informationisa-tion' of Shanghai, which include statements such as this one:

We believe that with our endeavours, all our dreams will come true in 2010. There will appear in digital Shanghai a platform for public services that is rich in content, highly shared and interconnected. The platform will be a milestone as Shanghai becomes one of the international, financial, economic, trade and shipping centres.

The language is hyperbolic, and the implementation woefully lacking in consultation with the people, but the scale of the vision is huge. The time frames are long – ten, fifteen years – and I find myself walking around the exhibition trying to catch the eye of the few other foreigners who are there, so I can just raise my eyebrows and say to them: 'This is quite scary, isn't it?' knowing they are likely to feel the same.

Once you've thought through *whether* all this could come to pass, you find yourself thinking what if it does? What will it all mean for the rest of us? If cities like Shanghai and Beijing and Tianjin and Chongqing remake themselves into the industrialised, informationised R & D hubs that they want to be, does it all add up to a threat to the West, and if it does, how should the West respond?

Economically, of course, China is in some ways a threat – if you are measuring it by the number of Western jobs lost to Chinese factories. China is still *the* main centre for global manufacturing, and if you are one of the people in Middle America (or Britain, or wherever) whose job is moved to Shanghai, China's development is inevitably a cause of anger.

In the light of this, it is right that Western governments try to protect their own industries as much as is possible and practical. It is also right to keep up the pressure on Beijing on issues such as the violation of Western intellectual property rights, and to keep pushing for improvement in China's labour rights, for the sake of the Chinese workers and in order to restore some kind of fairness to the competition. Such policies will create friction with Beijing, but a certain amount of economic friction is inevitable as China rises.

If the idea of 'the China threat' is pushed to far, however, and the language becomes too emtional and politicised (as it sometimes does in the US), there is a danger of creating a self-fulfilling prophecy of animosity beyond the inevitable friction caused by China's development. To allow the problems in the relationship to define our whole China policy is simplistic and dangerous, because so much of the Western economic boom of the 1990s and into the new century has been driven by China. Whether it is Chinese yuppies and companies buying Western goods and commodities – and giving a boost to Western stock markets and manufacturers – or the Chinese government buying US government bonds and thereby keeping US interest rates down. China's rise is undoubtedly benefitting the West in many ways.

In his brilliant book *China Shakes the World*, former *Financial Times* Beijing correspondent James Kynge illustrates this point by standing outside a Wal-Mart in Rockford, Illinois, and asking the shoppers of Middle America whether they feel like thanking the Chinese for all the cheap goods they can buy, and for the low interest rates they pay on their mortgages. Not surprisingly, he gets some funny looks. But his point, and mine, is that while China is certainly harming some areas of Western economies it is also doing a lot of good to Western pockets in much less visible ways. So we have to make sure that, while we continue to stand up to China in important areas, we do not damage our own interests in the process.

For instance, the West needs China to revalue its currency because at present the yuan's undervaluation gives it an unfair advantage in manufacturing. But proposing bills in Congress that would punish China with huge trade tariffs if it doesn't make a massive, immediate revaluation could end up being counterproductive, perhaps reducing the flow of Chinese finance to support the dollar, with very serious consequences for the American economy. Too sudden a revaluation could also slow down the Chinese economy, with all the potential social instability that could bring. A strong China may pose problems for the world, but a weak or collapsed China would be many times worse.

In short, I think we need to get out of the 'friend or foe?' line of questioning. In years to come, China could clearly become one of the two, depending on which way its domestic political situation plays out. For now, though, it is a mixture of both, depending on which area you look at. So it should be treated as a combination of the two, with a complex and nuanced foreign policy that looks to protect Western economic interests as much as possible, but also avoids the descent into overly emotional demagoguery that has sometimes characterised the relationship.

Militarily, China is growing fast too, though you won't see much public bragging about that. Beijing is spending roughly $50 billion on upgrading its military every year. (The US spends more than $400 billion annually.) But China is starting from a very backward position. Military experts say China is as many as thirty or forty years behind the US in its military technology. And even when it has bought or developed new technology, it has huge problems coordinating it all. China has no aircraft carriers, and the ships of its navy (whose official name, the People's Liberation Army Navy, gives you an idea of where its military priorities have always been) have only managed to cross the Pacific Ocean a few times, and even then with some difficulty.

The Chinese say they are simply upgrading their military to reach a level appropriate for a country of their size, and every Chinese person you speak to will tell you the same thing: philosophically, the Chinese are not an expansionary people. 'We build walls to keep others out,' they say, 'we don't go out invading others.'

I'm not convinced that China's rise will be completely peaceful. Certainly, history doesn't offer very reassuring lessons about the rise of new industrial powers. *If* China's leaders can hold the country together, and *if* the Chinese economy keeps booming, there is a possibility in the long term that the new Chinese nationalism *could* lead to some kind of military problems with its neighbours (especially Japan). But, at present, I don't think the leaders of China are waking up in the morning and wondering which countries in the region they can threaten, now or in twenty years. I think they are probably waking up and wondering, *How on earth are we going to hold this country together?*

That is why they are so (quietly) ecstatic about the terrorist attacks on the US in 2001. The new American enemy has been revealed, and it is *not* China, so Beijing can focus on making up the time economically that it wasted creating revolution under Chairman Mao. That is also why China has such an anodyne foreign policy in so many areas, wanting to avoid picking a fight with anyone (especially the US) so that it can focus on its domestic issues. Stability domestically and peace internationally are its watchwords, as it seeks to present itself as a responsible player on the world stage. So we should be careful not to exaggerate China's military threat (it has the right to have a modern military, after all), but at the same time we should cautiously monitor how it behaves towards its neighbours.

The wild card in the whole situation is Taiwan. Beijing considers the island of 22 million people off its southeast coast to be part of China, and if a Taiwanese president does something silly, such as declare official independence, there could be real problems. But, as I had seen in the town of Kunshan, just outside Shanghai, the $17 billion invested in the mainland by Taiwanese businessmen makes this unlikely, even though there are a growing number of Taiwanese who want to be separate from mainland China for ever.

Taiwan aside, in the short to medium term, I think a bigger threat than any that China poses militarily will be the threat to its own environment.

The degradation of China's land, air and water has reached critical levels. Deforestation, desertification, not to mention the rising rates of cancer and birth defects from the polluted water and air, are becoming increasingly pressing problems domestically. Pollution has also become a major cause of protest among farmers whose land is near factories. The lack of a effective legal system and the contradictions at the local level of needing the money that polluting factories produce mean that local implementation or enforcement of increasingly stringent central government laws is spotty at best. Once again, this problem comes back to the urgent need to keep the economy growing in order to stave off social discontent – a truth of which both local and central government officials are all too aware. And on top of the pollution, there is the chronic shortage of water in northern China. How can a country continue without water?

China's environmental problems are increasingly being exported. There is so much air pollution in southern China that Hong Kong is frequently enveloped in a shroud of smog. Even the effects of China's deforestation are being exported: the government has banned logging within China, but it still needs tons and tons of lumber, so forests in Southeast Asia, Africa and Latin America are being depleted to feed the Chinese economic monster.

China is also the world's largest importer of many metals and commodities, the consumption of which is single-handedly keeping parts of the world's economy afloat. Base metals, petrochemicals, foodstuffs, anything and everything is being sucked in to satisfy Chinese demand. Mines are being opened up in Australia simply to supply China.

Finally, added to all the noxious substances that China pumps out, there is the issue of what China pumps in: the need for oil, and the possibility of conflict arising from that need. To keep its economy going, and therefore to keep its population happy, China must continue to import more oil. It has already overtaken Japan as the world's second-biggest consumer of petroleum products after the US. Its demand is rising by 10 to 15 per cent per year; its own output of oil rises by only about 2 per cent. China's oil imports doubled between 2000 and 2005, and much of the reason for the huge hike in global oil prices during that time was increased Chinese demand.

The problem is that the world has become so reliant on Chinese demand and on the booming Chinese economy that we can't afford for China *not* to keep on consuming this way, even though it is playing havoc with the environment.

And so here is one final contradiction to add to the pile: we need the Chinese economy to slow down at the same time that we need it to keep booming.

Right in the heart of Shanghai, supporting the intersection of two of the city's busiest elevated motorways, is a massive steel pillar, about fifteen feet thick. Engraved on the pillar in relief is a huge, winding, weaving Chinese dragon. It stretches from the very bottom of the pillar to the very top, and must be at least fifty feet tall. The dragon looks somewhat incongruous. Almost any other part of Shanghai's new elevated road system could be in Los Angeles or Chicago, but it is unlikely you will see a dragon wrapped around a pillar like that in an American city. There seems to be a lot of history gathered around that pillar, a lot of memories, and the legacy of a whole civilisation caught up in the swirl of the dragon's long, slender body and its sweeping tail. In the midst of a city trying, and succeeding, to be so modern, the pillar seems to be saying, 'We're still here. We, the descendants of the dragon, are still here, and we are still Chinese.'

From the time the Western powers arrived and started bullying China in the nineteenth century, the country has been determined to stand up in the world and become strong again. The Chinese were willing to do this at any cost, and finally they seem to be succeeding. But the cost *has* been high. The Communist Party blamed traditional teachings and philosophies for the country's weakness, and launched an extraordinarily fierce assault on Chinese culture, practically wiping it out.

While some frustration at the debilitating power of Chinese tradition is understandable, they need not have launched such a furious assault. Taiwan, Japan and South Korea have all developed economically even though they too are Confucian-based societies. But the Communist Party believed that everything had to be thrown out. Now that the frenzied storm of Maoist destruction has passed, the Chinese economy is no doubt benefiting from the absence of ethical, religious and traditional objections that could slow its pursuit of wealth. But Chinese culture has been decimated, and sometimes, as an outsider, one wonders if anything is left of it after all. In trying to break the chains of history and restore China to its past greatness, has the Communist Party destroyed the very essence of Chineseness that they were supposedly trying to save?

I notice the dragon on the pillar again as I take a taxi underneath the elevated motorways to see Ye Sha, the radio talk-show host I had shared pizza with before I began my journey. We meet in a coffee bar in the lively Xujiahui district, just opposite the massive Catholic cathedral. I tell her about the dragon, and she smiles. I ask her about that indefinable Chinese essence, and whether it still exists or has all just disappeared. You don't feel it very much, I tell her, and for the outsider who comes wanting to experience China, and not a carbon copy of the West, that feels a little sad. Ye Sha has a different comparison.

'I think China is like a beautiful old house that is about to be knocked down,' she says. 'People are living in it, and some of them want to put on extensions or make renovations. But in the end they don't feel comfortable living in the old house: it doesn't suit them, so they decide to knock it down. The residents take one final walk through the house, and suddenly they find something very precious, some treasures that they didn't know were there before. It was only when they were going to knock the house down that they thought of looking. This is what I want to happen with China in the next few years, before we knock everything down – that we rediscover something precious in the rooms of the old house, something Chinese, something hidden that is waiting to be rediscovered.'

She can't quite put her finger on what it will be except to say that, despite all the westernisation, Chinese people will not be completely changed. She says simply that in a few years, once everyone has calmed down a little, when there is less frantic chasing after money, people will want to start rediscovering their Chineseness. She says it's already happening.

'A lot of Chinese people don't know what China is,' she goes on, concentrating on her words as she pauses to sip her fruit tea. 'They look at it through Western eyes. But I think that if we go a completely Western route, we will not succeed. We need to find a way that retains something of the Chinese essence. Lots of people agree with me. They just don't know where to look. I don't mean returning to the past, but I mean retaining an element of the Chinese approach. If we see what we are losing, then maybe we will recover it. We're in this very painful and difficult transition period, when the power of old values has declined and the system of new values has not yet taken hold. But I think we can find our own road, which will be specifically Chinese.'

Like so many Chinese people, Ye Sha takes the long view, talking in terms of decades. Despite being young, modern and apparently very westernised, politically she does not believe that China's future will follow the Western example, either. Nor does she think it should. 'I don't think that the democratic system, the multi-party system, is the best for China,' she says. 'I'm not saying it will never happen, but I just don't think it will *necessarily* happen.'

I ask her finally about all the new propaganda that the Communist Party is pushing out, and how much of it seems surprisingly Confucian, as though the Party has forgotten its hatred of Old China and is itself initiating something of a renaissance to try to instil some ethics in society. The concepts of moderate prosperity and harmony, and a recent campaign that encouraged officials to 'rule the nation by virtue', are all Confucian.

Ye Sha says she doesn't like the government slogans. 'They are external. They don't get inside a person, so that the person can act on them, and be transformed,' she says.

Ye Sha wants very much to be Chinese. She is Chinese, of course, but she wants that Chinese essence to be more a part of her and of her country's future, in a deeper way, in a way that seems to have been temporarily misplaced. While millions of rural people are still caught up in the basic needs of feeding their families, in the cities it seems as though more and more people are feeling this way, as a reaction to the blitz of Western materialism that has saturated China and the increased sense of nationalism and patriotic pride that has come with it.

A hundred years ago, many Chinese intellectuals believed that China had to destroy itself as a culture in order to save itself as a nation. Now, somehow, that feels reversed. After a century of cultural iconoclasm, many urban Chinese people are saying, 'Enough! We want to be Chinese again. We want to *save* ourselves as a culture, we want to *save* our Chinese identity, and perhaps only then can we rediscover ourselves as a nation.' It's still very much in transition, as the country itself is in transition, and it's hard to see what, or who, will come out the other end. But it's fascinating, and wonderful, to see some Chinese people trying to reclaim the heritage that their grandparents and parents were happy to (or told to) trash. Perhaps China in the end will not be so different from Japan and South Korea, full of modern people who are also proud citizens of their own country and proud inheritors of their own traditions, with a knowledge of who they are and where they're going. And hopefully that will be a kind of resolution to the century and a half of Chinese identity crisis that has claimed so many hopes and so many lives.

The next day I fly back to Beijing to say my final farewells. Before I fly to London, I run the Beijing marathon, staggering through in a less than impressive four and a half hours. Chinese people cheer me every step of the twenty-six miles through their city. 'Come on, *yang ren*! Come on, Ocean Person, you can do it! *Jia you!*'

I'm looking forward to seeing my family after a long summer apart, and in many ways, I know it's time to leave China.

But I know I will miss it: the zeal and optimism of the cities and the despair of the countryside, and the sheer excitement of a nation in tumultuous transition. I will miss the calls on my mobile phone late at night from angry peasants or laid-off workers. I will miss the energy and the dilemmas of life and death, of hope and tragedy, in which everything matters a great deal. I will also miss the hopefulness, the yearning for a better future. In the West, our better future is supposedly already here, so life is no longer as much of a journey. We have (so we think) reached our destination, so we've sat down, put our feet up and poured ourselves a large drink. In France, workers are restricted by law to a thirty-five-hour working week. Many Chinese people work that in two days.

Most of all I will miss the Chinese people, the wonderful Chinese people. The Chinese heart is so very, very big, but it has always been so very constrained, first by Confucian culture, and then by Communism. Now, amid all the problems, for the first time, it feels as if the big, big Chinese heart will have some space to expand and grow.

Chairman Mao once said that the Chinese people were a blank sheet of paper on which he could write the words of socialism. I've never agreed with that statement. Surely the whole point about the Chinese people before 1949 was not that they were blank, but that they had *too much* written upon them. Pages of history, pages of Confucian teaching that made it difficult for them to respond when the western powers arrived and tried to write their own, very different words upon them.

It is only after thirty years of militant Maoism and a total of sixty years of Communist Party rule that the Chinese people are a blank sheet of paper, because Mao did so much to erase (or tear up) what was written there before. Of course, there is much writing that still remains. You cannot erase everything from the past. But the point is that Chinese people are now writing on the paper themselves.

Can the government change the political system and still hold the country together? Can we have a strong, united China and a changed China?

I hope so, for the Chinese people's sake. Can there be any people in the world who deserve more to succeed, and to see and feel in their own lives the prosperity and freedom that we in the Western world take for granted? I do not think so. The Chinese people have suffered so long, *too* long, and now, in spite of all their country's imperfections, many of them are on the verge of tasting some kind of progress for the first time.

It's true, I have some major concerns about China and its future. I would go so far as to say I am rather fearful. China has more problems than people in the West realise, and the possibilities for progress are always tinged with the huge price that is paid by the losers in the whole economic reform process. Whatever happens in China, I have a feeling the country's development will continue to be a bumpy ride.

If the Communist Party does not start making political reforms, I fear that, looking towards 2020, that ride could become very bumpy indeed, as the pressures and the contradictions in Chinese society become too strong.

And always lurking at the back of my mind is the fear, that the weight of 2,000 years of imperial history is stacked against the possibility of democratic reform. I am afraid that the methods of holding the state together are incompatible with allowing the state to change, that a united China, a united empire, will continue to be more important to the leaders than the possibility of a changed China. And I fear that the Chinese state, which has always been more important than the individual, may end up betraying the Chinese people all over again.

But in the end I cannot be completely pessimistic and, on balance, I cannot end this book on a pessimistic note. Perhaps this is because I have seen with my own eyes over twenty years (and all along Route 312) how far China has come.

The great Chinese author Lu Xun asked all these questions back in the dark days after the collapse of the 1912 Revolution. In 1921 he wrote a short story called 'My Old Home'. In it, Lu describes how he returns to his hometown after twenty years away and meets his old playmate, who has remained stuck in the village while the narrator has gone off and become an educated urbanite. Lu Xun feels an invisible wall between them, and a sense of pessimism pervades the story, even though his nephew and his old friend's son get along well and he hopes they can have 'a new life, a life we have never experienced'.

Lu Xun worries that his hope may be misplaced, because he is so conscious of the pull of China's past, of its heritage and its inescapable history. But he heads back to the city from his old home, and as he goes he thinks what I have been thinking as I have travelled along Route 312: that yes, there is a difference now, and there is a cause for hope amid all the problems. Chinese people, even more so now than in the 1920s, are starting in a very small way to be in charge of their own destiny. They're writing their own words on the Chinese parchment, and their future will be less and less decided by fate or by the emperor or by the forces of nature. They are, as Lu Xun writes at the end of his story, making their own future, imperfectly, painfully, but hopefully along the road.

Hope cannot be said to exist, nor can it be said not to exist. It is just like roads across the earth. For actually the earth has no roads to begin with . . . but when many people pass one way, a road is made.

ACKNOWLEDGEMENTS

This book began life as a seven-part radio series for National Public Radio, which was broadcast in August 2004 (you can hear the series at: www.npr.org/programs/morning/features/2004/aug/china_road). A year later, just before I left China in the summer of 2005, I travelled Route 312 again. *China Road* is consequently the sum of two trips along the road, plus a brief return visit to Shanghai and Nanjing. Though it offended my journalistic sensiblities, that was the only way I could do it.

Like all authors, I have many debts of gratitude. My first is to my employer, NPR, and especially to its senior foreign editor, Loren Jenkins, whose support for the radio series and the book is typical of the encouragement he has always given me. I would also like to thank Barbara Rehm, Ted Clark, Kevin Beesley, Bob Duncan, the staff of the NPR reference library, and Hugo Boothby in the NPR London office. Thanks also to my editors at Bloomsbury, Bill Swainson and Emily Sweet; to my agent in Washington, Gail Ross, who took a chance on a first-time author; and to her creative director, Howard Yoon, who gave me crucial input at a critical time.

Many academics have helped me along the way, including Richard Baum at UCLA, Andrew Nathan and Robbie Barnet at Columbia, and Don Starr and Mike Dillon at Durham. I am particularly grateful to James Millward at Georgetown, who read the second half of the script, and John Flower of the University of

North Carolina at Charlotte, who read it all. Both gave invaluable comments. In China, I benefitted from conversations with many friends in the foreign press corps. I would especially like to thank James Kynge, Rupert Wingfield-Hayes, James Miles, Jim Yardley, Charles Hutzler, Joe Kahn, Holly Williams, Anthony Kuhn, Louisa Lim, Mike Lev, Henry Chu, John Pomfret, Adam Brookes, Duncan Hewitt and Frank Langfitt. Thanks also go to Patrick Fraser, Greg Barker, Kurt Selles, Caitrin McKiernan and Paul Gifford.

There are many Chinese people to thank, particularly those who opened up their homes and their hearts to me along Route 312. Some of them wish to remain anonymous, and there are several names in the book that I have changed to protect their identities. I live in hope for a day when we no longer need to do that. My assistant Liang Yan travelled the length of Route 312 with me for the radio trip, adding a huge amount to my understanding of everything, as she always does. I made the second trip on my own. Jasmin Gu gave me great research help in Shanghai.

I am forever grateful to my parents, Graham and Geraldine, who first put me on the right road. They made excellent suggestions about the manuscript, as did my wife's parents, Rosemary and Lloyd. My children, Amy and Daniel, gave me endless encouragement while I was planning and writing the book, even though it took me away from them for long periods of time. I am extremely proud of them, and confess that I love having children who were Made in China.

Most of all, my thanks to my wife, Nancy, who has lived through every moment of this book and everything that went before. Her love, faith, wisdom and patience, not to mention her skills as an editor, are infused into every page – every word – of what I have written, just as they are infused into every corner of my life. She has made so many things both possible and memorable, and this book is dedicated with much, much love to her.

London
March 2007

SELECT BIBLIOGRAPHY
AND SUGGESTIONS FOR
FURTHER READING

Barnett, Robert, *Lhasa: Streets with Memories* (Columbia University Press, 2006). A beautiful book about the many layers of Tibet's tragic history, as seen through the many layers of its ancient capital.

Buck, Pearl, *The Good Earth* (Simon & Schuster, 2004). The classic novel of one farmer's life and loves, set against the tumultuous, changing canvas of 1920s China.

Cable, Mildred (with Francesca French), *The Gobi Desert* (Hodder and Stoughton, 1950). One of the great China travel books, written by two middle-aged English missionaries.

Cable, Mildred, and Francesca French, *Through Jade Gate and Central Asia: An Account of Journeys in Kansu, Turkestan and Central Asia* (Houghton Mifflin, 1927). Another book of Gobi travels from two of the intrepid Trio.

Clissold, Tim, *Mr China: A Memoir* (Collins, 2006). Wonderful tale of trying to ride the China investment wave in the 1990s, and losing $418 million in the process.

Economy, Elizabeth, *The River Runs Black: The Environmental Challenge to China's Future* (Cornell University Press, 2004). Shocking summary of China's environmental meltdown.

Fleming, Peter, *News from Tartary: A Journey from Peking to Kashmir* (Jonathan Cape, 1936). Intrepid young journalist travels across a disintegrated China in the 1930s.

Goldstein, Melvyn, *The Snow Lion and the Dragon: China, Tibet and the Dalai Lama* (University of California, 1999). Excellent, short summary of the Tibet Problem from the doyen of Tibet-watchers.

Hessler, Peter, *River Town: Two Years on the Yangtze* (Harper Collins, 2001). Timeless, personal account of teaching for two years in the late 1990s in a town on the Yangtze River.

Hopkirk, Peter, *Foreign Devils on the Silk Road: The Search for the Lost Treasures of Central Asia* (Oxford University Press, 1980). The definitive account of Aurel Stein and the other 'robbers' of Dunhuang.

Jenner, W.J.F., *The Tyranny of History: The Roots of China's Crisis* (Penguin, 1992). Shockingly negative but staggeringly brilliant analysis of China's political culture.

Kynge, James, *China Shakes the World: The Rise of a Hungry Nation* (Houghton Mifflin, 2007). Award-winning analysis of how a hungry China is shaking the world economically.

Levathes, Louise, *When China Ruled the Seas: The Treasure Fleet of the Dragon Throne, 1405–1433* (OUP, 1997). The amazing story of Ming dynasty admiral Zheng He.

Lu Hsun, *Selected Stories*, (W.W. Norton & Co., 2003). A great introduction to some of Lu Xun's best short stories (using the old spelling of his name).

Macartney, Lord George, (ed. J. L. Cranmer-Byng), *An Embassy to China, Being the Journal Kept by Lord Macartney during his embassy to the Emperor Ch'ien-lung 1793–1794* (Folio Society, 2004). Beautiful reproduction of the original diary, including watercolours painted by the embassy's artist, William Alexander.

Millward, James, *Eurasian Crossroads: A History of Xinjiang* (Columbia University Press, 2006). The definitive academic history of Xinjiang, China's Muslim northwest.

Pei, Minxin, *China's Trapped Transition: The Limits of Developmental Autocracy* (Harvard University Press, 2006). Excellent, quite academic, analysis of why China won't be able to make the transition to multi-party democracy.

Pomfret, John, *Chinese Lessons: Five Classmates and the Story of the New China* (Henry Holt, 2006). The dean of China Correspondents tells the story of his twenty-five-year love affair with China.

Spence, Jonathan, *The Search for Modern China* (W.W. Norton & Co., 1999). The definitive modern history of China from the master of the genre.

Spence, Jonathan, *The Chan's Great Continent: China in Western Minds* (Penguin, 1998). Fascinating exploration of how westerners have seen China through the ages.

Studwell, Joe, *The China Dream: The Elusive Quest for the Greatest Untapped Market on Earth* (Atlantic Monthly Books, 2002). In-depth look at westerners' obsession with the China market.

Taylor, Dr & Mrs Howard, *The Biography of James Hudson Taylor* (Hodder and Stoughton, 1995). Biography of one of the greatest missionary figures in nineteenth-century China.

Terrill, Ross, *The New Chinese Empire, and what it means for the United States* (Basic Books, 2004). Very well-researched and well-written analysis, linking China's past, present and future.

Tu, Wei-ming, (ed.), *The Living Tree: The Changing Meaning of Being Chinese Today* (Stanford University Press, 1991). Academic but highly readable tome that digs deep into the search for a modern Chinese identity.

Tyler, Christian, *Wild West China: The Untold Story of a Frontier Land* (John Murray, 2003). A more journalistic history of Xinjiang.

And a couple of good websites:

http://afe.easia.columbia.edu/chinawh/ – Kenneth Pomeranz and Bin Wong's website about how China was far ahead of the West and how it fell behind.

http://xiakou.uncc.edu – John Flower's excellent, detailed website exploring the many layers of life in one village in the mountains of Sichuan province.

INDEX

NB: In China, surnames (e.g. Mao) traditionally come first, followed by the given name (e.g. Zedong). All Chinese names in this index have been listed by surname.

A NOTE ON THE AUTHOR

Rob Gifford first went to China in 1987 as a twenty-year-old undergraduate, to study the language. A fluent Mandarin speaker and former BBC producer, he has spent twenty years studying, visiting and reporting on China. From 1999 to 2005 he was Beijing correspondent for the US network National Public Radio. During that time he travelled all over China, from Tibet to the Russian border, and from the Muslim northwest to North Korea. He is now NPR's London bureau chief.